Flannery O'Connor's
Sacramer

Flannery O'Connor's Sacramental Art

Susan Srigley

University of Notre Dame Press

Notre Dame, Indiana

Manufactured in the United States of America

Library of Congress Cataloging-in-Publication Data
Srigley, Susan, 1967–
    Flannery O'Connor's sacramental art / Susan Srigley.
        p.   cm.
    Originally presented as author's thesis (doctoral)—McMaster University.
    Includes bibliographical references and index.
    ISBN 0-268-01779-4 (cloth : alk. paper)
    ISBN 0-268-01780-8 (pbk. : alk. paper)
    1. O'Connor, Flannery—Criticism and interpretation.   2. Christian
fiction, American—History and criticism.   3. Didactic fiction, American—
History and criticism.   4. O'Connor, Flannery—Religion.   5. O'Connor,
Flannery—Ethics.   6. Sacraments in literature.   7. Purgatory in literature.
8. Violence in literature.   9. Ethics in literature.   I. Title.
    PS3565.C57Z6868 2005
    813'.54—dc22

                                                          2004023683

∞ *This book is printed on acid-free paper.*

For my parents,
Ralph (1937–2000) and Joyce,
my sister Liz, and brother Ron

Without faith, we live with no sense of responsibility,
and we destroy our own bodies, our souls,
our families and our society.

—Thich Nhat Hanh, "For a Future to Be Possible,"
in *Thich Nhat Hanh* (Maryknoll, N.Y.: Orbis, 2001), 131.

CONTENTS

CW   *Collected Works*. New York: Library of America, 1988.

CS   *The Complete Stories*. New York: Farrar, Straus and Giroux, 1971.

HB   *The Habit of Being*. Edited by Sally Fitzgerald. New York: Farrar, Straus and Giroux, 1979.

MM   *Mystery and Manners: Occasional Prose*. Edited by Sally Fitzgerald and Robert Fitzgerald. New York: Farrar, Straus and Giroux, 1969

VBA   *The Violent Bear It Away*. New York: Farrar, Straus and Cudahy, 1960.

WB   *Wise Blood*. New York: Farrar, Straus and Cudahy, 1962.

ACKNOWLEDGMENTS

There are many people who deserve recognition for their support and encouragement with this book.

Travis Kroeker, my doctoral supervisor at McMaster University, inspired me to work on Flannery O'Connor and helped me to bring this work to fruition. He has been a formidable mentor to me for many years. I am now grateful for his friendship.

Richard Giannone deserves much admiration and respect. His work on Flannery O'Connor has guided and sustained my own, and his support of this book has been active and impressive. I feel fortunate to have been graced by his wise counsel.

For their guidance in various ways, I would like to thank Nancy Davis Bray, Zdravko Planinc, Valerie Sayers, and Peter Widdicombe.

I am indebted to the Erasmus Institute at the University of Notre Dame for a fellowship to participate in a seminar on "Faith and Fiction" in New York City, June 2002. I am also grateful for a LURF grant from Laurentian University in 2002. Nipissing University provided me with a grant to cover indexing costs, and I thank Andrew Mogg for compiling the index.

I would like to thank my editor, Susan Allan, and managing editor, Rebecca DeBoer, for their very careful attention to my manuscript. It has been a pleasure working with everyone at the University of Notre Dame Press.

I thank Ralph Wood and an anonymous reviewer at the University of Notre Dame Press not only for their helpful suggestions and ideas but especially for their interest in and engagement with my argument. Their questions about my reading of the ending of *Wise Blood* helped improve my interpretation of it. For this rethinking of Hazel's blinding I am also indebted to Richard Giannone.

I reserve special personal thanks for my husband, Bruce Ward, who read and edited innumerable versions of this manuscript. His willingness to engage in conversation about Flannery O'Connor, literature, and ethics on a daily basis, even during many memorable hikes and canoe trips, is deeply appreciated. His insights and suggestions have been invaluable to me. I would also like to acknowledge my stepsons, Ian and Graeme Ward; they have both been especially supportive and attentive to my work as they welcomed me into their family.

I offer my deepest gratitude to my parents and siblings and dedicate this book to them.

Introduction

All our values depend on the nature of our God.

—Jacques Maritain, *Art and Scholasticism*

In a letter written May 30, 1959, Flannery O'Connor clarified the order of events surrounding her protagonist's self-blinding in *Wise Blood*. After having put quicklime into his eyes, she says, Hazel Motes was "in no state to practice charity," and further, she questions in parentheses whether "he would have known to anyway" (*HB* 335). The reference to charity is crucial not only for an interpretation of this novel and its ending, but also for interpreting O'Connor's ethics. O'Connor's mention of love in the context of Hazel's blinding signifies its importance for her religious thought. Hazel's inability to practice charity is not simply the result of his blindness but an indication of a spiritual condition: he insists on human independence from all spiritual reality. Hazel Motes's quest for freedom from responsibility—to Christ's redemption, or to any other human being—has as its outcome his obsessive inward attention to acts of self-mortification. With his blinding, Hazel isolates himself from all community; it is an intrinsic effect of the absolute freedom he preaches. He is separated from others and unable to love because of his belief in an absolute spiritual and physical human independence from

God and from other human beings. Hazel Motes espouses a kind of penance that, instead of opening him to humility and to an awareness of human dependence, only reinforces his belief that responsibility can be measured by the calculation of debts.

The opening quotation from Jacques Maritain illustrates O'Connor's approach to ethical inquiry. The connection between the values of human beings and the nature of their God is portrayed in her understanding of Christian love. Charity, as a specific form of Christian love, is love that serves the other, a love for neighbor that equals or surpasses love of self. In O'Connor's religious thought this kind of love is the source of what I call her *ethic of responsibility*.[1] My concern is to demonstrate how O'Connor's ethics are inextricably linked to her role as a storyteller and how her moral vision is played out in the drama of her fiction.[2]

In a world of facts and statements, even in the discussion of ethical issues, O'Connor appeals to the power of stories for learning about who we are as human beings: "There is a certain embarrassment about being a storyteller in these times when stories are considered not quite as satisfying as statements and statements not quite as satisfying as statistics; but in the long run, a people is known, not by its statements or statistics, but by the stories it tells" (*MM* 192). O'Connor's moral vision is not discovered in statements or statistics, but in her stories. In her fiction, O'Connor's ethical vision transcends codified measures. She does not believe that human responsibility can be calculated; rather she understands self-sacrificing love to be the only way of understanding human accountability, a belief reminiscent of Father Zosima in *The Brothers Karamazov* by Fyodor Dostoevsky:[3] "There is only one salvation for you: take yourself up, and make yourself responsible for all the sins of men. For indeed it is so, my friend, and the moment you make yourself sincerely responsible for everything and everyone, you will see at once that it is really so, that it is you who are guilty on behalf of all and for all."[4] In a remark about her story "A Good Man Is Hard to Find," O'Connor notes the moment of grace as residing in a similar revelation of responsibility, finally understood by the grandmother at the moment of her death: "Her head clears for an instant and she realizes, even in her limited way, that she is *responsible* for the man before her and joined to him by ties of kinship which have their roots deep in the mystery she has been merely prattling about so far" (*MM* 111–12; italics mine).

My primary aim in this book is to elucidate O'Connor's sacramental vision with reference to her theological and philosophical sources and to show how this sacramental vision is embodied within her fiction as an ethic of responsibility. Many scholars, and indeed O'Connor herself, have identified her theological orientation as sacramental; I propose to develop the meaning of her sacramental view of reality further by exploring its ethical implications.

Flannery O'Connor identified herself as a prophetic novelist. But what is the substance, or better, the direction of her prophetic art? Is its prophetic aspect directly ethical, or is it related to a yet more fundamental vision of reality that in turn yields certain ethical implications? When O'Connor defines prophecy as "seeing near things with their extensions of meaning and thus . . . seeing far things close up" (*MM* 44) she affirms the inherent connection between visible and invisible reality and suggests that with careful observation, the prophetic eye will interpret the meaning of things both near (what is physical and sensible) and far (what is spiritual and intangible) by understanding the visible and invisible in relation to one another. The prophetic novelist has an important role to play, and by assuming this title for herself Flannery O'Connor sets the parameters for her own responsibility as an artist. She felt herself accountable to her readers, to truth, and to the good of the work made—the good that reflects God in art. The sacramental act of creating something good that expresses, in concrete circumstances, the divine beauty of God is what compels her as an artist. O'Connor's prophetic vision, theological and artistic, is directed toward drawing together the physical and the spiritual; that is, the lived sensible world and the mysterious unseen reality that is eternally present. For this reason, one of the principal questions animating her art is, as she voiced it, "How can the novelist be true to time and eternity both?" (*MM* 177). The responsibility of the religious literary artist, according to O'Connor, is to write without denying the reality either of time or eternity and to acknowledge their meaningful relation to human life. Her account of the prophetic novelist articulates her own ethic of responsibility.

The relation of time and eternity provides the animating focus for O'Connor's sacramental art. During a talk given in 1957 at the University of Notre Dame, she said that the "sacramental view of life is one that sustains and supports at every turn the vision that the storyteller must have if he is going to write fiction of any depth" (*MM* 152). O'Connor's "sacramental view of life" is Christian—centered on the Incarnation—and she insists that it is essential to her vocation as a writer. When she describes how the church is "mindful of the relation between spirit and flesh," she refers to "the double nature of Christ" (*HB* 365–66), as the basis for what it means to be true to time and eternity both. This explanation is not intended as a doctrinal formulation, nor is it a statement of faith; rather, O'Connor's point here is to emphasize the possibility of spiritual mystery being known and experienced in the flesh. That this sacramental view was central to her artistic impulse is evidenced in her numerous references to Joseph Conrad and his articulation of the inherent connection between the visible and the invisible: "Conrad said that his aim as a fiction writer was to render the highest possible justice to the visible universe. . . . It means that he subjected himself at all times to the limitations that reality imposed, but that *reality for him was not simply coextensive with the visible.* He was interested in rendering justice to the visible universe *because it suggested an invisible one"* (*MM* 80; italics mine). To be true to time and eternity both suggests more than their recognition; it requires that their reality be known and lived in the artist and that this be shared in some measure by those who experience her art.

O'Connor's prophetic impulse is not only about discerning the nature of human beings, but also about how human beings—as bodies and souls—are related to one another morally. Her ethical vision of responsibility opens a fruitful way of understanding her religious ideas as they are expressed in her fiction because the drama of how her characters choose to love and how they choose to act reveals an underlying religious meaning. Responsibility is living action, where the burden of moral choice is on the individual, not resident in an abstract code. For O'Connor, ethical choices are not simply a matter of codes of behavior dictated by religious doctrine; they are an engagement with and a response to reality. When O'Connor writes about the significance of the novelist's view of reality, she describes the inherent connection between how human beings understand the world to be ordered and how they choose to live in that order:

> It makes a great difference to the look of a novel whether its author believes that the world came late into being and continues to come by a creative act of God, or whether he believes that the world and ourselves are the product of a cosmic accident. It makes a great difference . . . whether he believes that we are created in God's image or whether he believes we create God in our own. (*MM* 156–57)

O'Connor's insight into the moral order of reality is revealed in stories, not in treatises on ethical questions. She is not an ethicist in a systematic sense; her approach is neither formulaic nor prescriptive. As a storyteller, she explores the moral complexities of life in their most concrete and dramatic form. Types of behavior that appear in her fiction—such as racism, sexism, and nihilism—are exposed as inherently irresponsible. O'Connor is not concerned with formulating codes to counter these but with bringing her characters to seek something more responsible. Approaching O'Connor's fiction from a moral perspective can often better illuminate the dramatic struggle of a story, not because it offers a religious or ethical solution to a particular issue, but because the choices each character makes reveal a vision of reality that is either meaningful and sustainable or narrow and destructive.

In *The Violent Bear It Away* O'Connor displays her ethic of responsibility under threat by its negative form, through the devil's choice in the stranger's words: "And that's the way it ought to be in this world—nobody owing nobody nothing" (*VBA* 51). The devil's choice is the moral opposite to O'Connor's ethical vision: it is a rejection of spiritual obligation to other human beings in life and in death, where responsibility is assiduously avoided rather than accepted. The positive thrust of the novel comes with its ending, after Tarwater has acted upon and experienced the consequences of his irresponsibility. O'Connor leaves her protagonist facing a new danger, but this time it is the danger and burden of responsibility: Tarwater, the murderer of the child Bishop, is now a prophet and responsible for the children of God who lie sleeping in the city.

My exploration of O'Connor's ethical vision will offer a counter-response to the claims made by those critics who suggest that her religious thought is dualistic or Manichean, a claim often illustrated by her use of the grotesque. To interpret the grotesque simply as a reflection of the worthlessness and ugliness of matter is to miss the moral dimension of O'Connor's understanding of what is grotesque. She saw the grotesque as implicitly revealing an ethical choice, because for her the grotesque is rooted in the desire for absolute human autonomy (represented by Hazel Motes in *Wise Blood*), for life lived independently of God. Without interdependence, and the connection to other human beings that God's love of creation implies, there is no obligation to human responsibility. An ethic of responsibility carries with it the implicit assumption that human beings, as spiritual and physical beings, no matter how limited they might be, are all worthy of love.[5] The moral choice that O'Connor consistently dramatizes in her stories is between a life of responsibility for others that is ordered by the love of God and other human beings and a life ordered solely by love of the self.[6] The struggle between the idea that human beings are morally interdependent, and therefore responsible for everyone (including the dead, the murderous, and the idiots), and the idea that as autonomous individuals human beings are not responsible for anyone unless they choose to be, is at the heart of O'Connor's ethical fiction.

To examine the ethic of responsibility in Flannery O'Connor's stories is to offer, from a different angle, an interpretation of her religious thought. It is to recognize in her fiction the less conventional meaning of compassion: "a sense which implies a recognition of sin; this is a suffering-with, but one which blunts no edges and makes no excuses. When infused into novels, it is often forbidding. Our age doesn't go for it" (*MM* 166). To understand O'Connor's ethics means to somehow get beyond the age in which we live. One can do this by engaging the biblical and ancient/medieval theological sources for her thought, to observe how they challenge and measure our own; but it is also true that one can simply be open to what the stories reveal about moral choices and their effects—in other words to approach ethics as fiction.

◻   ◻   ◻

This book is divided into four chapters. The first, which focuses on O'Connor's prose writing from *Mystery and Manners* and her letters from *The Habit of Being,* addresses her formulations about art drawn from theologians such as Jacques Maritain and Thomas Aquinas. The theoretical insights about art and morality that O'Connor gleaned from Maritain and Aquinas are not applied to the fiction as a template; the two kinds of writing—her prose essays and her fiction—have different purposes. What draws these two genres together is their shared vision of reality: O'Connor's moral response is grounded in an understanding of the meaning of human life, whether it is articulated in Thomistic language or in a Southern drawl. The difference of accent should not confuse their common ground.

While this collection of prose pieces by no means constitute a system of thought—instead, a variety of lectures, essays, and public addresses have been gathered into one volume—*Mystery and Manners* offers the most sustained statements made by O'Connor about religion, morality, and art. My discussion of O'Connor's prose will direct the reader to O'Connor's terminology and the subtle linguistic distinctions she makes to clarify her ideas. My aim is to foster a stronger appreciation for the artistic centrality of O'Connor's theological and philosophical ideas. Chapter 1 will also include an examination of O'Connor's Thomistic understanding of prophecy, which is crucial for grasping how the more philosophical, even scholastic, mode of expression in her essays can be related to her more biblically charged fiction.

My first chapter deals with the theological and artistic responsibilities central to O'Connor's art as they are expressed in her prose writing. Subsequent chapters are devoted to her fiction and offer close textual readings concerned with elucidating the drama of how her characters try to live within their visions of reality. Each of these three chapters will focus on one fictional work, examining the spiritual tensions and experiences in the central characters' lives: *Wise Blood, The Violent Bear It Away,* and the short story, "Revelation." In more concrete detail these stories reveal O'Connor's sacramental vision of reality. Since she believed fiction to be an incarnational art, her stories are the most appropriate means of discovering her sacramental view. Choices about freedom, love, and responsibility are enacted in dramatic form, which approximates the true complexity of moral choices; but the stories are also able to illustrate how the directions of human decisions bear ethical implications. It is crucial, however, to resist the temptation of absolutely identifying certain characters with O'Connor's views, theological or ethical. The reader must participate in the story as a whole in order to see all of its moral implications and where the characters' particular choices lead.

In these three works of fiction, O'Connor's characters struggle fiercely in relation to two claims: to discover the relation between self and other that is spiritual but lived out in concrete, physical existence, and to love others and God more than the self. They seek self-knowledge as well as knowledge of God. The moment of grace that O'Connor describes is often precisely the revelation of the interconnectedness of human lives and souls, and how that connection must be ordered by love in human life. The order of love that O'Connor perceives in reality directs her ethic of responsibility. For the Christian writer O'Connor it is not a theological formula that dictates an ethic, but a sacramental orientation that sees human beings as inherently worthy of love and thus morally interconnected. To see the ethical dimension in these stories is to grasp the immense power of O'Connor's writing, which points to "mystery that is lived" (*MM* 125). The fiction writer, says O'Connor, is "concerned with ultimate mystery as we find it embodied in the concrete world of sense experience" (*MM* 125).

CHAPTER ONE

Sacramental Theology & Incarnational Art

Mystery and Manners

God is infinitely more lovable than art.

—Jacques Maritain, *Art and Scholasticism*

Religious Ethics

Flannery O'Connor stated the issue herself in a letter dated March 17, 1956: "Many of my ardent admirers would be roundly shocked and disturbed if they realized that everything I believe is thoroughly moral, thoroughly Catholic, and that it is these beliefs that give my work its chief characteristics" (*HB* 147–48). How to interpret the relation between her religious orientation and her art remains a central issue in O'Connor scholarship. What O'Connor says certainly assumes that her writing is and can be admired by those who do not know or share her religious beliefs. Nonetheless, O'Connor confirms the connection, and in the same letter she tries to clarify how she understands the relation between religious ethics and fiction. In response

9

to an essay written about her stories, O'Connor replies: "I don't write to bring anybody a message . . . this is not the purpose of the novelist; but the message I find in the life I see is a moral message" (*HB* 147). The point is extremely significant: O'Connor clarifies her understanding of ethics by distinguishing between humanly created or projected moral beliefs and the experience of a moral order present in reality. Her ethics are inherently religious.

This letter deserves serious attention, not only because it defines O'Connor's approach to moral issues, but also because it outlines her religious self-understanding in relation to her role as a novelist. She resists being characterized as imparting or intending a message, a function incompatible with her art; but more specifically, she wants to convey that her religious beliefs are not moralistic, in the negative sense of moralizing to others. O'Connor will not subordinate her art to her religious ideas: "Whatever the novelist sees in the way of truth must first take on the form of his art and must become embodied in the concrete and the human" (*MM* 175–76). That being said, what O'Connor says in her letter also affirms the moral dimension in her fiction while explaining the specific manner in which this happens: she finds *in the life she sees* a moral message. There is no denying the inherently ethical thrust of her fiction, but what needs amplification is the nature of that ethical vision. O'Connor argues that fiction "must carry its meaning inside it," and this includes moral ideas: "Any abstractly expressed compassion or piety or morality in a piece of fiction is only a statement added to it" (*MM* 75). Her point is not just about morality in fiction, but morality in life.

The purpose of this chapter is to show how Flannery O'Connor's sacramental theology and her incarnational art are connected and how *both* reveal her moral vision. The sacramental character of O'Connor's Christian aesthetics means that, for her, spiritual reality is present and experienced in the material world; her fiction as an incarnational art is the embodiment of this understanding, but she also explores the inherent moral meaning of the connection between the spiritual and the physical. O'Connor consistently denies the charges of Manichean dualism in her thought and work, and in her essays she argues against the separation of nature and grace, reason and imagination, and vision and judgment. An analysis of these separations and of how O'Connor overcomes them will also demonstrate the connection between her theology and her art. While O'Connor claims to have no "foolproof aesthetic theory," her aesthetic conviction, borrowed from Thomas Aquinas, is firmly expressed in a series of letters to Betty Hester: the moral basis of fiction and poetry is "the accurate naming of the things of God" (*HB* 123–31).[1] The substance of O'Connor's moral vision, as I suggested above, can be interpreted in the stories as an 'ethic of responsibility,' and thus the two aims of theology and art come together in her Christian aesthetics. O'Connor's theology is sacramental and Christ centered, and her ethic of responsibility is rooted in Christ's model of love as service to others. What this theological position means for O'Connor is a very practical matter of judgment in her art: "So far as I am concerned as a novelist, a bomb on Hiroshima affects my judgment of life in rural Georgia, and this is not the result of taking a relative view and judging one thing by another, but of taking an absolute view and judging all things together" (*MM* 134). The implications of her comment are ethical. O'Connor sees human responsibility for others as something that cannot be relative, but at the same time her language of "an absolute view" is not used to herald one religious position over another. The interdependence of all human life and the ethic of responsibility are measured by love.

Those who lack any interest in O'Connor's religious orientation assume that O'Connor's fiction can be interpreted and analyzed without the aid of the explicitly religious commentary found in her essays. Often what scholars find objectionable are religious interpretations of O'Connor's work that use her prose as a religious template to determine or finalize the meaning of her fiction.[2] Certainly this is a reasonable objection. Statements of religious ideas should never be substituted for careful analysis and interpretation. On the one hand, using theological ideas as if they were formulas distorts the often subtle philosophical orientation of O'Connor's religious thought in *Mystery and Manners*. On the other hand, those who radically separate her theological inquiry from her fictional landscapes refuse to acknowledge how profoundly the two are connected. What is commonly argued is that *Mystery and Manners* is not important for illuminating O'Connor's ideas as they are expressed within her fiction. It is accepted that while she does in her essays refer specifically to the religious meaning of certain gestures or actions within her stories, many of her comments about art and fiction generally can be read separately from her own artistic work.[3] This tendency to emphasize the independent worth of her essays as personal theological commentary, in addition to a closer scrutiny of and growing skepticism about authorial intention in literary theory, has led to the assumption that O'Connor's theological-philosophical reflections are not necessarily pertinent to an interpretation of her art.[4] In my view, it seems quite possible to discover the inherent connection between O'Connor's theological and philosophical thought—as found in the essays and letters—and her fictional art.

Mystery and Manners, the collection of Flannery O'Connor's essays and lectures, was published posthumously by her literary executors the Fitzgeralds as "occasional prose"; it seems wise to keep this subtitle in mind. The essays and lectures do not provide us with a complete or even systematic account of O'Connor's theology or theory of art, nor were they intended to be published as such. Nevertheless, the theological, moral, and artistic ideas that O'Connor was working through as she wrote these essays form a coherent vision of reality that can, even in the form of brief commentaries and anecdotes, help us to interpret her fiction. The theological concerns in O'Connor's essays are explicitly linked to and revealed through her art. The question remains how best to determine and clarify the nature of the relation. I interpret these essays in light of the tradition of thought that O'Connor herself acknowledges in her prose writing. While her own ideas about religion, art, and ethics may not always be fully developed in these occasional essays, O'Connor draws on writers who are indeed systematic, like Jacques Maritain and Thomas Aquinas. O'Connor's theology was largely influenced by Thomas Aquinas, but much of her knowledge of Thomas came through the Thomistic philosopher Jacques Maritain. By pursuing O'Connor's references to these philosophers we can better evaluate the focus of O'Connor's theological-philosophical ideas. She developed her religious and aesthetic sensibilities in dialogue with a Thomistic tradition, and true to this theoretical background her theological formulations are directly linked to her artistic pursuits.[5]

O'Connor made her Thomistic views about art very clear: the artist is "wholly concerned with the good of that which is made" (*MM* 171), she says, clarifying her opposition to the modern view that art must have some "utilitarian value," even and including a religious one. O'Connor's religious aesthetic is not concerned with imposing a religious message on her readers. She states the relation between her artistic impulse and her religious orientation quite simply: creating good art is the business of the artist, and yet, "what is good in itself glorifies God because it reflects God." The artist makes the good art, but the measure of art's goodness comes from God, not the artist. As if to further clarify what kind of religious writer she is, O'Connor explains that the artist "can safely leave evangelizing to the evangelists" (*MM* 171). O'Connor aligns her self-understanding as an artist with Aquinas's definition, revealing how one can have a religious approach to art that is not primarily concerned with evangelizing. O'Connor's theology is not forced onto the fictional works but envisioned sacramentally in them, and for this reason she argues that her religious vision does not, in some programmed sense, determine what or how she sees. Christian dogma "is not a set of rules which fixes what [the writer] sees in the world"; O'Connor explains that it affects her writing primarily by "guaranteeing [her] respect for mystery" (*MM* 31). This is not the guardianship of doctrine, but the recognition of and the openness to reality, which does not enshrine fact without mystery, or separate nature from grace, or spiritual reality from the physical world, but sees all of these as integral to the mystery of existence.[6]

The impulse to separate physical and spiritual reality is a problem O'Connor perceives both in fictional art and the religious imagination, and in response, she focuses her attention on writing fiction that is grounded in the sensible world yet that also points toward the experience of mystery. O'Connor's concern to draw together the various separations of spirit and matter is related to another tension between the Catholic artist's vision and that of the church, where it might be assumed that what the artist sees is secondary to the spiritual ideas of the church. O'Connor insists on the freedom of the artist to see and interpret reality as she experiences it, but she also admits to the Catholic artist's obligation toward the church's teaching about that same reality. What needs to be addressed, argues O'Connor, is the fact that the tension exists *because* the religious artist is always free to look at and observe reality as an individual and further, that the goal is not the removal of the tension: "When the Catholic novelist closes his own eyes and tries to see with the eyes of the Church, the result is another addition to that large body of pious trash for which we have so long been famous" (*MM* 180). The obvious problem with such deference to the "eyes of the church" is that the artist sacrifices reality as it is known and seen through lived experience in favor of a doctrinally formed vision. O'Connor's concern is not to dissolve this tension between what the church sees and what the artist sees; rather, she wishes to understand the nature of the Catholic artist's responsibility to be aware of both poles within the tension. The fact that the "eyes" are central to O'Connor's discussion of this issue suggests that the real task of the prophetic artist is to achieve and communicate a wholeness of vision, rather than to determine which side in the conflict is correct or more appropriate. This can only be done through the artist's willingness to look at what is there to see—and further, to what is not seen.

O'Connor did not separate her religious views as a Catholic from her artistic intentions, nor did she see one as simply in the service of the other. Instead, she acknowledged some of the difficulties of writing as a Catholic and also of the reception of her work by Catholic audiences, whose desire for "positive literature" was rooted, according to O'Connor, in a "weak faith and possibly also from this general inability to read" (*MM* 188–89). It is important to note that, for O'Connor, art has its own demands, and these govern her writing more so than the church does: "Our final standard for [the novelist] will have to be the demands of art, which are a good deal more ex-acting than the demands of the Church. There are novels a writer might write, and remain a good Catholic, which his conscience as an artist would not allow him to perpetrate" (*MM* 183–84). O'Connor's comment here is re-vealing because, while she refers to the "more exacting demands of art" as the final standard for the novelist, she does so using the religious language of conscience.

O'Connor's response to the problems associated with writing religious fiction was to maintain a careful balance between her religious views and the demands of art. It is important to emphasize that being true to her artistic vocation was essential to her religious orientation, and her concern to inte-grate the two was influenced by her careful reading of Jacques Maritain.[7] She took him seriously, and she repeated his ideas in her own prose writing about being a Christian artist. Maritain says in *Art and Scholasticism:*

> Do not make the absurd attempt to dissociate in yourself the artist and the Christian. They are truly one, if you are truly Christian, and if your art is not isolated from your soul by some system of aesthetics. But apply only the artist to the work; precisely because the artist and the Christian are one, the work will derive wholly from each of them.[8]

The tone of Maritain's words is educative, offered as counsel and guiding the Christian artist to balance the integrity of religious faith and art. There is no mistaking O'Connor's reception of this guidance, which she repeats in her own essays: "Novelists who are deeply Catholic will write novels which you may call Catholic if the Catholic aspects of the novel are what interest you. Such a novel may be characterized in any number of other ways, and per-haps the more ways the better" (*MM* 193). Her point is that what is em-bedded in the vision of the artist will be apparent to some extent in the art, but that it is not the art's sole or defining characteristic.

Taking her lessons from Maritain, O'Connor would not compromise the good of her art or her religion. She makes her argument forcefully:

> They say the reader knows nothing about art, and that if you are going to reach him, you have to be humble enough to descend to his level. This supposes either that the aim of art is to teach, which it is not, or that to create anything which is simply a good-in-itself is a waste of time. Art never responds to the wish to make it democratic; it is not for everybody; it is only for those who are willing to undergo

the effort needed to understand it. We hear a great deal about humility being required to lower oneself, but it requires an equal humility and a real love of the truth to raise oneself and by hard labor to acquire higher standards. And this is certainly the obligation of the Catholic. (*MM* 189)

The demands of art need not be opposed to the demands of religion. For O'Connor, artistic pursuits, like religious ones, are not simply didactic but require the effort of raising oneself—on the part of the artist and the reader—to the perception of truth. Further, while the writer "has to write at his own intellectual level," she says that "this doesn't mean that, within his limitations, he shouldn't try to reach as many people as possible, but it does mean that he must not lower his standards to do so" (*MM* 186). Again, her argument is an echo of Maritain's, who regards the habit (*habitus*) of art as incompatible with egalitarianism. The modern mind instead prefers the more inclusive approach to art that is interpreted according to methodology, Maritain laments: "Now it cannot be admitted that access to the highest activities depend on a virtue that some possess and others do not; consequently beautiful things must be made easy." Both Maritain and O'Connor reveal their preference for the "ancients," who "thought that truth is difficult, that beauty is difficult, and that the way is narrow; and that to conquer the difficulty and the loftiness of the object, it is absolutely necessary that an intrinsic force and elevation—that is to say, a *habitus*—be developed in the subject."[9]

O'Connor identifies this love and pursuit of the truth, which is the work of artistic creation, with the religious obligation of the Christian. To designate the religious artist as one who simply humbles oneself—in the sense of simplifying, or democratizing, the art—to accommodate the readers' level of understanding is to force an inadequate understanding of religion on the artist. O'Connor acknowledges that the ascent to truth is a concern *equally* important to religion and art. In this sense, the artistic and religious quest is more appropriately designated as one undertaken in dialogue. A more precise understanding of the relation between O'Connor's religious insights and her artistic motivation, however, needs to be achieved in order to meet directly the claim that the former is a matter of personal opinion, while the latter is an object of literary interest alone. O'Connor takes seriously the relation between religious insight and artistic motivation, and her comments reveal their proximity: "We reflect the Church in everything we do, and those who can see clearly that our judgment is false in matters of art cannot be blamed for suspecting our judgment in matters of religion" (*MM* 190).[10] With this statement O'Connor addresses specifically those critics who separate her art from her religion, and in it she suggests that if the measure and judgments of art are ignored (for the purposes of religious propaganda or evangelizing) there would be reason to suspect her religious insight also. Of course, this could also indicate the opposite; false religious insight could produce artistic propaganda and ideology. It is "the sorry religious novel," according to O'Connor, in which "the writer supposes that because of his belief, he is somehow dispensed from the obligation to penetrate concrete reality" (*MM* 163).[11] The problem tends to be perpetuated in the interpretation of religious fiction, especially by coreligionists, since "every given circumstance of the writer is ignored except his Faith. No one taking part in these discussions seems to remember that the eye sees what it has been given to see by concrete circumstances, and the imagination reproduces what, by some related gift, it is able to make live" (*MM* 195).

O'Connor suggests that "the main concern of the fiction writer is with mystery as it is incarnated in human life" (*MM* 176). The artist's task is to see the spiritual through the physical, an emphasis that applies both to her fiction and her theological orientation: "The real novelist . . . knows that he cannot approach the infinite directly, that he must penetrate the natural human world as it is. The more sacramental his theology, the more encouragement he will get from it to do just that" (*MM* 163). O'Connor identifies the essential link between her understanding of fiction and her sacramental theology. She calls fiction an "incarnational art," because it "operates through the senses" (*MM* 91). In using this term, she also points to the connection between the Incarnation of Christ and the work of the literary artist: her theology is sacramental, her fiction incarnational. Both affirm the goodness of creation and the centrality of love to her religious vision, whether expressed in her prose or in her fiction. For O'Connor, "this physical, sensible world is good because it proceeds from a divine source" (*MM* 157). As Maritain says, "The artist has to love, he has to love *what he is making,* so that his virtue may truly be, in Saint Augustine's words, *ordo amoris*" (italics in original).[12]

Incarnational Art

Art requires what O'Connor calls "a delicate adjustment of the outer and inner worlds in such a way, that without changing their nature, they can be seen through each other" (*MM* 34–35). The aim of O'Connor's art is not to use one in the service of the other but to explore the interpenetration of physical and spiritual reality. In light of this, the Catholic novel would be "one that represents reality adequately as we see it manifested in this world of things and human relationships. Only in and by this sensed experience of the world and human relations does the fiction writer approach a contemplative knowledge of the mystery they embody" (*MM* 172). What this means for O'Connor is that fiction draws together mystery and manners: "There are two qualities that make fiction. One is the sense of mystery and the other is the sense of manners. You get the manners from the texture of existence that surrounds you" (*MM* 103). Fiction is an incarnational art because it offers a concrete representation of life and human existence in the facts of the story, but within these representations it can also reveal spiritual mysteries and meaning. Meaning, in this sense, is not disembodied in fiction as abstracted principles or ideas but is always incarnate: "The meaning of a story has to be embodied in it, has to be made concrete in it. . . . The meaning of fiction is not abstract meaning but experienced meaning" (*MM* 96).

O'Connor's description of art as incarnational can be described as religiously rooted in her understanding of the Incarnation of Christ; her vision is ordered by the images of creation and the Incarnation. O'Connor's use of the phrase "incarnational art," as John Desmond explains it, "implies a whole way of seeing reality, from the immediate concrete to the farthest reaches of human history and beyond. More important, it implies an intrinsic relationship between the historical event of Christ's Incarnation, present-day reality, and the creative act of fiction writing as O'Connor attempted to practice it."[13] The Incarnation is the climactic divine incursion into the drama of temporal creation; O'Connor models her fictional art from this understanding of the divine presence in the drama of everyday life:

> I see from the standpoint of Christian orthodoxy. This means that for me the meaning of life is centered in our Redemption by Christ and what I see in the world I see in its relation to that. I don't think that this is a position that can be taken halfway or one that is particularly easy in these times to make transparent in fiction. (*MM* 32)

To interpret O'Connor's fiction and theology sacramentally is to acknowledge her understanding of the Incarnation as the perfect expression of spiritually embodied existence ordered by love.

In an important passage from *Mystery and Manners*, O'Connor writes that "Christ didn't redeem us by a direct intellectual act, but became incarnate in human form" (*MM* 176). The Incarnation of Christ expresses the nature of the human experience of the divine: spiritual reality is experienced in concrete human existence, and God relates to human beings in the flesh. Christ represents the joining of the visible and the invisible: this is the central Christian mystery for O'Connor, and it is a reality that human beings experience themselves as spiritually embodied beings. When O'Connor says that Christ did not redeem by an intellectual act, she intentionally uses the word *direct,* which suggests an experience of Christ that is entirely spiritual or intellectual without bodily significance or presence. Rather than a rejection of the intellect, O'Connor is affirming the connection of the spiritual/intellectual life with bodily existence. The Incarnation, therefore, represents the mystery of embodied spiritual life, both by mirroring the human condition of an interwoven physical and spiritual existence and by revealing the connection of human beings to God that is known through love and lived in both body and soul.

When O'Connor discusses her writing, she often draws parallels between the difficulty of writing fiction and the human experience of limitation. Self-knowledge is crucial for writing fiction, and about this self-knowledge she identifies two important facts: "To know oneself is to know one's region," and "To know oneself is, above all, to know what one lacks. It is to measure oneself against Truth and not the other way around" (*MM* 35). The writer cannot escape the specific details of her region or country, and at the same time the writer's region is always known in relation to something that transcends it. The latter is a measure that points to limitation, of writer or region, but at the same time it points to the experience of mystery. Instead of being taught "how to write," O'Connor argues that what needs to be taught in the art of writing are "the limits and possibilities of words and the respect due them" (*MM* 83). Her statement here is not simply a description of writing habits; it is also a religious comment. Just as the writer needs to learn respect for words and their limitations, the human experience of mystery is fundamentally an experience of human limitation in the face of something transcendent: "If a writer is any good, what he makes will have its source in a realm much larger than that which his conscious mind can encompass" (*MM* 83). The artist "must first of all be aware of his limitations as an artist," says O'Connor, "for art transcends its limitations only by staying within them" (*MM* 171). In a letter to Cecil Dawkins she says, "Vocation implies limitation but few people realize it who don't actually practice an art" (*HB* 221). The experience of limitation is related to another example that O'Connor uses to draw together the habits of the artist with her basic religious orientation: poverty.

O'Connor describes her own situation as working "from such a basis of poverty" (*HB* 127), but she also writes about being interested in the poor, not out of curiosity about their economic situation but because poverty is also a condition that afflicts the soul.[14] The artist's focus is spiritual need: "His concern with poverty is with a poverty fundamental to man. I believe that the basic experience of everyone is the experience of human limitation" (*MM* 131). The poor, therefore, symbolize the central spiritual condition of human life, and because they live in a more immediate sense "with less padding between them and the raw forces of life" (*MM* 132). O'Connor finds in them a revealing touchstone for the universal human experience of limitation and need. However, the novelist is also looking at himself, says O'Connor, and in seeing the depths of himself he comes to know "the bedrock of all human experience—the experience of limitation or, if you will, of poverty" (*MM* 132). O'Connor's artistic discussions of limitation and of poverty communicate her religious understanding of the human experience of incompleteness and the corresponding desire in human beings to seek out and attain completion.

O'Connor, in her prose, is attempting to reveal that the religious question of human limitation and the desire for completion or wholeness are indeed the question of art. In her fiction, O'Connor takes up this question and expresses it through her characters and their actions and experiences of life. However, the sometimes bleak picture that emerges out of these human experiences does not mean that her religious vision of life is hopeless or negative. Commenting on her stories, she remarks that they are "about people who are poor, who are afflicted in both mind and body, who have little—or at best a distorted—sense of spiritual purpose, and whose actions do not apparently give the reader a great assurance of the joy of life" (*MM* 32). The comment is followed by her own question: How does this portrayal of afflicted characters in her fiction relate to her belief that the meaning of life is centered in "our Redemption by Christ"? I think that O'Connor's answer links her understanding of poverty to her sacramental view of reality: "Redemption is meaningless unless there is cause for it in the actual life we live." The "cause" to which she refers is sin, and O'Connor believes that sin and poverty of spirit are spiritual experiences that are also manifest in the specific details of human life. Sin is not an abstraction but an experience, albeit a negative one, that is both spiritual and physical. O'Connor is aware, however, that the secular belief animating the culture in which she lives and writes is not centered so much on the rejection of the Redemption as it is on a "belief that there is no such cause" (*MM* 33). While O'Connor acknowledges that sin is implicit in the idea of redemption, the focus of her sacramental vision is the human response of love to the reality of poverty and sin. The Incarnation and Redemption of Christ, as the model of love, guides O'Connor's theology and her art.

It is my intention to discuss the nature of O'Connor's dependence on ancient and medieval philosophical and religious traditions, not as an exclusive guide for interpreting her concerns as a theological artist but to deepen our understanding of the separations in art and life that she identified: between nature and grace, reason and imagination, and vision and judgment. A closer investigation of O'Connor's essays and lectures will help to clarify and in fact reconcile some of the various relations among aesthetics, ethics, philosophy, theology, and religion in her writing.

Nature and Grace

To silence the dialogue between O'Connor's prose and her fiction inevitably reduces the possibilities for judging certain actions within the fiction; when the fiction is interpreted without reference to O'Connor's understanding of the relationship between nature and grace, for instance, any episode that describes the body with grotesque attributes is interpreted automatically as O'Connor's repulsion at the physical world.[15] The relation between nature and grace is central to O'Connor's work because it provides the background for interpreting her characters' struggles within the world and the tensions of spiritual experiences as they are lived in physical circumstances. O'Connor's sacramental fiction addresses not only the Protestant view of the (lack of a) relation between nature and grace; she also stresses in her writings how this relation has been nearly obliterated in the modern period by a Manichean tendency that separates spirit and matter, and consequently the human and the divine.[16] In some of her essays on the church O'Connor goes so far as to suggest that most modern Catholics are no longer sensitive to these distinctions, and so they have more in common with her secular and Manichean audience than with the teachings of the church. She says: "If the average Catholic reader could be tracked down through the swamps of letters-to-the-editor and other places where he momentarily reveals himself, he would be found to be more of a Manichean than the Church permits. By separating nature and grace as much as possible, he has reduced his conception of the supernatural to pious cliché" (*MM* 147). O'Connor specifies one of the immediate effects of the separation of nature and grace here: their separation ends up *reducing* the conception of the supernatural to pious cliché.

The separation of nature and grace makes the reality of grace irrelevant to the natural world, akin to a magical act rather than something inherent within creation,[17] and makes nature simply dead matter to be acted upon. In O'Connor's view, the separation of the physical and the spiritual divides our existence as embodied beings capable of spiritual experience and negates the meaning of our connection to a larger spiritual reality. The supernatural becomes nothing more than a cliché because its reality within the natural world is denied, relegating it to a matter of opinion or belief. The further consequence is that human beings are also reduced: they become nothing more than bodies, disconnected from any larger order of spiritual meaning

The separation between nature and grace as O'Connor describes it above is a pivotal issue for the fiction writer, and one that is central for religious fiction particularly. Whether or not the question is explicitly addressed, the effect of assuming human beings to be radically separated from God—cut off from grace and not naturally disposed to the experience of anything divine transcending human consciousness—is going to make itself apparent in the fictional work. O'Connor notes the shift in modern fiction that marks this type of separation: "In twentieth-century fiction it increasingly happens that a meaningless, absurd world impinges upon the sacred consciousness of author or character; author and character seldom now go out to explore and penetrate a world in which the sacred is reflected" (*MM* 158). The separation must have one of two obvious outcomes. Either the spiritual experience is drawn wholly into the human, initiated and exhausted in its meaning by human needs and ends; or an external, divine being is seen as separate from the human and, because of this separation, is ultimately unable to penetrate human life and be known sacramentally in the world.

These are two examples of what O'Connor calls "spiritually lopsided" modern tendencies, and their significance for this discussion is related to O'Connor's insistence that the separation of nature from grace will inevitably result in art that is no longer true to reality. In fact, such art simply ends up mirroring the distorted image of human existence within this lopsided spiritual condition. One result of this trend in modern fiction, O'Connor sees, is evident in universities, where you find "departments of theology vigorously courting departments of English" (*MM* 158). The modern novel is of interest to religious or theological schools because it presents the plight of the modern unbeliever, who is nonetheless seeking out the possible meanings of his or her spiritual experience.

This separation between nature and grace was not affirmed by O'Connor, either artistically, or in her prose writing about religion and art. Her artistic and religious preoccupations are centered within the firm conviction that human beings are not cut off from grace, and although human nature is imperfect, or sinful, O'Connor maintained consistently the Catholic view that nature is perfected by grace.[18] The difficulty in portraying this experience artistically was nonetheless an issue for O'Connor: "It's almost impossible to write about supernatural Grace in fiction. We almost have to approach it negatively. As to natural Grace, we have to take that the way it comes—through nature" (*HB* 144). "The Christian novelist lives in a larger universe," she explains, believing that "the natural world contains the supernatural. And this doesn't mean that his obligation to portray the natural is less; it means it is greater" (*MM* 175). Her convictions affirm that the world is not meaningless, but full of meaning that is larger and extends further than human knowledge. The confrontation of the individual with this experience of the limits of human knowing is deeply embedded in her fiction. For O'Connor, reality is divinely ordered, not subject to human will or changed by human belief. Human beings are not self-created or autonomous; in the midst of their experiences within the world the meaning of their existence is found in something larger than themselves, namely, the power that created human beings and the world and holds everything together.[19]

Some scholars persist in claiming, despite O'Connor's statements to the contrary found throughout *Mystery and Manners* and *The Habit of Being*, that her understanding of the relationship between nature and grace was not the traditional Catholic one. Or, more commonly, they misunderstand what her Catholic position means. In her essay on O'Connor, for instance, Mary Gordon remarks that "like most contemporary Catholics, O'Connor found that nature didn't matter very much, and that although individual humans could achieve redemption, the race remained, in this world, unredeemed."[20]

Lorine Getz, who has written a study devoted to the question of nature and grace in O'Connor's fiction, argues that O'Connor did not have a "single theology of grace" but instead offers "several theologies of grace."[21] Getz's analysis offers a breakdown of the three theologies of grace that she perceives in O'Connor's fiction: Thomistic, Augustinian, and Jansenist. According to Getz, Thomistic grace affirms the natural and "perfects and expands the meaning of nature"; Augustinian grace reveals that the "natural meaning is shown to belong to the order of sin," so that "grace opposes nature"; and finally, in Jansenist grace, "the natural level is altogether displaced by the supernatural."[22] Although O'Connor read and was influenced by Augustine, her language is often more obviously Thomistic, especially on the issue of the relation between nature and grace. Getz's Thomistic definition is probably the most consistent with O'Connor's own formulations on this topic. However, the application of Getz's model can be rigid and tends to reduce the portrayal of the mystery of grace and nature to formulaic codes in O'Connor's fiction.

One helpful source for clarifying this issue is Baron Friedrich von Hügel, whose writings O'Connor read and reviewed. There are many convergences between von Hügel's thought and O'Connor's, and in her 1956 book review of his *Letters to a Niece,* her discussion is focused explicitly on his ideas of nature and grace.[23] In the letter, which O'Connor quotes in her review, von Hügel's warning to his niece mirrors precisely what O'Connor says concerning the separation of fact and mystery, which often occurs as the consequence of a single-minded preoccupation with things religious. Von Hügel tells his niece to fight vigorously against the mentality that considers nonreligious subjects boring. He concludes: "If there is one danger for religion— if there is any one plausible, all-but-irresistible trend which, throughout its long rich history, has sapped its force, and prepared the most destructive counter-excesses, it is just that—that allowing the fascinations of Grace to deaden or to ignore the beauties and duties of Nature."[24] An excessive concern with the spiritual will eventually "lose the material for Grace to work in and on."[25] What is central to this discussion is that for both O'Connor and von Hügel the separation of the physical world—of nature and bodily existence from spiritual reality for the purposes of glorifying one or the other— is a separation that reduces the meaning and purpose of each. In O'Connor's Christian sacramental vision the physical and spiritual are inherently connected, and her fiction dramatically represents the tension of this human experience of living as embodied spiritual beings, not to exalt either the physical or the spiritual but to reveal the meaning and nature of their union.

The significant drama of O'Connor's fiction is found within the human response to the encounter with spiritual reality, and, given the nature of that reality, what the consequences of differing responses to it might be. Her approach is not dogmatic but insightfully imagined according to her understanding of human nature and the reality of a divinely ordered creation. O'Connor does not assume that because there is a connection between human beings and the divine, or nature and grace, that somehow this connection is programmed in a specific way. The workings of grace and the mystery of the human response to the divine are not determined or inevitable, and this is evident in O'Connor's insistence on human freedom: "The novelist does not write about general beliefs but about men with free will, and that there is nothing in our faith that implies a foregone optimism for man so free that with his last breath he can say *No"* (*MM* 182). The most one can say is that there are patterns of response within spiritual experience that we see mirrored in O'Connor's fiction. But patterns should not be confused with programmed responses, a confusion often at the root of O'Connor criticism: she is characterized as a godlike controlling narrator who forces her characters into spiritual experiences against their own inclinations.[26] Contrary to this view, and more in tune with O'Connor's own thinking, the idea of patterns of response suggests shared human experiences of reality that lead to a better understanding of both human nature and the spiritual reality in which that nature participates. O'Connor does not see her Catholic faith as somehow determining that free participation and serving as a "theological solution to mystery" (*MM* 184); instead she sees her religious faith as one of the few things in the modern world that guarantees a respect for mystery.

The sacramental orientation of O'Connor's religious thought holds, in tension, the spiritual experience of mystery together with the lived order of life. However, O'Connor also recognizes that, despite her conviction that the Catholic faith helps to guarantee a respect for mystery, there exists the further temptation (on the part of Catholics and writers with theological interests) to separate the facts of life from the mystery that abides in those facts by focusing on mystery to the exclusion of facts:

> We Catholics are very much given to the Instant Answer. Fiction doesn't have any. It leaves us, like Job, with a renewed sense of mystery. St. Gregory wrote that every time the sacred text describes a fact, it reveals a mystery. This is what the fiction writer, on his lesser level, hopes to do. The danger for the writer who is spurred by the religious view of the world is that he will consider this to be two operations instead of one. He will try to enshrine the mystery without the fact, and there will follow a further set of separations which are inimical to art. Judgment will be separated from vision, nature from grace, and reason from imagination. (*MM* 184)

O'Connor here recognizes the desire, stemming from the religious mindset, to "enshrine mystery" and thereby disregard fact, or the concrete experiences of life, in favor of a more spiritualized existence. The separation of fact and mystery is linked to those other separations that O'Connor considers "inimical to art": between nature and grace, reason and imagination, and judgment and vision. O'Connor's point is an artistic one, but it is also theological: she makes it by indicating a particular theological view that interferes with art, namely, the separation of mystery from fact. Her comparison between sacred texts and fiction is an obvious indication of her sacramental vision and how it is embodied in her writing. Just as "every time the sacred text describes a fact, it reveals a mystery," O'Connor suggests that the fiction writer "begins . . . with the senses, [in order to] go through it into an experience of mystery itself" (*MM* 41–42). O'Connor's artistic and theological vision is combined here in that her sacramental view is seen as best represented fictionally, insofar as fiction, like the revelation of mystery in sacred texts, is rooted in the sensible world. The spiritual mystery of existence is revealed in and through that world. O'Connor's use of the word "mystery" should be clarified given its role in relation to the discussion on reason and imagination I pursue below. John Desmond, quoting Tresmontant, points out that mystery should not be confused with the modern assumption of "something impenetrable to the mind, something never to be understood." Instead, Desmond stresses that "mystery is intelligible; it is a proper subject of knowledge; it can be known *as* mystery." With this account of the intelligibility of mystery in view, as something that is spiritual and yet sought for the "delectation of the mind,"[27] we can turn the discussion to the spiritual experience of reason.

Reason and Imagination

My philosophical notions don't derive from Kierkegaard . . .
but from St. Thomas Aquinas.

—Flannery O'Connor

The central role of reason in O'Connor's understanding of art is undeniable, and several scholars have noted her usage of the Thomistic phrase—"art is a virtue of the practical intellect" (*MM* 81).[28] The intellect, along with the reasoning process, is integral to her definition of art. What needs further explanation for interpreting O'Connor's account of reason is the influence upon her of Jacques Maritain's Thomistic account of art.[29] How is art a virtue? What is the practical intellect? What is the habit of art? In her use of these terms O'Connor assumes the Thomistic/Aristotelian division of the intellect into its speculative and practical orientations. For O'Connor, art is a virtue, and thus inclined always toward the good; as a virtue of the practical intellect it is ordered by the reasoning power of the soul directed toward action, or, more specifically, the action of making. These distinctions contribute to O'Connor's careful articulation of a philosophical anthropology, informed by classical philosophy and medieval Christian traditions, which extends to her fiction.[30] My discussion of the relation between reason and imagination will focus on three themes that emerge in O'Connor's comments about reason/mind/intellect: the habit of art as a virtue of the mind, art as a virtue of the practical intellect, and the revelatory experience of reason in art and ethics. Reason is understood by O'Connor to play an active role in the discernment of spiritual reality and this has converging rather than diverging implications for her thinking about both artistic creation and religious ethics.

Art as a Virtue of the Mind

When O'Connor gave lectures about art, especially when she was addressing those who were interested in writing fiction, she would usually provide a definition and even a brief explanation of that definition. She was noticeably careful with words like *art* and *reason,* most likely because she knew that her Thomistic definitions might sound unfamiliar or even odd to modern audiences. Even in letters she wrote to friends, she expressed the importance of definitions so as to be clear about whatever underlying assumptions they held. Her religious views were often the focus of such clarifications: "I am one, of course, who believes that man is created in the image and likeness of God. I believe that all creation is good but that what has free choice is more completely God's image than what does not have it; also I define humility differently from you. . . . I think it is good to have these differences defined" (*HB* 104). In the same letter, O'Connor quotes Maritain about the intellectual habits of the mind in order to highlight that there must be some critical distance between the artist and the art created: "Maritain says that to produce a work of art requires the 'constant attention of the purified mind,' and the business of the purified mind in this case is to see that those elements of the personality that don't bear on the subject at hand are excluded" (*HB* 105). The habit of art, for O'Connor, was an intellectual activity directed to the good of the art made, but she qualified this activity by distinguishing between the external habits of the artist and the spiritual element of what Maritain means by habit. She writes: "He explains that 'habit' in this sense means a certain quality or virtue of the mind. The scientist has the habit of science; the artist, the habit of art" (*MM* 64–65). O'Connor is trying to convey the belief that the creation of art is sustained by the cultivation and discipline of the mind "over a long period of time," but this belief is also, she notes "a way of looking at the created world and of using the senses so as to make them find as much meaning as possible in things" (*MM* 101).

The virtue or quality of the mind is thus a spiritual capacity, related to seeing or to vision. Maritain distinguishes habit (*habitus*) from the "modern sense of the word," which is "mere mechanical bent and routine," by explaining that although the habits of intellectual and moral virtues are acquired through "exercise and use" they are an "activity of the spirit" residing "principally in an immaterial faculty, in the intelligence or the will."[31] While open to the fact that the artist works toward the expression of mystery in concrete form, O'Connor kept an ordered view of the experience of the mind in its relation to truth; she was wary of language that misunderstood the direction of the creative impulse. In a letter to Betty Hester she writes, after asking for an impression of Maritain's work: "Strangle that word *dreams*. You don't dream up a form and put the truth in it. The truth creates its own form. Form is necessity in the work of art. You know what you mean but you ain't got the right words for it" (*HB* 218). Truth is the measure of art for O'Connor: "The basis for art is truth, both in manner and in mode" (*MM* 65). She does not understand truth, however, as some abstract form, and she rejects this meaning in a follow-up letter to Hester: "The last thing I would like to convince you of is that form is an absolute lying somewhere in an esoteric mist to which only the artist has access. Heavens no. That is to me what the world 'dreams' used untechnically summons up" (*HB* 219).

Maritain clarifies the spiritual movements of the creative process in *Creative Intuition in Art and Poetry,* which was a source for many of O'Connor's ideas. He delineates the mysterious process of the creative impulse and how this manifests itself in the production of art. Neither art nor poetry can do without the other, and yet the words are not synonymous: by art he means "the creative or producing, work-making activity of the human mind" and by poetry, he does not mean the art of writing verse, but the more general and primary experience of "the intercommunication between the inner being of things and the inner being of the human Self which is a kind of divination."[32] What Maritain is describing as "poetry" is the spiritual discourse that is known in the soul through its connection to the spiritual world, and this discourse is characterized as "a kind of divination" because it can be a revelatory experience. The connection of the poetic to the divine was a common feature of the ancient world, with the Latin term *vates* describing both a poet and a diviner.

Art as a Virtue of the Practical Intellect

O'Connor introduces her comment that "art is a virtue of the practical intellect" by describing the artist as having a gift. She does this in order to explain how the intellect works in relation to that gift. The gift is not automatic; it requires the habit of art and the work of the intellect to make it live. The practice of any virtue, she explains, "demands a certain asceticism" (*MM* 81), and the language she uses suggests that the discipline of the artist means being attuned to how the work of art relates to truth, which measures both the art and the mind of the artist. The distinctions within the intellect implied by the particular virtue of art are helpful for understanding the relationship of reason to art and imagination, and also, for clarifying the relation between art and ethics. First it is necessary to explain the division of the intellect into the theoretical and the practical in order to understand the different spheres of intellectual activity.

Maritain understands the main division of the activity of the intellect in terms of Aristotle's account of the speculative, or theoretical, intellect and the practical intellect. Maritain reiterates that this does not refer to two separate powers of the soul but to two different ways in which the same power works.[33] The speculative intellect is the soul's desire to know what is; it is the conformity of the intellect with being itself. Its end is knowledge and the understanding of first principles. This is what Maritain describes as knowing for the sake of knowledge alone. The practical intellect differs in that it tends more toward action and seeks something other than knowledge itself.

Within the realm of the practical intellect there is a further distinction between making and doing. Art is the virtue of making, while prudence is the virtue of doing. The difference between these two lies in their ends: art inclines itself toward the good of the work done, whereas prudence is directed toward the good of the worker, namely, human beings themselves. One is an intellectual virtue (art) and the other is a moral virtue (prudence). One further consideration that Maritain addresses is the role of the will in relation to truth. The speculative intellect is driven by the will, or as Maritain suggests, the will as "man's energy of desire or love" is what "intervenes . . . to bring the intellect to the exercise of its own power."[34] Beyond this, however, the will is not part of the intellectual pursuit. The will plays a different, but more essential, role in relation to the practical intellect. Since the practical intellect is oriented toward action, the will works with reason in order to make or perform some action. Truth, therefore, for speculative knowledge, is "the adequation or conformity of the intellect with Being, with what things are," whereas the concern with truth in practical knowing is the conformity of the reason and the will, whether that conformity occurs in human doing or in the making of a work of art.

These distinctions are helpful not only because they recognize generally the different human experiences of contemplation and action, but also because they clarify the difference between art and ethics, or between making and doing. It is a subtle difference because ethical (or moral) action, like art, is a practical virtue; it is grounded in the everyday experiences of human action and thought. For O'Connor, ethical deliberation is grounded not in abstract theory, but in the reasoned working of the mind to discern and measure the good of concrete human acts in relation to their ultimate end, which is God. In order to appreciate O'Connor's approach to art, and also how her theological position informs this approach, it is important to note that in the classical understanding morality and art are not opposed; they merely have different proximate ends.

O'Connor draws the two together in relation to her fiction thus: "There is no room for abstract expressions of compassion or piety or morality in the fiction itself. This means that the writer's moral sense must coincide with his dramatic sense" (*MM* 125). For this to happen, O'Connor says that the artist's "moral judgment is part of the very act of seeing" (*MM* 31), suggesting that the ethical and artistic direction of her work cannot be separated from the reason's spiritual vision. In Maritain's discussion of reason's role in the creative act, at the preconscious level and through to the work of art, he is also presenting his view of the inherently visionary nature of reason:[35] "Reason possesses a life both deeper and less conscious than its articulate logical life. For reason indeed does not only articulate, connect, and infer, it also *sees;* and reason's intuitive grasping, *intuitus rationis,* is the primary act and function of that one and single power which is called intellect or reason."[36] O'Connor affirms that the ability to see and discern spiritual reality is central to how reason informs her art, and she explicitly connects seeing with moral insight. She conveys this experience by explaining her view of the artist's intellectual and ethical aims: "Those who believe that art proceeds from a healthy, and not from a diseased, faculty of the mind will take what [the artist] shows them as revelation, not of what we ought to be but of what we are at a given time and under given circumstances; that is, as a limited revelation but revelation nevertheless" (*MM* 34). The health of the mind determines the clarity of the artist's vision and how well the artist is able to reveal not a prescriptive ethical code, but an account of the human condition.

The artist's intellect, in O'Connor's view, participates in a larger order of meaning through the reasoning process; the creation of the work of art can be understood as a revelation because it is not simply created out of the artist's own consciousness. Reason, says Maritain, "must be understood in a much deeper and larger sense than is usual. The intellect, as well as the imagination, is at the core of poetry. But reason, or the intellect, is not merely logical reason."[37] Maritain quotes Aristotle for his description of God as the ordering source of reason: "As in the universe, so in the soul, God moves everything. The starting point of reasoning is not reasoning, but something greater. What, then, could be greater even than knowledge and intellect but God?"[38] God is connected to the reasoning powers of the soul as that which draws out and moves the intellectual pursuit. O'Connor and Maritain both interpret reason according to its classical and Thomistic meaning, and both refer to the inherently spiritual and participatory nature of the soul's power of intellection. In a book review of Maritain's *The Range of Reason,* O'Connor signals the difference between the modern view of reason and the one she shares with Maritain:

> The age of Enlightenment substituted reason for revelation, with the result that confidence in reason has gradually decayed until in the present age, which doubts also fact and value, reason finds few supporters outside of Neo-Thomist philosophy. Maritain's has been one of the major voices in modern philosophy to reassert the primacy of reason. . . . He puts it in the proper perspective, where it serves and not substitutes for revelation."[39]

Maritain locates the modern shift away from the classical understanding of reason toward a reduction of its scope in Descartes, who, "with his clear ideas, divorced intelligence from mystery. . . . The Schoolmen, when they defined beauty by the radiance of the form, in reality defined it by the radiance of a mystery."[40] As Maritain notes, the intellect's perception of beauty was, for the Schoolmen, integral to the experience of mystery. He quotes Aquinas to suggest the transcendent measure of beauty and how human beings come to know it: "Beauty of anything created is nothing else than a similarity of divine beauty participated in by things," so that, in the last analysis, "the existence of all things derives from divine beauty."[41] The language of participation is central to the question of beauty and the human experience of the divine. Maritain explains the participatory nature of the human relationship to beauty by making a distinction between aesthetic and transcendental beauty. He defines transcendental beauty as "the beauty that God beholds," whereas aesthetic beauty is the beauty that is perceived through the human senses. Maritain accounts for the relation between the two: "I would say that aesthetic beauty, which is not all beauty for man but which is the beauty most naturally proportioned to the human mind, is a particular determination of transcendental beauty: it is transcendental beauty as confronting not simply the intellect, but the intellect and the sense acting together in one single act; say, it is transcendental beauty confronting the sense as imbued with intelligence, or intellection as engaged in sense perception."[42]

For O'Connor, the separation of reason and imagination (which Maritain identifies as one of the effects of the Cartesian reduction of reason to the autonomy of the *cogito*) threatens "an end to art," because in the experience of aesthetic beauty it is the *intellect*, combined with the powers of sense perception, that fuels the imagination (*MM* 82). Reason is neither independent nor merely abstract but integral to the soul's movement toward mystery. As Maritain states: "It is by virtue of this transcendental nature of beauty, even aesthetic beauty, that all great poetry awakes in us, one way or another, the sense of our mysterious identity, and draws us toward the sources of being."[43] O'Connor makes a similar comment in regard to her fiction as *poesis*, or poetry: "The fiction writer presents mystery through manners, grace through nature, but when he finishes there always has to be left over that sense of Mystery which cannot be accounted for by any human formula" (*MM* 153).

Reason in Making and Doing: Art and Ethics

O'Connor emphasizes throughout her prose writing that the modern understanding of reason has tended to reduce it to the autonomous calculative workings of the human mind alone. One of the primary effects of this reduction is the divorce of reason from the imagination—which she understood as the imaging faculty of the soul—not only in the realm of art but also in the realm of ethics. O'Connor was interested in the general difference between ancient and modern accounts of reason (the explicit subject of her review of Maritain's book *The Range of Reason*), an interest evident in her concern with distinguishing between the participatory or revelatory experience of reason and an autonomous reasoning power located in the human mind.[44] Her specific concern with the modern, reductive conception of reason and its separation from the imagination was that it inevitably limited the meaning of the experiences of both art and ethics, or making and doing. If the processes of reason are understood to be independent from the envisioning of the imagination, then creativity and moral action are also affected, since, according to O'Connor, both reason and imagination are essential to art and ethical discernment.

O'Connor states that the separation between reason and imagination is one of the separations that are "inimical to art" (*MM* 184). According to O'Connor's aesthetics, art is not simply a product of the human imagination; it is also a product of reason. The difficulty associated with explaining this connection, however, is that the general modern notion of reason is already reduced in scope, as outlined above—reason is understood according to an abstract and autonomous definition of rationality. This is not what O'Connor means when she is speaking about reason, unless of course, she is using the term in a way critical of the modern reduction of the reasoning power of the soul. In fact, O'Connor is often critical of this modern type of rationality in her fictional characters, but her criticism of their excessive rationality is a criticism of the kind of reasoning they employ, not of reason itself. Given this, how reason is defined is crucial for properly interpreting O'Connor's approach to art and the art itself. She has frequently been categorized as an anti-intellectual, or as a religious (i.e., irrational) thinker, because the distinctions she makes between reductive accounts of reason and her Thomistic definition of reason are not fully appreciated. What often happens is that, when one of her characters is presented as an intellectual, the character is misunderstood because the type of rationality he or she expresses is misinterpreted by the reader. It is usually assumed that O'Connor is highly critical of her intellectual characters because they order their lives according to reason instead of faith.[45] But how can it be that O'Connor calls art and what she does as a novelist "reason in making" (*MM* 82) if her fiction is entirely concerned with rejecting reason and the intellect?[46] Precision about the meaning of reason is crucial for understanding O'Connor's intellectual characters, providing one very important example of how a proper understanding of her philosophical-theological ideas can be crucial for the interpretation of her fiction. The intellectual Rayber, in *The Violent Bear It Away,* is not at odds with Mason Tarwater because Rayber lives according to reason and Mason lives according to faith; Rayber's problem lies in his idea that his reasoning powers are entirely human and autonomous without connection to any revelatory or spiritual insight. It is a reductive form of rationality that forces Rayber to fight against the love he feels for Bishop. O'Connor is not critical of the fact that Rayber is an intellectual; her criticism is focused on his belief that rationality is autonomous and completely within his control.

O'Connor tries to restore the classical account of reason in her theoretical discussions in order to describe its relation to imagination in her art.

What she wants to convey is reason's role in creative intuition. She views reason not as a faculty of the mind opposing the imaginative and sensible powers of the soul, but instead as one that needs to be distinguished from and yet related to these other powers. Such a description indicates quite clearly that O'Connor speaks about reason in a profoundly unmodern way. In referring to Aquinas's definition of art as "reason in making" (*MM* 82), she describes it as "a very cold and very beautiful definition" and one that is likely to be an unpopular definition today, owing to the fact that reason "has lost ground among us" in the modern period.

In O'Connor's view, the emphasis on art fed solely by emotion and imagination without due consideration for the role of reason has produced an unbalanced vision of human nature, and this in turn has reduced the perception of mystery. Reason, in its reduced capacity, is no longer understood as necessary for artistic creation, and O'Connor notes that instead of a recovery of the fuller meaning of reason and its relation to art, reason is effectively abandoned in artistic endeavor. She makes this view explicit in her comment about artists who try to rid themselves of reason, and it is obvious that she has little tolerance for the artist's desire to free him- or herself from intellectual integrity:

> If you have read the very vocal writers from San Francisco, you may have got the impression that the first thing you must do in order to be an artist is to loose yourself from the bonds of reason, and thereafter, anything that rolls off the top of your head will be of great value. Anyone's unrestrained feelings are considered worth listening to because they are unrestrained and because they are feelings. (*MM* 82)

O'Connor's discussions of art usually include combined references to both reason and imagination. Primarily she wishes to establish their connection for artistic creation, but at the same time perhaps she hopes to expand the modern understanding of reason. She says, again in a discussion of Maritain and Aquinas on art, that "the person who aims after art in his work aims after truth, in an imaginative sense" (*MM* 65). The pursuit of higher truth—which is the direction and goal of the ancient classical understanding of reason—is coupled with the imagination in the artistic creation. The artist, according to O'Connor, "uses his reason to discover an answering reason in everything he sees. For him, to be reasonable is to find in the object, in the situation, in the sequence, the spirit which makes it itself" (*MM* 82). O'Connor is describing the participatory nature of reason and how this is crucial to the artist's work: reason is not simply the calculative workings of the mind alone, as it creates out of the mental processes of the brain; it is a spiritual faculty that seeks and responds to an order outside the mind. The action of reason is described both in terms of its pursuit and the ensuing dialogue, since what is discovered is the "answering reason" of a spiritually ordered universe.

The spiritually ordered universe that O'Connor discovers is also a morally ordered universe, and so the experience of reason is not only applicable to her aesthetics; it is also formative for her religious ethics.[47] The modern reduction of reason has also affected the expression of religious ethics by assigning all moral deliberation to an unthinking faith, or an inspired but unreasoned vision. In a letter to a college student who was confused about the role of reason in religious faith, O'Connor writes: "Learn what you can, but cultivate Christian skepticism. It will keep you free—not to do anything you please, but free to be formed by something larger than your own intellect or the intellects of those around you" (*HB* 478). Her emphasis is on the cultivation of the intellect in religious inquiry and the exercise of doubt, but at the same time she urges her correspondant to recognize that the intellect participates in a life larger than the human mind. She counsels him to avoid narrowing his intellectual focus, especially in a restrictive anti-Christian intellectual climate: "For every book you read that is anti-Christian, make it your business to read one that presents the other side of the picture" (*HB* 477).

Ethical deliberation is not restricted to the autonomous workings of the individual human mind. Because it recognizes human dependence, the ethic of responsibility in O'Connor's fiction is based in community, and this means that the very nature of moral decision making must transcend individualistic interests. Characters such as Buford Munson and the woman at the filling station in *The Violent Bear It Away* remind Tarwater of his responsibilities on the most immediate and local level. O'Connor's religious ethics are not primarily concerned with the right or wrong view of ethical matters; instead, she is interested in the question of how human beings are spiritually and morally interconnected and thus responsible for others in view of that connection. To emphasize the importance of a larger intellectual and spiritual framework is, for O'Connor, to expand the role of reason in ethics beyond individualistic and selfish motivations.

As a religious artist with ethical concerns O'Connor was aware of how a reductionist view of reason affected the moral imagination. The human experiences of God are not understood by her to be unreasonable or without the active role of both reason and imagination.[48] Keeping in mind the reductionist account of reason in relation to art discussed above, it seems obvious that this reduction will have similar effects on the understanding of religious ethics and that O'Connor would have comparable objections. If reason is narrowly defined as calculative rationality, or autonomous cogitation, there is little that unites it with concrete moral experiences: it is limited to logic or calculation, and centered on independent human thought. The effects, according to O'Connor are stifling to the artistic and the ethical imagination:

> One of the effects of modern liberal Protestantism has been gradually to turn religion into poetry and therapy, to make truth vaguer and vaguer and more and more relative, to banish intellectual distinctions, to depend on feeling instead of thought and gradually to come to believe that God has no power, that he cannot communicate with us, cannot reveal himself to us, indeed has not done so, and that religion is our own sweet invention. (*HB* 479)

To limit the reasoning power of human beings to their own resources, as if reason were an autonomous faculty, has negatively affected modern ethical reflection, according to O'Connor, because it relativizes religious experience by situating it entirely in the human consciousness. The implication for ethics is obvious: the loss of "intellectual distinctions," as O'Connor notes, has the effect of rooting moral discernment in individual, feeling-centered judgments. To focus on the role of reason in ethics does not mean that moral deliberation is entirely ruled by the intellect. Instead, O'Connor's Thomist-inspired discussions of art and morality assume the combined action of reason and love: while art is the imaginative 'making' of the practical intellect, morality, or ethics, is the 'doing' of the practical intellect through love. Although reason is central to religious thought, love is what connects human beings to each other and to God: "Satisfy your demand for reason always but remember that charity is beyond reason, and that God can be known through charity" (*HB* 480).

O'Connor elaborates this experience of knowing God through love in another letter: "Bridges once wrote Gerard Manley Hopkins and asked him to tell him how he, Bridges, could believe. He must have expected from Hopkins a long philosophical answer. Hopkins wrote back, 'Give alms.' He was trying to say to Bridges that God is to be experienced in Charity (in the sense of love for the divine image in human beings)" (*HB* 476–77). O'Connor adds her own interpretation to Hopkins's account with her parenthetical remark: God is experienced through the love of other human beings who are created in the image of God. Most significantly, O'Connor identifies charity as a responsibility for others *because* the divine image is in them. The spiritual worth of every person is confirmed by this spiritual communion that all human beings share. As *virtues* of the practical intellect, both art and ethics are ultimately about love. Says Augustine, "Virtus est ordo amoris"—virtue is the order of love,[49] meaning that all virtues are expressions of the divine order of love. When O'Connor uses the word *virtue* to describe the intellectual activity of the artist, she understands virtue to be an expression of the love of God. Love is what orders reality, and for O'Connor, making good art and the ethic of responsibility are both informed by the order of love. Just as O'Connor does not want to separate the experience of reason and imagination, or reason and love, Maritain states that "undeviating love is the supreme rule . . . love presupposes intellect; without it love can do nothing, and, in tending to the beautiful, love tends to what can delight the intellect."[50]

Finally, for O'Connor, love is the ordering force of reality, and though transcendent, it is found and experienced in human relations. O'Connor's prophetic art is an investigation into the mystery of reality as it is lived through love; her religious ideas are not applied as formulas to the experiences of her characters or used to interpret them. Instead, her characters discover the ordering of love and the ethic of responsibility in their experiences of reality. O'Connor appeals to the transcendent order of reality to clarify her understanding of what makes good art and good religious ethics:

> The virtues of art, like the virtues of faith, are such that they reach beyond the limitations of the intellect, beyond any mere theory that a writer may entertain. If the novelist is doing what as an artist he is bound to do, he will inevitably suggest that image of ultimate reality as it can be glimpsed in some aspect of the human situation. In this sense, art reveals, and the theologian has learned that he can't ignore it. (*MM* 158)

O'Connor does not simply present the order of love as her particular religious view, but as a way of seeing into the nature of the human experience of reality. While she sees reality as morally ordered, she is not concerned with formulating her ideas doctrinally because she is a novelist, not a theological ethicist. Yet while she does not attempt to convert her readers to her religious understanding, she does not thereby abandon all judgment about such matters. She acknowledges how she can, as an artist, be of interest to the theologian, insofar as the insights of art contribute to theological and ethical reflection. As a prophetic novelist, O'Connor makes a claim about her insight into reality, which requires the visionary capacities of reason as well as the imagination. For her, the good novelist not only "finds a symbol and a way of lodging it," she will also be implicitly suggesting "to the intelligent reader whether this feeling is adequate or inadequate, whether it is moral or immoral, whether it is good or evil. And [her] theology, even in its most remote reaches, will have a direct bearing on this" (*MM* 156).

Prophetic Vision

In addition to the separations between nature and grace and reason and imagination noted by O'Connor, she describes another common separation, which "we see in our society and which exist[s] in our writing," between vision and judgment (*MM* 184). O'Connor's response to the separation of vision from judgment is found in her account of prophetic vision, which combines the act of seeing with judging what is seen. In O'Connor's writing there is an implicit recognition that prophetic insight is not just about observing: what is seen is also measured by something greater than itself. This account of prophetic vision shifts our discussion to O'Connor's understanding of the artist's responsibility in the creation of art. As a prophetic novelist, O'Connor considers herself accountable for her insight into the nature of reality and for the judgments implicit in describing what she sees. The responsibility she feels in this role is a moral one, insofar as her vision of reality is shared with others to whom she is in some measure accountable, but this does not mean that the prophetic artist must be morally perfect (a topic I will address shortly in Aquinas's discussion of prophecy). O'Connor knew that the moral responsibility of the artist could not be understood absolutely. She does not claim that the novelist can somehow prevent "corrupting those who are not able to understand what he is doing," because "to force this kind of total responsibility on the novelist is to burden him with the business that belongs only to God" (*MM* 187). O'Connor's advice is for the writer to return to the good of the art, where he can focus on the "order, proportion, and radiance" of what he is creating (*MM* 189).

As a novelist who saw herself in a prophetic role, O'Connor's sacramental theology is expressed ethically in her desire to bring vision and judgment together. Unlike her aesthetically focused discussions of Maritain, O'Connor's use of the term *prophecy*—both in a novel like *The Violent Bear*

It Away and in her essays about the novelist's vision—marks a shift in language: here, she places less emphasis on philosophical formulations about the intellect and more on the biblical world of prophets, sin, and morality. In order to appreciate how O'Connor understood the prophetic novelist's responsibility, I will consider the Thomistic account of prophecy that she read in the *Summa Theologiae*. Unlike her discussions about art, which are often focused on Maritain's Thomistic thought, O'Connor's references to prophecy derive largely from her direct reading of Aquinas. It is also appropriate to focus on O'Connor's reading of Aquinas because of his use of biblical references, which are less common in Maritain. Aquinas's account of prophecy combines philosophical discussions of the intellect—the knowing that accompanies prophecy—with images and examples from the biblical prophetic tradition. In this way Aquinas's writing provides a helpful model for understanding O'Connor's ability to blend together her philosophical, theological, and biblical ideas.

Since the focus of the prophetic function is, for O'Connor, centered on the drawing together of vision and moral judgment, ethical questions are at the heart of her work as a novelist. In the conversation between O'Connor's sacramental theology and her incarnational aesthetics, the notion of prophetic vision provides a focus for understanding her morally imbued stories. She acknowledges that her fiction incorporates the spiritual nature of vision or insight, which Maritain attributes to reason's intuitive powers, and the prophetic, a biblical term referring to the communication and ordering of relations between God and human beings. Her self-description as prophetic novelist implies a connection between her insight into the nature of reality and her presentation of how human beings choose to live within that reality. Philosophical and biblical concerns are united in O'Connor's thought because her art, like her theology, is incarnational. Art is never portrayed as an abstract entity in either Maritain's or O'Connor's aesthetics.[51] As Maritain describes it, art is related to human life insofar as it is the product of the human mind, imagination and desire:

> Art does not reside in an angelic mind; it resides in a soul which animates a living body . . . [and so] art is therefore basically dependent upon everything which the human community, spiritual tradition and history transmit to the body and mind of man. By its human subject and its human roots, art belongs to a time and a country.[52]

For Maritain—and for O'Connor, who regularly mentioned the importance of regional manners in a writer's work—this is the reason that "the most universal and the most human works are those which bear most openly the marks of their country."[53] O'Connor also refers to the significance of the writer's country in terms that are both physical and spiritual, again reflecting her sacramental view of reality. For her, the word *country* "suggests everything from the actual countryside that the novelist describes, on to and through the peculiar characteristics of his region and his nation, and on, through, and under all of these to his true country, which the writer with Christian concerns will consider to be what is eternal and absolute" (*MM* 27).

Since the prophetic novelist both sees and judges what is seen, according to O'Connor, the novelist is never neutral: "The fiction writer is an observer, first, last, and always, but he cannot be an adequate observer unless he is free from uncertainty about what he sees" (*MM* 178). O'Connor recognizes that regardless of the artist's beliefs, neutrality is impossible in the writing of fiction: "Those who have no absolute values cannot let the relative remain merely relative; they are always raising it [i.e., the relative] to the level of the absolute" (*MM* 178). It should be noted that O'Connor does not interpret her prophetic role as her own; she felt her responsibility not only in relation to her readers and her own imagination, but also in relation to the church:

> For the Catholic novelist, the prophetic vision is not simply a matter of his personal imaginative gift; it is also a matter of the Church's gift. . . . It is one of the functions of the Church to transmit the prophetic vision that is good for all time, and when the novelist has this as part of his own vision, he has a powerful extension of sight. (*MM* 179–80)

The responsibility that the gift of prophetic vision requires is the willingness to measure what the artist sees in light of what is unseen; it is to see in relation to what is "good for all time."

During a 1955 television interview with Harvey Breit, O'Connor explained that "a serious novelist is in pursuit of reality."[54] The pursuit of reality may not sound like much of a claim, but for O'Connor discerning the nature of reality was central to her profession as a prophetic novelist. O'Connor is aware that her approach to writing might be unpopular, since the idea "that reality is something to which we must be returned at considerable cost, is one which is seldom understood by the casual reader, but it is one which is implicit in the Christian view of the world" (*MM* 112). As a self-described "Christian realist" (*HB* 92), O'Connor often faced the assumption from critics that her Christian belief hindered her freedom to see and to penetrate the meaning of reality. She resists this assumption regularly in her writing, arguing instead that "there is no reason why fixed dogma should fix anything that the writer sees in the world. On the contrary, dogma is an instrument for penetrating reality" (*MM* 178). O'Connor emphatically proclaims that religious belief extends rather than diminishes the artist's prophetic insight into reality.

She argues that, while "the Catholic fiction writer is entirely free to observe" (*MM* 178), the incarnational nature of fiction is binding: "By the time we are able to use our imaginations for fiction, we find that our senses have responded irrevocably to a certain reality. This discovery of being bound through the senses to a particular society and a particular history, to particular sounds and a particular idiom, is for the writer the beginning of a recognition that first puts his work into real human perspective for him. . . . He discovers that the imagination is not free, but bound" (*MM* 197). Interestingly, what O'Connor describes as binding for the religious writer is not religion as much as region and the commitment to portraying the texture of life known through the senses.[55] Her point is, again, sacramental and her argument is voiced against "those Manichean-type theologies which sees the natural world as unworthy of penetration." A sacramental theology will encourage the writer to "penetrate the natural human world as it is" (*MM* 163). O'Connor argues that writers cannot rid themselves of the constraints of matter in order to convey the spirit of what they want to express: "They would like to eliminate the region altogether and approach the infinite directly. . . . This is not even a possibility" (*MM* 198). The responsibility of the prophetic artist is to remain true to the texture and matter of life as well as its spiritual meaning, without reducing reality to either one or the other.

How, then, does O'Connor understand her *Christian* sacramental vision in relation to her description of the artist's pursuit of reality? She believes in one "Reality" that transcends all distinctions, and yet at the same time she identifies her position with the term "Christian Realism" (*HB* 92). This attempt to be precise about language raises some interesting questions about how her Christian vision relates to her prophetic art. Is her Christian realism part, or all, of the one Reality she attempts to describe? O'Connor argues that reality transcends the human beings who participate in it, although what the writer is trying to see and understand is that reality:

All novelists are fundamentally seekers and describers of the real, but the realism of each novelist will depend on his view of the ultimate reaches of reality . . . if the writer believes that our life is and will remain essentially mysterious, if he looks upon us as beings existing in a created order to whose laws we freely respond, then what he sees on the surface will be of interest to him only as he can go through it into an experience of mystery itself. (*MM* 41)

O'Connor argues that the "Catholic novel can't be categorized by subject matter, but only by what it assumes about human and divine reality (*MM* 196).[56]

Without a doubt, O'Connor's "view of the ultimate reaches of reality" is Christian and sacramental. Rather than seeing this as a narrowing of her prophetic vision, it is worth the effort to consider how complex and expansive that vision is. O'Connor's religious thought incorporates philosophy, theology, biblical symbolism, ethics, and aesthetics, and any serious appreciation of her thought cannot avoid this diversity. Her language concerning aesthetics is philosophical, following Maritain, yet she also writes with a powerful prophetic voice in her essays and her fiction. The difference in language, however, may sometimes be perceived as a disjunction between her ideas and her art. It is certainly difficult to fathom how her elevated Thomistic accounts of art can be connected to her portrayal of characters like Mason Tarwater in *The Violent Bear It Away*. How are we to relate O'Connor's use of the classical philosophical account of the intellect's role in the creation of art to the less mediated biblical images in her stories? There is an emphasis on action, judgment, vision, and biblical prophecy in O'Connor's fictional work, and yet, as we have seen in the preceding section, her discussion of art as a virtue of the practical intellect in her essays is formulated in relation to the philosophical influences of Maritain and Aquinas.

Rather than interpreting this apparent difference of language as indicative of a divide between O'Connor's aesthetics and her religious ethical concern—already problematic if one is mindful of the fact that for her both art and ethics operate under the rubric of the practical intellect—we should consider how O'Connor interprets the prophetic novelist as joining these together. To use Maritain's philosophical language, we can say that O'Connor's prose writing about art is focused on the 'making' aspect of the intellect, whereas the actual stories she writes, portraying human lives, requires the artist's judgments to enter the ethical realm of 'doing.' The difference is a matter of ends, but both are related as virtues of the practical intellect. The basis for O'Connor's philosophical aesthetics is ultimately to create the good work that reflects God, and this is in no way opposed to the religious ethics discernible in her fiction; both are about seeing, but the seeing cannot be, in O'Connor's view, separated from a judgment about what is seen. As a

Christian writer, O'Connor is not willing to provide "something a little more palatable to the modern temper," where all judgment is withheld in favor of a more relative view: "We are asked to form our consciences in the light of statistics, which is to establish the relative as absolute" (*MM* 30). Instead O'Connor argues that "moral judgment is part of the very act of seeing" (*MM* 31). O'Connor speaks directly about this combined action of seeing and judging in her essays and letters, but her stories render that combination in the lives and choices of her characters.

O'Connor's prophetic insight is especially directed toward the human experiences of limitation, which is essential to her work as a writer: "Drama usually bases itself on the bedrock of original sin. . . . For this reason the greatest dramas naturally involve the salvation or loss of the soul" (*MM* 167). In the aesthetic works of Maritain used by O'Connor, he rarely addresses the limitation of human knowing in relation to sin, but when he does, he does not explain human limitation negatively, as a lack or a willful deficiency, but positively, as the human confrontation with mystery. In O'Connor's view, sin is one such human mystery. On this question, O'Connor and Aquinas are more closely aligned: both speak more directly to the defect in human knowing, attributable to human fallenness through sin brought about by the conscious choice of the will.[57] Art is an experiential encounter with the mystery of existence, and, as O'Connor reminds one of her correspondents: "Part of the mystery of existence is sin. When we think about the Crucifixion, we miss the point of it if we don't think about sin" (*HB* 143).

What O'Connor wants to pursue dramatically in her fiction is not just the limitation of human knowing in the face of mystery, but the willful refusal even to look at or consider that mystery. The free human choice, however, is always a real choice, with real consequences. O'Connor's stories expose the nature of human sin by portraying how human beings fail to love God, themselves, and each other. The ethic of responsibility, far from being a dogmatically prescribed code, is rooted in love. O'Connor's understanding of responsibility is grounded in her two main sources on prophecy: the biblical prophets themselves and Thomas Aquinas. The Hebrew prophets were less interested in displays of religious conduct than they were in the imperatives of righteousness: providing for others who were in need. Isaiah 58:6 states clearly the ethic of responsibility: "Is not this the fast that I choose; to loose the bonds of wickedness . . . to let the oppressed go free, and to break every yoke? Is it not to share your bread with the hungry, and bring the homeless poor into your house?"[58] The prophetic tradition, according to the sources with which O'Connor was familiar, is directed toward how the relationship between Creator and creature is best ordered and lived out in human relationships.

O'Connor's understanding of the biblical prophetic tradition is extremely important for dispelling the idea that she had a morally rigid or legalistic approach to justice. In Kathleen Feeley's book on O'Connor, our attention is helpfully drawn to the many theological texts and biblical studies that were influential for O'Connor's thought.[59] Feeley notes some of the various sources for O'Connor's study of prophecy: Bruce Vawter's *The Conscience of Israel,* Eric Voegelin's *Israel and Revelation,* Martin Buber,[60] and, as already mentioned, Thomas Aquinas's *De Veritate* and parts of the *Summa,*[61] One of these texts, namely Voegelin's *Israel and Revelation,* is reproduced in part by Feeley in *Voice of the Peacock,* and she indicates that this passage is reproduced as it was marked by O'Connor in her own copy. The passage from Voegelin is significant for our discussion here because it redirects the focus of the prophetic call away from a moralistically legal orientation, toward an account of existence ordered by love and humility under the Creator. Voegelin says that it is the particular prophetic insight of Israelite history that "existence under God means love, humility and righteousness of action rather than legality of conduct."[62] This expression of the prophet's concern is also echoed in O'Connor's reading of Thomas Aquinas. In a succession of letters to Betty Hester written in 1959–60, O'Connor makes it clear that she depends on Aquinas not only for her use of the prophetic voice as a novelist, but also for her portrayal of the prophet in *The Violent Bear It Away*: "I have found a lucky find for me in St. Thomas' sections of the *Summa* and the *De Veritate* on prophecy. . . . Thomas says that prophetic vision is dependent on the imagination of the prophet, not his moral life; and that there is a distinction that must be made between having prophetic vision and the proclamation of the same" (*HB* 367).[63]

Prophetic knowing, or revelation, according to Aquinas, is a manner of seeing things that not only relate to human beings but also to God. In the *Summa Theologiae,* Aquinas describes the substance of this kind of vision: "Prophetic revelation is about things pertaining to spiritual substances, by whom we are urged to good or evil; this pertains to the discernment of spirits."[64] But, for both O'Connor and Aquinas, the discernment of spirits is not a disembodied act, and our corporeal nature guarantees that the experience of sight, both spiritual and physical, is connected to our experience in the sensible world. The prophetic novelist is, as O'Connor puts it, "a realist of distances" (*MM* 44) who seeks to widen the view of the imagination to include and reveal the hidden spiritual realities that are present in the everyday of human experience.[65] F. C. Copleston suggests that Aquinas's account of the human dependence on sense perception and the imagination does not thereby limit or "destroy its openness to reality in a wider sense than material reality"; instead "it means that in its present life the human mind can know spiritual or super-sensible reality only in so far as it is manifested in the material world."[66] As a prophetic novelist with a sacramental theology, O'Connor sees her writing as the discernment of reality within the sensible experiences of her characters' lives: "Every serious novelist is trying to portray reality as it manifests itself in our concrete, sensual life" (*MM* 170).

In order to understand in more detail O'Connor's debt to Thomas Aquinas on prophecy, and to suggest how that influence might contribute to an ethical interpretation of O'Connor's fiction, it is useful to engage further particular aspects of Aquinas's account of prophecy. I would like to focus on three specific questions regarding prophecy: (1) Is prophecy only a matter of faith, or does it pertain also to knowledge? (2) Is prophecy to be understood primarily as a means of forecasting the future? and (3) Must the prophet be of a particular moral standing as a prerequisite for prophesying? While the third question is most often mentioned by O'Connor, Aquinas's answers to all three questions accord with her basic views: prophecy does not assume a separation between faith and knowledge, it is not about predicting future events, and the prophet does not have to be a paragon of virtue. Implicit for Aquinas in the connection between knowledge and faith is a more expansive meaning of knowledge, defined in the sense of spiritual insight and wisdom rather than the acquisition of information or facts. The cultivation of wisdom requires the active participation of the intellect, the exercise of discipline, and the willingness to bear the responsibility that such insight carries with it. Insight into spiritual reality, as opposed to the forecasting of events to come, means that the prophet is present in the spiritual experiences of daily life as they are seen beneath the surface. The prophet's gaze is not directed toward the future so much as it is directed to the spiritual mystery of the present. Finally, the ethical view of the prophetic novelist suggests most forcibly that there is no prescriptive or determinative relation between the imaginative vision of the artist and the exercise of moral judgment.

The first question to address, since it affects all of the others, is the relation of prophecy to knowledge and faith. Aquinas does not separate faith from knowledge; in fact, he incorporates faith under prophetic knowing. Aquinas categorizes prophecy as the encompassing term for all kinds of knowing, including the spiritual vision of the mind, faith, and the pursuit of wisdom: "Now all things pertaining to knowledge may be comprised under *prophecy,* since prophetic revelation extends not only to future events relating to man, but also to things relating to God, both as to those which are to be believed by all and are matters of *faith,* and as to yet higher mysteries, which concern the perfect and belong to *wisdom*" (II–II, q. 171). To understand the connection between prophecy and knowledge and, further, the nature of prophetic knowledge, we can begin with the first article of question 171, where Aquinas asks whether prophecy pertains to knowledge.[67] After the objections, his answer begins with a quotation from 1 Kings 9:9, which suggests the connection between prophecy and vision because an older description of the prophet used the term "seer" to refer to those who had spiritual insight or vision. Aquinas adds to the quotation from Kings by asserting the correlation among sight, knowledge, and prophecy: "For he that is now called a prophet, in time past was called a seer. Now sight pertains to knowledge. Therefore prophecy pertains to knowledge" (II–II, q. 171, art. 1). The vision of the seer or prophet is characterized by the knowledge of things unseen or invisible, and the language of sight in relation to what is unseen refers to spiritual vision, or insight, known through the intellect and otherwise hidden to common sight. As Aquinas states: "Prophets know things that are far removed from man's knowledge. Wherefore they may be said to take their name from *apparition,* because things appear to them from afar . . . , in the Old Testament, they were called Seers, because they saw what others saw not, and surveyed things hidden in mystery" (II–II, q. 171, art. 1).[68] To survey "things hidden in mystery" suggests that the seer or prophet can know, and hence convey, something about that mystery. The insight is not simply a vision that the prophet possesses in isolation; it is meant to be expressed and shared because the mystery that the prophet seeks to know ultimately is God.

Thus, the knowledge of the prophet is not without purpose or expression. Aquinas notes that "prophecy consists secondarily in speech" in order to instruct others with "the things [the prophets] know through being taught of God." Prophetic knowledge, rather than being the prophet's own wisdom, is "taught by God," and therefore an important part of the prophet's task is to teach the knowledge of his vision. Prophetic knowledge, according to Aquinas, necessarily comes from God, in contrast to the knowledge of the false prophet, who speaks for himself rather than for God. In his account of the false prophets' error, Aquinas quotes from Jeremiah and Ezekiel: "They speak a vision of their own heart, and not out of the mouth of the Lord" and "Woe to the foolish prophets, that follow their own spirit, and see nothing." The implication is that the source of all prophetic knowledge is God, but this fact should not be understood simply, as though the prophet plays the role of a mouthpiece only.

The fourth objection in article 1 addresses this issue with a discussion of inspiration, which questions the active role of the prophet's intellect. The objection states that because inspiration, denoting motion, concerns the affections and because revelation concerns the intellect, if prophecy is characterized as inspired speech, then "it would seem that prophecy does not pertain to the intellect more than to the affections." Aquinas responds to this objection by suggesting that both inspiration and revelation are part of prophecy, insofar as "inspiration is requisite for prophecy, as regards the raising of the mind," and revelation is necessary "as regards the very perception of Divine things, whereby prophecy is completed" (II–II, q. 171, art. 1). What can be understood from this discussion is that the experience of the prophet is an intellectually active one because, as Aquinas says, the mind of the prophet must be raised and receptive to the revelation of divine things. It is a participatory action. The false prophet acts independently, without the intellectual ascent, by speaking his own truth and not participating in the truth of God. For both Aquinas and O'Connor, all knowledge of the mysteries of human beings and God is included, to various degrees, in the activity of prophecy. The difference between true and false prophets is not simply that one has the knowledge of God and the other does not; the difference lies primarily in the orientation of the knowledge of these prophets—that is, the manner in which the mind of each type is directed. The false prophet, says Aquinas, speaks out of a claim to his own knowledge, independently of divine revelation, whereas the true prophet understands that the knowledge revealed to him comes from his participation in the truth of God. This language of orientation fits with those lines from Aquinas above (II–II, q. 171), where knowledge is described as something received in faith (acknowledging the limitations of human knowing) and as something pursued in the ascent to wisdom (knowing understood as a participation in God's perfection, not as a human possession).

Aquinas's second point concerning prophecy addresses its association with predicting the future. This is probably the most common assumption about prophecy, and although prescience does play a role in the biblical prophets, in Aquinas's account the purpose of prophecy is not limited to forecasting future events.[69] O'Connor says that the writer must "make his gaze extend beyond the surface, beyond mere problems, until it touches the realm which is the concern of prophets and poet" (*MM* 45). It is necessary to distinguish how for O'Connor prophetic vision is about seeing in a different way, not simply about seeing into the future. She describes the prophet as "seeing near things with their extensions of meaning and thus of seeing far things close up" (*MM* 44–45). The question of how prophecy is related to seeing what is distant, not with regard to time but with regard to spiritual reality, is at the heart of O'Connor's interest in the significance of what the spiritual insight of the prophet can reveal: "Prophecy is a matter of seeing, not saying" (*HB* 372).

In the third article of question 171, Aquinas asks whether prophecy is only about future contingencies, and he replies that prophecy is not limited to the future, but can refer to the past and the present also. Given this, he explains how the diversity of prophetic revelation extends to many things: "Now prophetic knowledge comes through a Divine light, whereby it is possible to know all things both Divine and human, both spiritual and corporeal; and consequently the prophetic revelation extends to them all" (II–II, q. 171, art. 3). The reason, however, that prophetic knowledge is often associated with the future is because one of the prime characteristics of prophetic knowledge is that it concerns things "remote from our knowledge." Clearly, the future is remote temporally, but there are things remote from our knowledge spiritually and intellectually as well. Aquinas clarifies the various levels of remoteness and suggests that "the more remote things are from our knowledge the more pertinent they are to prophecy." There are three degrees of remoteness according to Aquinas: (1) things remote from the knowledge, either sensitive or intellective, of some particular man, but not from the knowledge of all men; (2) things that surpass the knowledge of all men without exception, not because these things are in themselves unknowable, but because of a defect in human knowledge; (3) things remote from the knowledge of all men, through being in themselves unknowable; such are future contingencies, the truth of which is indeterminate (II–II, q. 171, art. 3).

Given these varying degrees of human knowledge, the question of whether prophecy is natural to the soul arises as an issue of human-divine relations. How does the human mind perceive and know spiritually? O'Connor's discussion of the participatory experience of spiritual and intellectual knowing is related to Aquinas's account of prophetic knowing, of what is natural to human knowledge and what is revealed through divine revelation. In the first article of the *Summa* (II–II, q. 172), Aquinas asks whether prophecy can be natural. The objections, in their positive responses, point to the powers of the soul to see into the future and to sometimes know what is to come. Aquinas's primary reply is that prophecy cannot be willed by man at any time and that the source of prophetic knowledge comes not from nature but "through the gift of the Holy Ghost." The language of the "gift" of her prophetic vision and her art is often used by O'Connor: "There is no excuse for anyone to write fiction for public consumption unless he has been called to do so by the presence of a gift" (*MM* 81), and "for the Catholic novelist, the prophetic vision is not simply a matter of his personal imaginative gift" (*MM* 179). Here she acknowledges both the source and orientation of the "gift" of prophecy.

Prophetic knowledge, defined generally as that which is remote from human knowledge, always proceeds from a divine source. Aquinas elaborates his answer, however, by referring to the possibility of "prophetic foreknowledge" (II–II, q. 172, art. 1), occurring in two ways, as befits divine and human knowing. It is proper to the divine intellect, according to Aquinas, that future things are known "as they are in themselves," whereas "future things can be foreknown in their causes with a natural knowledge even by man: thus a physician foreknows future health or death in certain causes." From this, Aquinas explains that the natural foreknowledge proper to human beings can be experienced in two ways. First, he describes the way the soul knows, as understood by Plato, "who held that our souls have knowledge of all things by participating in the ideas; but that this knowledge is obscured in them by union with the body." He agrees more explicitly with Aristotle, however, and echoes the argument that "the soul acquires knowledge from sensibles." Aquinas suggests that instead of assuming that the body hinders the soul's knowing, it is through the body and sensible experience, joined with man's imaginative power, that a human being can acquire some knowledge of the future. Above all, and this is Aquinas's final point, the prophetic foreknowledge that is natural to human beings is secondary to the prophetic foreknowledge of divine revelation for two reasons: first, divine revelation can be about anything, and infallibly so; second, divine prophecy is "according to the unchangeable truth" (II–II, q. 172, art. 1).

Finally, in addressing this issue of the distinction between human knowing (through natural reasoning) and divine communication through revelation, Aquinas asks whether the prophet always distinguishes the insight of his own spirit from his instruction by the prophetic spirit. He responds by arguing that "the prophet's mind is instructed by God in two ways: in one way by an express revelation, in another way by a most mysterious instinct" (II–II, q. 171, art. 5). In order, then, to establish the different degrees of certainty in the prophet's knowledge, Aquinas specifies two ways in which the prophet participates in the knowledge of God: by divine revelation and by the knowledge gained through a "mysterious instinct." According to Aquinas, an express revelation of God would necessarily be known with certainty, because otherwise someone like Abraham would not have been willing to sacrifice his only son in response to the command. He contrasts the certainty of a divine revelation with things known by a mysterious instinct, and sometimes those things, being mingled with the thoughts of one's own spirit, "are not all manifested with prophetic certitude, for this instinct is something imperfect in the genus of prophecy" (II–II, q. 171, art. 5). In response to those who wonder why she writes about violence and ugliness, O'Connor says, "though the good is the ultimate reality, the ultimate reality has been weakened in human beings as a result of the Fall, and it is this weakened life that we see. . . . What one sees is given by circumstances and by the nature of one's particular kind of perception" (*MM* 179). Here we have O'Connor's specific mention of the "defect" in human knowing, voiced in the biblical language of the Fall, to which Aquinas also refers, and we have her awareness of the fact that, despite this weakened human vision, she can affirm that "the good is the ultimate reality." The pivotal question for O'Connor is the responsive choice and the manner in which the human being approaches divine knowledge. The "mysterious instinct" is mysterious primarily insofar as it can be ignored, pursued, or rejected, and O'Connor is aware of the fact that some seek its source and others do not. The issue is not a matter of knowing differently according to different natures, but of the direction or orientation of one's knowledge.

The third and final question in our consideration of Aquinas's account of prophecy is whether the prophet must be morally good. In order to clarify the relation between prophecy and ethics in O'Connor's thought, some attention should be drawn to her regular use of Aquinas's idea that prophetic vision is not primarily a moral faculty, but an imaginative one (*MM* 179). This clarification is important in two respects: first, for O'Connor's claim to be a prophetic novelist, and second, for her presentation of prophecy in her fiction, particularly in *The Violent Bear It Away*. In the first instance, Aquinas's distinction means for O'Connor that the ends pursued in her fiction are not solely moral ones; the primary task is seeing the nature of reality so that the moral implications will be evident in the vision itself. O'Connor writes that "the fiction writer should be characterized by his kind of vision. His kind of vision is prophetic vision," and she adds that "prophecy, which is dependent on the imaginative and not the moral faculty, need not be a matter of predicting the future" (*MM* 179). When O'Connor adopts Aquinas's description of prophetic vision as imaginative rather than moral, her point is not to remove the ethical dimension from seeing, but to deepen the mystery of moral order through our experience of sight. O'Connor interprets this idea in Aquinas: what the artist sees in the world and how the artist sees that world ordered are both dependent upon imaginative vision, which draws primarily upon the artist's sensed experience of the world.[70] The ethical implications, judgments, and interpretations of what is seen are combined with the artist's imaginative expression and representation of the vision. O'Connor believes that with the artist's capacity to see—as it is experienced through the senses and known through spiritual insight—comes the need for moral discernment about the value of what is seen. Moral judgment is a central job of the novelist:

> I think the novelist does more than just show us how a man feels. I think he also makes a judgment on the value of that feeling. It may not be an overt judgment, probably it will be sunk in the work but it is there because in the good novel, judgment is not separated from vision.[71]

O'Connor's reference to Aquinas's distinction between the imaginative and the moral faculty of the artist's prophetic vision is essential to this discussion because O'Connor's Catholic beliefs are often interpreted simply as introjections determining her moral judgments in the fiction.[72] Instead, O'Connor explicitly rejects the idea that she operates with some kind of theory concerning the moral basis of fiction:

> The subject of the moral basis of fiction is one of the most complicated and I don't doubt that I contradict myself on it, for I have no foolproof aesthetic theory. However, I think we are talking about different things or mean different things here by moral basis. I continue to think that art doesn't require rectitude of the appetite but this is not to say that it does not have (fiction anyway) a moral basis. I identify this with James' *felt life* and not with any particular moral system. (*HB* 123–24)

O'Connor always distinguishes between the personal morality of the artist and the ethical meaning embedded within the art. As she writes, simply: "St. Thomas' remark is plain enough: you don't have to be good to write well. Much to be thankful for" (*HB* 103).

The artist's personal moral status is unimportant for producing good art, but that fact does not diminish the ethical implications of the fiction itself. The difference is that one approach to interpreting the moral basis of fiction is to see it rooted in the author's personality, while the other recognizes the author's search for and experience of a larger moral order that is then reflected in the fiction. O'Connor's lack of concern with the artist's personal morality is not a statement of modesty; she is attempting to relocate the order of moral experience as grounded in reality and perceived through the artist's vision of the world rather than through a projection of the artist's beliefs.[73] To dismiss the particular morality of the novelist does not mean that one must no longer contend with the ethical implications of the art; O'Connor insists repeatedly that the imaginative vision of the artist has moral significance,[74] whether it is acknowledged or not.

For O'Connor, the artist's vision, which is always tied to the power of intellection and directed to the "image of its source, the image of ultimate reality" (*MM* 157), is occupied with the good that is made, and this good reflects that image of reality most perfectly. Her prophetic vision should be characterized neither as a religious projection that is morally prescriptive nor as the product of an artistic imagination severed from moral relevance. As a novelist O'Connor understands her prophetic vision in such a way that the moral ends of her work are crucial, but they must remain subordinate to the ultimate end of the art. But, given our earlier discussion, if the virtues of art and prudence are both within the order of the practical intellect, why would art be seen as not contributing specifically to moral instruction or inspiration? The decisive point is that any effects, moral or otherwise, of the artist's vision are grounded in the artist's focus on the source and image of ultimate reality; yet when art is understood as being intended for moral instruction, the focus is centered on human action. For O'Connor, art transcends usefulness, even in a moral sense, in that the good of what is made reflects the divine source of goodness, God. O'Connor's understanding of prophetic vision and its relation to art and ethics explains why the separation between reason and imagination, or between religious belief and art, is not valid for her self-understanding as an artist. She makes this self-understanding clear in her reference to Aquinas, by reaffirming that her purpose as an artist is to make something good in itself:

> St. Thomas Aquinas says that art does not require rectitude of the appetite, that it is wholly concerned with the good of that which is made. He says that a work of art is a good in itself, and this is a truth that the modern world has largely forgotten. We are not content to stay within our limitations and make something that is simply a good

in and by itself. Now we want to make something that will have some utilitarian value. Yet what is good in itself glorifies God because it reflects God. The artist has his hands full and does his duty if he attends to his art. (*MM* 171)

The question of how the prophet measures up morally is also relevant to the interpretation of O'Connor's fictional characters. In *The Violent Bear It Away*, Tarwater's prophetic call begins after he has murdered an innocent child: Does this preclude taking seriously O'Connor's claim that he has now understood and is ready to fulfill his prophetic calling? One of the "objections" in Aquinas's article on prophecy makes the argument that moral purity is necessary for prophecy: "For it is written (*Wis.* vii.27) that the wisdom of God through nations conveyeth herself into holy souls" (II–II, q. 172, art. 4). Yet, according to Aquinas's reply, to focus on the prophet's individual or personal goodness is potentially to separate the prophet from the source of that goodness, whereas to address the goodness that the prophet sees or imagines in creation is to recognize its presence as a reality in which all human beings can participate, though none may possess.

Aquinas makes a distinction between the good life in terms of the soul's inward root (which is sanctifying grace) and the soul's passions and will (II–II, q. 172, art. 4). Sanctifying grace is given so that "man's soul may be united to God by charity," and yet, according to Aquinas (quoting St. Paul), "prophecy can be without charity" because "prophecy pertains to the intellect, whose act precedes the act of the will, which power is perfected by charity." Aquinas concludes that since prophecy is not "directly intended to unite man's affection to God, which is the purpose of charity," then "prophecy can be without a good life, as regards the first root of this goodness." He does suggest further, however, that a consideration of the good life in terms of the soul's passions and external actions would require him to say that an evil life from this point of view "is an obstacle to prophecy." He argues this because prophecy requires the mind to be raised up to the contemplation of spiritual things, which is an activity hindered by strong passions (II–II, q. 172, art. 4). The inward good life of the soul, rooted in God's grace, is not required for prophetic knowledge, since prophetic knowing is determined largely by the intellect, but the soul's passions and external habits can prevent the attainment of the prophetic life if they block the mind from spiritual ascent.

O'Connor's claim to be a prophetic novelist, and her belief that as such she is not required to be morally pure, is directed to the former distinction that Aquinas makes about the inward root of the soul. She is not concerned with the issue of her own passions or external habits, nor is she concerned with the passions or external habits of those of her characters who are struggling to become prophets. The primary issue regarding the prophet's vision, according to O'Connor, is the discernment of what is spiritual as it is seen and experienced in the natural world. She is less occupied with questions of moral habits than with making her spiritual vision apparent in an age peculiarly closed to spiritual reality as it can be perceived in the physical world:

> The problem of the novelist who wishes to write about a man's encounter with this God is how he shall make the experience—which is both natural and supernatural   understandable, and credible, to his reader. In any age this would be a problem, but in our own, it is a well-nigh insurmountable one. Today's audience is one in which religious feeling has become, if not atrophied, at least vaporous and sentimental. . . . When the physical fact is separated from the spiritual reality, the dissolution of belief is eventually inevitable. (*MM* 161–62)

What is O'Connor's response to this disjunction between artist and audience? The task of the Christian artist, according to Maritain, is a formidable one: "It is difficult to be an artist and very difficult to be a Christian . . . for it is a question of harmonizing two absolutes. Say that the difficulty becomes tremendous when the entire age lives far from Christ, for the artist is greatly dependent upon the spirit of his time."[75] For O'Connor, the separation between religious artist and secular audience is a matter of ethical discernment:

> I don't believe that our present society is one whose basic beliefs are religious, except in the South. In any case, you can't have effective allegory in times when people are swept this way and that by momentary convictions, because everyone will read it differently. You can't indicate moral values when morality changes with what is being done, because there is no accepted basis of judgment. (*MM* 166)

Until there exists a "happy combination of believing artist and believing society," O'Connor admits that "the novelist will have to do the best he can in travail with the world he has. . . . He may find in the end that instead of reflecting the image at the heart of things, he has only reflected our broken condition. . . . This is a modest achievement, but perhaps a necessary one" (*MM* 168). O'Connor's attempt to overcome the separations between grace and nature, reason and imagination, and vision and judgment, is part of her response to the modern lack of shared moral values. O'Connor is not suggesting that everyone must have the same beliefs in order to understand her fiction, but what she does see as necessary is the common desire to penetrate and understand the mystery of existence. Not belief, but openness to reality is paramount. The willingness to trust the prophetic insight of the artist means the reader must not be prejudiced against what is being shown simply because it does not correspond with his or her belief.

Although O'Connor writes that "what St. Thomas did for the new learning of the 13th century we are in bad need of someone to do for the 20th" (*HB* 305), this task was not hers. She was dependent on Thomistic thought because for her there was no comparable intellectual synthesis available in the modern era; her prose essays are not an attempt to establish a new synthesis, but simply her acknowledgment of a tradition of interpretation and religious thought that definitively informed her understanding of art and theology. O'Connor is primarily an artist who is writing in such a way that her fiction is an invitation to all to see what she sees, an experience that is possible even without reading about the Thomistic distinctions concerning art and theology in her theoretical essays. Certainly she is critical of the loss of intellectual distinctions and of the way in which the intellect has become sterile, but the intellect here is not the privilege of an educated elite—it is the human experience of the soul's ability to know its divine source and to be confronted with mystery in the midst of concrete existence. O'Connor sees only a need for a certain openness on the part of her audience, a willingness to see what is being shown, and a willingness to be changed by it: "The type of mind that can understand good fiction is not necessarily the educated mind, but it is at all times the kind of mind that is willing to have its sense of mystery deepened by contact with reality, and its sense of reality deepened by contact with mystery" (*MM* 79).

And what does O'Connor strive to show, through her sacramental theology, incarnational aesthetics, and prophetic vision? She illustrates that reality is morally ordered by love and that the response to love is the moral basis of all action. Such is the ethical dimension of her fiction. In the next three chapters I will embark on an analysis of O'Connor's novels, *Wise Blood* and *The Violent Bear It Away*, and her short story "Revelation." The difference between the philosophical language of her prose essays and the language of her fiction will be immediately obvious. Nonetheless, her sacramental and moral basis remains the same as delineated in the essays and letters: all of her characters make choices and act in response to their experience of reality. Since for O'Connor love is the ordering force of reality, it can be stated more precisely that everything they do is measured by love.

CHAPTER TWO

Moral Vision & the Grotesque

Wise Blood

The Moral of the Story

In his book *Christian Ethics and Imagination,* Philip Keane has noted that one of the significant changes in Catholic moral theology since Vatican II is that it has become more conversant with biblical themes.[1] In relation to this, there has been a shift away from discursive, logical, and positivistic forms of moral argument toward a discussion of ethics as embodied in story, narrative, and drama. The connection that Keane and others have recognized between the biblical stories and our modern moral discourse seems to be rooted in our need for a common mythic literature, or *mythos,* where new stories continue to resonate with the stories of old that are already shared, as some kind of measure.[2] Understood in this way, O'Connor's use of biblical imagery in her fiction is not so much owing to a religious preference—over her more systematic readings of classical philosophy—as it is a recognition of the inherent value of stories for illuminating the nature of moral choices. To discuss a shared measure for moral discourse, however, presumes a number of things, one of which is the fact that O'Connor is not speaking of a neutral universe where human beings create and project their ethical concerns out of various individual motivations and needs. She is presuming a moral order present in creation, known and intuited in human experience, and, ultimately, shared.

For many modern ears, however, the use of biblical stories presents a problem, because the common, biblical mythos is no longer necessarily "common." And when communities—the groups who hold such mythic stories in common—disperse, the common mythos is forgotten and soon abandoned. The consequence of this loss is the impoverishment of the imagination in the realm of ethical judgments; when moral reflections cannot be grounded in any common drama within creation, there is an increased dependence on the abstract rather than on lived experience for moral reasoning. This is not to say that moral reflection is rooted only in the imagination, but O'Connor realized that the type of reasoning that often serves as its alternative is abstract, calculative reasoning. O'Connor sees abstract reasoning as an impediment to engaging in good fiction as well as unsupportive of good moral questioning. The relation between a shared moral vision and a common sacred literature is notable because, as a Southern writer in the 1950s and early 1960s, O'Connor occupied an interesting position. Her often repeated phrase—that while the South is not perhaps "Christ centered" it is clearly "Christ haunted" (*MM* 44)—points to the existence of a community that still recalls the images of its collective, religious past: "In the South the Bible is known by the ignorant as well, and it is always that *mythos* which the poor hold in common that is most valuable to the fiction writer. When the poor hold sacred history in common, they have ties to the universal and the holy, which allows the meaning of their every action to be heightened and seen under the aspect of eternity" (*MM* 203). The biblical stories themselves are not necessarily prescriptive for those who remember them, but they do reflect the imaginative encounter of human beings with ethical questions and choices. Nonetheless, while O'Connor knew that the South was unusual in its continued familiarity with the biblical stories, she understood that a shared biblical culture was diminishing even there.

As O'Connor noted, "It takes readers as well as writers to make literature" (*MM* 181), and this symbiosis between writer and reader means that the sacred stories of the past, which have shaped and defined human communities, require a continued life as the common mythical measure. Without this measure, O'Connor foresaw the degeneration of the life of fiction because of the inability to ground its meaning in anything greater than itself. On the level of fiction, allusions to other stories make a new story resonate through different layers of meaning, and this is paralleled on the level of moral choices, where each new thing that is done has some connection with past attempts to understand what must be done. To make fiction or ethics entirely self-referential is to lose not simply one meaning that determines everything but the larger idea that our stories, like our moral choices, do not exist in a vacuum. When the value of something is defined simply by what is being done, whether it is fiction or ethics, there is no sense of a common or shared measure of what is good: "You can't indicate moral values when morality changes with what is being done, because there is no accepted basis of judgment" (*MM* 166).

But according to O'Connor, the fiction writer needs more than a moral code, and this is where storytelling and ethical reflection are seen as intrinsically linked. She explains that "to be great storytellers, we need something to measure ourselves against, and this is what we conspicuously lack in this age. Men judge themselves now by what they find themselves doing. The Catholic has the natural law and the teachings of the Church to guide him, but for the writing of fiction, something more is necessary" (*MM* 202). Even as a Catholic, O'Connor sees church doctrine as insufficient for moral questioning in fiction, but her critical position here is not so much directed toward doctrines as it is toward the separation of fiction or stories from the moral life. O'Connor not only identifies the need for a measure but also suggests something unique about the nature of fiction itself: in this realm she recognizes that the "teachings of the Church" are not enough. Something beyond such teaching is required to give life to the ethical dimension of the drama. The distinction between the measure of the Church and the measure of the artist does not imply that there are two measures; rather, O'Connor understands that the means of representing the measure in fiction must answer to the demands of art, the demands of both the intellect and the imagination. She clarifies this measure by saying:

> For the purposes of fiction, these guides have to exist in a concrete form, known and held sacred by the whole community. They have to exist in the form of stories which affect our image and our judgment of ourselves. Abstractions, formulas, laws will not serve here. We have to have stories in our background. It takes a story to make a story. It takes a story of mythic dimensions, one which belongs to everybody, one in which everybody is able to recognize the hand of God and its descent. (*MM* 202)

The stories about which O'Connor is speaking are mythic in the sense that they address religious and ethical realities that abstract formulas only serve to reduce in the process of containing their meaning. Stories in which "everybody is able to recognize the hand of God and its descent" require the participation of the reader's intellect and imagination as well as the author's, and this means that there must be sufficient space for interpretation and understanding, a space wherein the story can unfold and reveal itself in different ways. This is the good of art, according to O'Connor, who believes (like Aquinas) that art should be a good in itself, not forced into some utilitarian purpose. Her reasons for saying this are at the heart of her understanding of art, and, essentially of reality, because for O'Connor, "What is good in itself glorifies God because it reflects God" (*MM* 171).

O'Connor insists that fiction has to "have value on the *dramatic* level, the level of truth recognizable by anybody. The fact that many people can't see anything *Christian* about my novel doesn't interfere with many of them seeing it as a novel which does not falsify reality" (emphasis mine).[3] These comments raise two important points. O'Connor insists that the truth of reality transcends a particular Christian teaching when she says that, on the dramatic level, the truth can be recognized by anybody. Further, she argues that even if the Christian elements in her novels are not perceived by the reader, the novel does not falsify reality. This would suggest that the truth of the story is not limited to its Christian images or that reality is any less present in her stories when those images are not understood. The second point must be made, however, that for O'Connor the "truth of reality" is best understood and represented in Christian language and symbol, and that to do this is also not to falsify reality. Both the dramatic episodes of life and her Christian understanding of them share in reality, as well as account for it and describe it. While O'Connor acknowledges that her Christian symbolism does not contain all of reality, she does not separate the two in her fiction. When they are not seen together—and for the modern reader the failure to apprehend both is less a matter of not being a Christian than it is a lack of familiarity with Christian traditions, scriptures, and symbols—then appreciation of the depth of O'Connor's symbolic representation of reality is limited by the reader's level of perception. The result is usually that the reader considers the Christian symbolization irrelevant or, more often, does not even relate the symbolization to reality.

Given this, O'Connor also recognized that while the South provided her with the religious landscape for her fiction, the knowledge of those religious themes in the South was already diminishing. The common measure was disintegrating, and as a novelist she was confronted with the task of writing fiction for a community that held less and less in common in regard to religious/mythic stories. She says of this disjunction between the writer and his audience:

> I am often told that the model of balance for the novelist should be Dante, who divided his territory up pretty evenly between hell, purgatory and paradise. There can be no objection to this, but also there can be no reason to assume that the result of doing it in these times will give us the balanced picture that it gave in Dante's. Dante lived in the thirteenth century, when that balance was achieved in the faith of his age. We live now in an age which doubts both fact and value which is swept this way and that by momentary convictions. Instead of reflecting a balance from the world around him, the novelist now has to achieve one from a felt balance inside himself. (*MM* 49)

In saying this, O'Connor does not mean that she creates this balance, or that it is hers alone. She expresses the larger dimension of this balance through her use of the word "felt"; the experience is not projected but intuited, and although it is no longer acknowledged publicly in shared symbols, it has not disappeared.

The balance of which she speaks is an experience of the moral order of reality, but it is one that is noticeably absent in the context of modern, liberal culture, where order (moral or otherwise) is understood to be determined by individual opinion. Her comment suggests that, as a novelist lacking the means from the age in which she lives, she must reflect this order of reality through her own perception and recognition of it. The result is often a conflict between reader and author, because when the vision of reality is not shared, it is rejected as being simply the imagination of the artist. This is especially true when the vision suggests a spiritual order of reality that is understood by the author to be more encompassing than personal opinion. For O'Connor, this precipitated the use of sometimes "violent literary means to get [her] vision across to a hostile audience" (*MM* 185). The name given to this moral vision in O'Connor's fiction is "the grotesque."

Ethics and the Grotesque

A brief account of some of the different meanings of the grotesque as it is employed by O'Connor seems in order. Peter Hawkins, in his book *The Language of Grace,* offers a helpful description of the grotesque: "[It] incarnates the illness of the human condition, the extent to which we have fallen from the image of God in which we were created," and yet it also "expresses the tension and discrepancies that arise when grace is at work in a nature that either resists it or is struggling to comply."[4] These are certainly the central intentions of O'Connor's use of the grotesque. Hawkins also notes that the grotesque is a matter of writing style for O'Connor; the grotesque is her imaginative talent. Yet, to avoid reducing O'Connor's philosophical and religious insights, it is important to emphasize that she does not consider the grotesque to be indicative of the human condition in any complete sense, nor is it the sole expression of spiritual disorder or sickness.

O'Connor is aware of her particular artistic ability with the grotesque, but she insists that the grotesque need not be understood as indicative of the writer's outlook on human life. In fact, it is the opposite, insofar as the novelist writing about the grotesque, especially with moral concerns, must be aware of the good by which the grotesque is measured: "Those who believe that art proceeds from a healthy, and not from a diseased, faculty of the mind will take what he shows them as a revelation, not of what we ought to be but of what we are at a given time and under given circumstances" (*MM* 34). O'Connor is not interested in the grotesque for its own sake. Despite some readers' assumptions, her fiction is not the result of a diseased mind with a penchant for ugly things. In her comment above she clearly indicates that art proceeds from a healthy faculty of mind and that by virtue of a healthy mind the order of spiritual reality is revealed. O'Connor repeats François Mauriac's advice to "purify the source" (*MM* 149), but not in some moralistic sense, whereby the author's sanctity is expected to protect all readers from scandal. Rather, O'Connor recognizes that the health of the mind is itself the ordering force for one's artistic vision. Her ability to see the nature of specifically modern, spiritual perversions and name them as such requires a spiritually healthy mind that can know the difference between what is beautiful and what is ugly.

For O'Connor, the grotesque is both a means of countering the loss of a common vision of the Good that is the ground of all ethical discussion and a judgment on the outcomes of this blindness. As John Desmond says so well in his book *Risen Sons,* "O'Connor saw her special problem as a writer to be rooted in the fact that the age speciously believed in its own capacity for achieving wholeness exclusive of the divine, a situation she found truly grotesque."[5] Desmond's comment about the spiritual condition of the modern age aptly summarizes the character of Hazel Motes in O'Connor's first novel, *Wise Blood,* considered to be her most grotesque work. There are several ways in which Hazel Motes's character might be interpreted as grotesque, but my analysis will focus on Motes's limited search for meaning within his self-constructed vision of autonomous reality. Motes's belief in his ability to "achieve wholeness exclusive of the divine" is what O'Connor finds grotesque, because in constructing his own measure of meaning he fails to understand both himself as a human being and the nature of his relation to God and the order of reality. The grotesque in this novel reveals O'Connor's ethical vision in that Hazel Motes's insistence on his spiritual autonomy, from God and from other human beings, prevents him from recognizing his connection to others, the spiritual bond that would help him to see his responsibility for others,

In her preface to the second edition of *Wise Blood*, O'Connor makes the problem of human autonomy explicit, using the language of integrity. For most readers, says O'Connor, "Hazel Motes' integrity lies in his trying with such vigor to get rid of the ragged figure [Jesus] who moves from tree to tree in the back of his mind. For the author, Hazel's integrity lies in his not being able to" (*WB*, preface). O'Connor's reference to integrity in this context is often interpreted as a vaguely moralistic comment, where the character of Motes only serves to show the inevitability of Jesus prevailing over human resistance. When integrity is simply equated with goodness, O'Connor's comment can even be regarded as praise for Motes's struggle against Christ, and his perverse rebellion made into a virtue.

Without suggesting that O'Connor's mention of integrity is devoid of moral significance, it is perhaps more to the point to reflect on the meaning of the word as *wholeness*. According to O'Connor, the general response to the novel has been to see Motes's integrity, or wholeness as a human being, in his strength to be himself against the forces of the Jesus figure haunting him from his strict familial indoctrination. Yet O'Connor's theological anthropology is different: she is critical of both Motes's religious upbringing and his response to it. In declaring that Motes's integrity lies in his inability to resist the divine figure, O'Connor means that Motes's wholeness depends on something more than himself. His integrity requires divine completion, due to the lack in himself. If wholeness cannot be achieved exclusive of the divine, as Desmond suggests of O'Connor's vision, then it is true to say that Motes's integrity or wholeness lies in the fact that he cannot do it himself. O'Connor asks finally, "Does one's integrity ever lie in what he is not able to do? I think it usually does" (*WB*, preface). Hazel Motes is unable to make himself whole independently of a divine source; more important, he refuses to acknowledge this and instead seeks wholeness in his own creation of meaning. The effect of this vision in the novel is that characters like Hazel appear to be "two-dimensional": closed off from the transcendence of the divine. Desmond describes O'Connor's use of this two-dimensional scale as a strategy "to develop the theme of a world that has largely abandoned any interest in the divine. . . ." In a world such as this, "its dominant images reflect that reduction to the natural order which is a logical result of its view of reality."[6]

In an unpublished manuscript O'Connor refers to Sherwood Anderson as part of her introduction to a discussion of the grotesque. Anderson's account of what is grotesque in human beings clearly influenced O'Connor's understanding. She notes that Anderson was the first modern writer to apply the word "grotesque" to his characters with a conscious intent: "He saw them as grotesque because each one embraced a single truth to the exclusion of other truths. Being what we are, finite, no man is able to embrace all truth and every man can be seen as, in part, grotesque who embraces with passion any truth at all."[7] From O'Connor's description, therefore, we can see how Anderson's point is related to the question of integrity or wholeness. Human nature is marked by finitude, and this finitude defeats any attempt to embrace truth in a comprehensive way. To claim the ability to wholly know the truth is what Anderson categorizes as grotesque primarily because it disregards the limitations of human knowledge and experience. O'Connor adds an explicitly religious interpretation of the nature of human finitude to Anderson's account: the notion of sin. Anderson's recognition of finitude does not attend to the specifically willful occasions of the radical rejection of God and the impulse to "embrace all truth" autonomously. While we could argue that human finitude is something for which human beings are not entirely responsible, O'Connor sees sin as a willful choice of offence against God. She suggests that both the natural limitations of human knowledge and the existence of sin contribute to the condition she calls grotesque: "If you add to our finite nature, original sin, or whatever reasonable facsimile you substitute for that doctrine, you have enough to account for the grotesque as a realistic factor in the human condition."[8]

The issue of limitation raises the same question I ask in the preceding chapter. How does O'Connor understand human beings as limited? Maritain's analysis of the intellect acknowledged the limitations of human reason, but O'Connor (using Aquinas and the biblical texts) also addressed the willful rejection of God, and presumably, of human limitation itself. In *Wise Blood* the struggle of Hazel Motes is rooted in his willful rebellion against the reality of a divinely established order. Motes wants to create an alternative order of reality and become his own measure for truth. One of the novel's symbolic expressions of Motes's desire to be whole—independently of any divine source—is represented by his belief in a new kind of Jesus, one who is "all man and ain't got any God in him" (*WB* 121). While the image of Christ reveals human limitation in O'Connor's fiction, it also expresses the connection between what is physical and spiritual in human beings—another matter of wholeness. O'Connor's ethical vision presumes that human beings are created in the image of God and that this spiritual image is what connects human beings to each other through love. Motes's rejection of spiritual reality implicitly negates the spiritual connection that makes human beings responsible for one another. Freed from accountability to God and without need of redemption, we are also effectively cut off from each other as spiritual creatures. The key to interpreting these questions of human limitation and spiritual orientation is found in the novel's images of sight or vision.

In his analysis of Hazel Motes's name, Richard Giannone explains that *hazel* in Hebrew means "God sees."[9] In *Embodying Forgiveness,* L. Gregory Jones takes both names, Hazel and Motes, and suggests that the name Hazel Motes "indicates the problem of lack of vision and judgment."[10] Jones argues that in addition to Hazel being an eye color, in the form of "Haze" it can suggest the lack of clear vision; "Motes" hearkens back to Matthew 7:1–5 (King James Version), where Jesus criticizes those who see "motes" (i.e., specks) in others' eyes without seeing the "beams" in their own. Both of these etymologies of Hazel's name seem true and relevant to our discussion, although they are not precise about the nature of Hazel's specific problem of vision. What does it mean to say that Hazel's name means "God sees"? In what way does Hazel Motes lack clarity of vision? Jones's analysis of Hazel's last name might indicate that it has something to do with Hazel's judgments of others, but this does not appear to be the main preoccupation of Hazel Motes. If we take the two explanations together, however, the moral implications of the grotesque and of the novel as a whole begin to emerge. The name Hazel Motes could suggest simultaneously that God sees but that Hazel does not see clearly. However, it is *Hazel* that is the verb for God's seeing, and so there is still an implicit connection between the two—the measure is God's vision and not independent of Hazel himself.

The "mote" described in Matthew 7:1–5 is essentially something that deflects from the more obvious and blinding "beam," signifying that part of Hazel's problem is precisely that he does not see his own condition as grotesque, that he is unaware of his limited or hazy vision. More specifically, to use the contrasting image of "God seeing," Hazel does not recognize the relation between God's vision and human vision; wherein God provides the light by which human beings see. The tension of the novel resides in Hazel's attempt to see as God sees, but through his own narrow human vision and without any recognition of a divine source. But perhaps because of the beam in his eye, Hazel never does see clearly in the novel; at least he does not see the problem inherent in his quest for spiritual autonomy. Even after blinding himself (and including his reasons for doing it) Hazel does not acknowledge his dependence on God for wholeness. This act does not bring about a conversion or any reassessment of his spiritual condition, and he continues to understand God as disconnected from his own intellect and imagination. Hazel's physical self-blinding does effect a kind of inward reflection or "seeing," however limited, and what he sees might only be the realization that "God sees." There is an unspecified sense of accountability in Hazel's desire to "pay," but he does not see it clearly enough to confess the nature of his connection to God as anything other than that of debt and debtor. In fact, Hazel's final desire to be rid of any debt he might owe, which dominates his thinking throughout the novel, is directed almost entirely toward gaining his autonomy rather than acknowledging his dependence.[11]

Given that O'Connor knew that most readers saw Motes's integrity as rooted in himself and in his resistance to any divine measure—rather than seeing his integrity as requiring divine completion—she also used the grotesque as a kind of literary technique to bring home to the reader the perversity of his spiritual condition. Motes's moral position is rooted in his idea of complete self-sufficiency. His murder of Solace Layfield dramatizes the image of absolute human freedom and independence and represents the moral opposite of O'Connor's belief in human accountability and responsibility. Hazel cannot even tolerate the idea of conscience, symbolized by Layfield, because he understands it as something other than himself that measures or judges his actions. O'Connor's concern was to emphasize and to reveal what is actually grotesque about Hazel's spiritual condition, without mistaking the grotesque for Hazel himself, or for the world, or for reality. It takes some effort on the part of readers to see precisely what is grotesque in Hazel's self-understanding in relation to God and others. O'Connor's now famous and often-quoted line about her use of the grotesque—"to the hard of hearing you shout, and for the almost-blind you draw large and startling figures" (*MM* 34)[12]—indicates a challenge to her readers' habits of thinking. The grotesque is a technique that uses extreme images to illustrate how the lack of accurate understanding concerning what is grotesque actually stems from a lack of understanding of what is good.

The presence of what O'Connor refers to as the "order of the universe" is another factor for Hazel's rebellion, which continually measures his actions throughout the story. O'Connor's description of the sky at the beginning of chapter 3 implies a transcendent, spiritual reality to which human beings must respond or relate. When Hazel Motes first arrives in Taulkinham, "The black sky was underpinned with long silver streaks that looked like scaffolding and depth on depth behind it were thousands of stars that all seemed to be moving very slowly as if they were about some vast construction work that involved the whole order of the universe and would take all time to complete. No one was paying any attention to the sky" (WB 37). The spiritual reality that hangs overhead and permeates creation is present, but it is ignored by everyone, including Hazel. This passage establishes the central importance of sight and the direction of one's vision in the story, because it suggests the human freedom of soul to choose to look where it will. If there is a connection between transcendent spiritual reality and the human soul—a possibility ignored, if not explicitly rejected, by Motes—the process of understanding and perceiving the nature of that connection requires clarity of vision, which presupposes a willingness to look at what is there to see. Although Hazel Motes is free to choose or ignore any larger conception of reality, his vision is diminished by his refusal to consider what is unseen. With his willful self-blinding at the end of the story Hazel Motes follows his closed vision to its logical conclusion, and while he thus imitates Asa Hawks in order to see what Hawks claims to see, Motes does so without any spiritual perception. His final observation of the sky before he blinds himself, when he takes the time to look up at it, is dimmed and blank, still suggesting a depth upon depth. But because Motes has narrowed his vision so radically to take in only physical objects and facts, he is unable to see beyond his own small universe (WB 209). No amount of blinding to the physical world around him will remedy his spiritual blindness at this point. Physical vision is not immediately replaced by the spiritual; spiritual vision must be cultivated, and Hazel Motes has only succeeded in rejecting its reality.

It is worth mentioning the narration concerning the sky and the implications of a transcendent order as they stand in relation to the characters' understanding of what they see. In the passage quoted above, the sky is represented as reflecting an eternal, transcendent order that goes completely unnoticed by the people in Taulkinham. It would seem that a complete interpretation of the symbols of sight and blindness in the novel would include these instances of the refusal to see something that is there. The theme of this willful blinding is crucial to the movement of Motes's rebellion and final act. Marshall Bruce Gentry argues that this passage about the sky is "ridiculous" and "fanciful" because the imposed set of standards that it represents goes unnoticed by the characters.[13] I would suggest to the contrary that this image of the sky reflects an experienced order of creation, fundamental to O'Connor's sacramental vision of the world, and that, specifically, Hazel's efforts to separate himself from this order—which is the tension of the whole novel—are indicated by this early description of his particular kind of spiritual blindness. If we are to interpret the novel only through the actions and intentions of the characters' individual ideas and opinions, we would become subject to the same limiting features of Hazel Motes's positivism.

Blind Seers and False Preachers

With the only precise date evident in her fiction, O'Connor sets the day of Asa Hawks's revival meeting and intended self-blinding on "the fourth of October" (*WB* 112), the feast day of St. Francis of Assisi and the anniversary of his death in 1226.[14] Richard Giannone characterizes the contrast between St. Francis and Hawks: "Where Francis gives up great wealth to live by the will of God, Hawks tries to tell God what to do by imitating Paul for personal profit."[15] This contrast serves as an appropriate analogy for the inner struggle of Hazel Motes, although for Motes the contrast has less to do with money than with the choice between submission or resistance to God. I suggest that Hazel Motes is not compelled by Asa Hawks's concern for economic gains; rather, his interest is sparked by Hawks's apparent spiritual authority and autonomy, which seem all the more mysterious because of his dark glasses and blindness. Motes's imitation of Asa Hawks, as opposed to someone like St. Francis, suggests the pattern for his actions: a negative appropriation of God's will.

What Hazel Motes resists in *Wise Blood* is symbolized by the frequent references to the blood sacrifice of Christ as the atonement for human sinfulness. Hazel rejects the need for atonement by rejecting the idea of sin. His first encounter with the preacher Asa Hawks solidifies this response in Motes and establishes the order of his rejection. When Hawks tells Motes to repent, Hazel replies, "If I was in sin I was in it before I ever committed any. There's no change come in me. . . . I don't believe in sin" (*WB* 53). Motes's rejection of sin rather than of God reveals the particular nature of his religious rebellion, and it can be traced back to what he has learned from his family's religious ideas. The severe religious upbringing of his youth, which emphasized human sinfulness at the expense of human goodness,[16] causes Motes to attempt to finalize the human/divine rupture by arguing for the elimination of the only apparent thing that makes the connection between human beings and God necessary: sin.

Hazel spurns his *family's* religious ideas of human beings and their relation to God, a severed relation at best, because he finds the idea of redemption meaningless when human participation is limited to the external acts of sin. Motes rightly criticizes a relation to God that revolves solely around the passive acceptance of Christ's atonement for human sin. For Hazel, if the human experience of God is rooted solely in the debt of sinfulness without an experience of God's redeeming power, then there is no compelling reason to desire redemption.[17] The question remains, however, as to whether Hazel Motes is ever able to overcome his early religious indoctrination sufficiently to reach a more meaningful understanding of redemption through his rebellion. It should be noted that Hazel's resistance to redemption and atonement is framed and defined by his own narrow vision, learned from his mother, and it is not therefore indicative of O'Connor's understanding of redemption. His resistance is necessarily limited in this regard, as I will demonstrate throughout my analysis.

Wise Blood begins with Hazel Motes's train ride to the city to begin his new life of independence from his family life and the army. As the train moves forward, Hazel thinks back, and in his recollection we can observe the preoccupations of his past that will inform and shape his actions in the future. When his fellow traveler, Mrs. Hitchcock, asks Hazel if he is going home (*WB* 13) he emphatically replies, "No, I ain't," suggesting perhaps not only a new location but a rejection of what "home" represents. Moreover, he insists on this rejection in religious terms to another passenger: "Do you think I believe in Jesus? . . . Well I wouldn't even if He existed. Even if He was on this train" (*WB* 16). This outburst provokes Motes to reflect on his childhood, when he accompanied his grandfather as he preached from the hood of his Ford automobile. The seeds of Motes's religious rebellion are planted in his youth, and the decisive emphasis on sin in relation to Jesus makes Hazel wary of both. Watching his grandfather as a boy Motes recalls that "there was already a deep black wordless conviction in him that the way to avoid Jesus was to avoid sin" (*WB* 22).

To ensure that he avoids sin as an adult, the only two things that Hazel Motes takes with him from his home in Eastrod when he is drafted into the army are a "black Bible and a pair of silver-rimmed spectacles that had belonged to his mother" (*WB* 23). Given his religious background, he presumes that the Bible will protect him from sin, and he reads it through his mother's glasses to remind himself of that fact. These references are suggestive of the kind of religious views Hazel's family espoused. The "wordless conviction" that Hazel has about religious matters indicates the religious education he experienced: "He had gone to a country school where he had learned to read and write but that it was wiser not to; the Bible was the only book he read. He didn't read it often but when he did he wore his mother's glasses. They tired his eyes so that after a short time he was always obliged to stop" (*WB* 23). Hazel Motes's religious instruction and education are severely limited; the only thing he reads is the Bible, but he reads it with his *mother's* glasses. The symbolic effects of home are significant: using his mother's prescription distorts his reading of the Bible, which is considered, furthermore, to be the only book worth consulting. Another relevant detail concerning Motes's limited religious understanding is that the fatigue from his blurred vision inevitably restricts how much he can read; therefore, he never actually reads much of the Bible. O'Connor clearly intends these inferences to be critical of Hazel Motes's religious upbringing. As she says in a letter to Carl Hartman about *Wise Blood,* "I have directed the irony against this Protestant world or against the society that reads the Bible and the Sears Roebuck catalogue wrong" (*CW* 921).

The army offers Motes an alternative vision to that of his family's religious strictures, and in so doing challenges his already troubled understanding of sinful human nature. Hazel's comrades present him with the possibility that there is no moral significance to existence, and subsequently they try to convince him that he has no soul. The introduction of this radically new idea suggests to Motes that he can resist corruption (sin) by resisting the idea of any spiritual meaning to his existence. The development of his religious thought moves one step further with this newly discovered alternative: he progresses beyond the avoidance of Jesus by avoiding sin, to the avoidance of both sin and Jesus by rejecting anything spiritual in him that would connect him to either. For Hazel Motes, this meant "to be converted to nothing instead of to evil" (*WB* 24), and it becomes obvious that his thinking does not extend much further than this throughout the course of the novel, except that in his later preaching he does realize that he cannot effectively preach "nothing." The reason for this restricted development is that, despite Hazel's desire to transcend his religious upbringing, it has already decisively narrowed and dimmed his vision.

Asa Hawks perceives Motes's spiritual condition on their first meeting, echoing Isaiah 6:9–10: "You got eyes and see not, ears and hear not, but you'll have to see some time" (*WB* 54).[18] What Hawks's reference to Isaiah suggests is that Motes's lack of vision stems from his refusal to acknowledge the ultimate source of spiritual vision. His vision is limited to external sense perceptions, and his sight and hearing are made blind and deaf because, fat and bloated with his own self-sufficiency and importance, he is unable to understand with his heart—the spiritual center from which real understanding comes.[19] The implication in the Isaiah passage is that to be healed, or made whole, is to understand with the heart that God *is* and that God is the only source of human completion. But Hazel Motes cannot get beyond his own narrow vision, because he has nothing by which he can measure his view other than his rejection of what has guided his own sight until now.

The two primary issues that are pivotal to Motes's rebellion are his youthful preoccupation with sin and—owing largely to the desire to escape the oppressive religious teaching of his youth—his later conviction that he has no soul. Thus, the impulses that dominate his escape in the city from his religious past are the refusal to accept sin as real and the complete severance of human beings from any relationship to God, and in particular, to Christ. But even the most vehement rejection of the past cannot liberate one entirely from the influences of that past; Motes, because he is contending with the religious influence of his mother and grandfather, remains firmly subject to the impact of that influence. As a consequence, Hazel Motes takes on the role of preaching an alternate view of reality for which he seeks believers, but he cannot help defining his ideas in response to, or in negative proportion to, the religious ideas he rejects.

The significance of the familial influence on Motes's actions is revealed in an external way by his relation to the profession of preaching, a profession he both rejects and embraces in his departure from his deserted family home and his entry into the city of Taulkinham. To be a preacher is to be tied to his religious past, and Motes, by denying his religious heritage, feels compelled to deny also the profession that is expected of him, and indeed, which his outward appearance suggests to everyone who sees him.[20] Preaching is an integral part of his family's religious background—his grandfather was a preacher and Hazel remembers listening to him as a young boy, knowing at the age of twelve that he would be a preacher too (*WB* 22). But it is also the case that despite Hazel's resistance to his assumed place in a line of preachers, he is deeply affected by the actions and the lessons of his grandfather, whose power as a preacher made an impression on him: "Every fourth Saturday [the grandfather] had driven into Eastrod as if he were just in time to save them all from Hell, and he was shouting before he had the car door open. People gathered around his Ford because he seemed to dare them to" (*WB* 21).

Hazel's encounter with the blinded preacher in Taulkinham, Asa Hawks, presents a more compelling series of questions. Ironically, it is the possibility of spiritual sight or vision that Asa Hawks introduces to Hazel

Motes. Motes is perplexed by a blind man who claims to see more than a sighted person: How and what could a blind man see? While his grandfather had physical sight, Hazel thought he was "blind"; now he must confront someone who is "blind" and yet says that he can see more than someone who possesses healthy vision. There is little spiritual subtlety in Hazel Motes; he limits his perception of reality to the sensual world and, in particular, to what he can see with his physical eyes alone. Nonetheless, Asa Hawks's challenge to that sight gets his attention. The first few exchanges with Asa Hawks reveal the growing tension in Motes's soul. He almost instinctively follows Asa, "keeping his eyes on the blind man" (*WB* 45), just as he followed his grandfather around as a child. But his grandfather only ever told him his religious fate as an immutable decree: "That boy had been redeemed and Jesus wasn't going to leave him ever" (*WB* 21). Once in the city Motes takes to following Asa Hawks, but Hawks leaves room for some freedom in Hazel's religious life, releasing him from the predetermined cage of his grandfather's making. Asa knows of the struggle in Hazel and simply asks him which pull he intends to follow: "'Some preacher has left his mark on you,' the blind man said with a kind of snicker. 'Did you follow me to take it off or give you another one?'" (*WB* 51). Hawks identifies the critical issue: Hazel Motes has been marked by his grandfather's preaching, and Asa Hawks, as the fraudulent, blind preacher, can disabuse Motes of his religious background for good or become a different kind of mentor to him. Sensing the confusion in Motes and his inability to transcend his past indoctrination, Hawks provides Motes a model of rebellion. Hazel Motes's actions in the novel, and specifically the progression of his preaching, make it clear that O'Connor knows Hawks to be the only possible paradigm for Motes.

In this situation, Hazel Motes does the only thing he can do. His rejection of his family's religious ideas is acted out by him through the very professional calling that he resists: he preaches his rebellion. His response to the redemption through Christ preached by his grandfather can only become a negative version of the message of salvation that he rejects. His response is of a parasitic nature, unimaginative, which simply mimics with a proffered salvation from salvation. This form of negative preaching prevents Motes from moving beyond preaching a church without Christ. Because Hazel Motes does not want to acknowledge that his wholeness as a human being is tied to anything beyond himself and his perception of the physical world, he is forced to manipulate the reality he lives in to be as he would envision it, drawing on his limited understanding and experience. Asa Hawks's character is important in this regard, representing not only the calling to be a preacher (he is the first city preacher Hazel encounters) but also the perversion (Asa is a fraud) of the deeper question of Motes's rejection of God. Hazel Motes, in his desire to surmount the truth that Asa Hawks preaches, realizes that he must preach his own truth, although he can only formulate it as a response to Hawks's version. In particular, Hawks presents him with an obstacle against which Hazel Motes begins to formulate his rebellion: "You can't run away from Jesus. Jesus is a fact" (WB 51). Consequently, Motes's truth is always rooted in a disputation of the facts as well as how the facts are determined. The connections between fact and truth form the basis for Hazel Motes's preaching, and the three different names he gives to his church are indicative of his struggle to understand the relation between truth and fact.

From the point when Hazel Motes decides to set up his own church to preach in response to Asa Hawks, the name of the church changes subtly, three times, and approximately every fifty pages. The first church is the "Church of Truth without Jesus Christ Crucified" (WB 55); the second is the "Church without Christ" (WB 105); and the third, the "Church of Christ without Christ" (WB 151). They are all proclaimed as churches by Motes, and they all include varying references to Christ, but the nature of the changes indicates his confusion in articulating his rebellion. The variations are worth considering in detail, since they reveal the progression of Motes's under-standing of, and confrontation with, the consequences of the negative version of Christian redemption that he preaches. In addition, a few words about the corresponding symbol of the car are necessary.

Although the progression of his church names suggests the struggle of the intellect that Motes experiences, the images of the car he buys, drives, preaches from, and eventually loses, suggest the freedom, movement, and choice of his soul.[21] Hazel Motes's preaching and driving parallel each other, as the church he preaches can only develop in relation to the movements of his soul. Essentially, the car symbolizes freedom for Hazel, and this includes the freedom to interpret and preach his own version of reality. Reacting against the deterministic preaching of his mother and grandfather—"Jesus would have him in the end!" (WB 22)—Hazel discovers his ability to refuse. John Desmond suggests that "Haze is torn between his rejection of a purely mechanistic view of things—the redemptive vision of history represented by his mother—and his own inner sense of the spiritual and of freedom to act."[22] However, Desmond argues that the car is essentially a "negative image" and that Motes invests it falsely with a spiritual meaning. To see the car rep-resenting entirely the negative direction of Motes's rebellion, however, leaves no room for the possibility that Hazel is or can be aware of his spiritual condition. His internal struggle could be elaborated by interpreting the images of the three churches in relation to his experiences with the car—that is, when the car is seen as affording Motes freedom, and when it is limited, hesitating, or breaking down. In Desmond's analysis, the car represents a determined will to absolute freedom, but instead of defining the tension of Motes's conflict as solely between his mother's religious views and his freedom to act, I argue that the tensions are more complex. Motes has the freedom to act as though his freedom were absolute, but he is equally free to recognize the limitations on that freedom.

I diverge from Desmond's interpretation of the car because Hazel's resistance to his mother's views cannot overcome her influence, and therefore he never quite escapes his past completely, even in his pursuit of absolute freedom. Further, he cannot transcend reality, and various experiences, in the car or otherwise, remind him of the limitations to his freedom. Thus, the tension resides both in his rejection of his religious upbringing and also in himself, insofar as he can reject his past yet also embody it. The three variations on the church are offered in direct response to his *mother's mechanistic view*, as Motes wants to remove the only reason for Christ's redemption of human beings—human sinfulness, a spiritual idea that is meaningless in a world of facts. The car, however, can potentially represent both the positive and negative movements of Hazel's freedom; it can symbolize the choice of the soul in the freedom to act, either with the idea of a freedom that is absolute or with the recognition of one's limits. Desmond sees the car as depicting exclusively the former, an "emblem of a desacralized world rendered with comic exaggeration,"[23] whereas I suggest that the car, while often symbolizing Motes's misguided notions of freedom, also introduces moments of real spiritual freedom, wherein his movement in the car allows him to see where he is in relation to other things.

When Motes drives along the highway after purchasing his car, he observes the various fields and notices that "the sky leaked over all of it and then it began to leak into the car," and when a string of pigs cross the road and Hazel has to stop for them to pass, he has "the feeling that everything he saw was a broken-off piece of some giant black thing that he had forgotten had happened to him" (*WB* 74). These passages indicate the possibility of recognition in Motes of some kind of spiritual interconnectedness with a larger reality, although obviously vague and inarticulate, "some giant black thing that he had forgotten." But the sky connects him to the pigs and the fields, and indeed even "leaks" into his car, suggesting also that the freedom of the car is not absolute: it is limited by the sky, the pigs crossing, and the boundary of the fields bordering the highway. Rather than eliminating the true tension of human freedom, therefore, the car serves more revealingly as a symbol of the condition of Motes's soul, and these movements are related to the various modifications he makes while preaching his church. To put it simply, the preaching of his church marks his rebellion, while the car gauges his soul's struggles and possibilities in the process.

The Church of Truth without Jesus Christ Crucified

Hazel Motes's preaching career is sparked by Asa Hawks's insistence that he repent when Motes is already defensive after his night with Leora Watts. When Hawks says to him "I can smell the sin on your breath," Hazel draws back in shock (*WB* 49). It is no accident that the first church he preaches centers on the crucifixion and specifically on his rejection of the crucifixion as salvific. What he rejects is the idea that God's blood atones or makes human beings whole, although his understanding of atonement, given his religious background, is rooted in an idea of absolute human sinfulness largely equated with sex.[24] To reject Christ's redemption, therefore, one must first reject the need for it, and in Hazel's view, this means that he must proclaim human cleanliness. Even though Hazel posits human cleanliness primarily as a negation of sin as sex, he is nonetheless attempting to eliminate the only human connection to Christ that he knows from his religious background: redemption from sin through the crucifixion. If there is no sin, then there is no need for redemption and the crucifixion serves no purpose. Just before naming his first church, when he overtakes the exiting auditorium crowd where Asa Hawks and Sabbath Lily are about to distribute leaflets, Hazel assures everyone that they are clean: "Every one of you people are clean and let me tell you why if you think it's because of Jesus Christ Crucified you're wrong. I don't say he wasn't crucified but I say it wasn't for you" (*WB* 55). What Hazel Motes rejects is the personal need for Christ's act of atonement; at this point he does not want to refute the fact of the crucifixion, only its meaning for individual human beings. He accepts the historical fact, but not the interpretation of the crucifixion as an act of God that is offered for the sake of humanity.

After his encounter with Asa Hawks, Motes limits his preaching to the facts of his experience: "'Don't I know what exists and what don't?' he cried. 'Don't I have eyes in my head? Am I a blind man?'" (*WB* 55). Hazel opposes this blind man's claim to spiritual sight by preaching the facts as *he* sees them, shunning all paradox or subtlety of vision. His Church of Truth without Christ Crucified is a rejection of the only remnant left of his religious understanding of Jesus. It is an effective removal of the connection between human beings and the divine that makes way for a purely human salvation. It also serves to defeat the notion of human beings as spiritually connected and interdependent. Enoch Emery's appraisal of Motes after this first round of preaching suggests that it begins and ends entirely in the preacher himself: "You act like you think you got wiser blood than anybody else" (*WB* 59). This *is* what Motes thinks; because he denies the idea of redemption, he denies any link between human beings and God, and because he sticks to the facts, there is no spiritual reality. Enoch sees that, as a consequence, Hazel Motes considers all meaning to be centered in himself, dependent on nothing wiser and purer than himself. Hazel Motes rejects Christ crucified because it suggests atonement, or being "at one" with the divine.

To follow through with his plan, Hazel Motes needs a car. He says to the car dealer: "I wanted this car mostly to be a house for me. . . . I ain't got any place to be" (*WB* 73). With his attempt to sever the human-divine relation, Hazel is confronted by the problem of place. By locating all meaning within himself, Hazel's car-as-soul becomes his only place to be, and he preaches the independence of his place with increasing insistence: "I'm going to take the truth with me wherever I go. . . . I'm going to preach it . . . at whatever place" (*WB* 105); and, "if there's no Christ, there's no reason to have a set place to do it in" (*WB* 106). In Hazel's desacralized world, he must invest his independent place with truth, since no spiritual meaning inheres in the world beyond his own creation of meaning. He understands place as rooted entirely in the self, and this understanding indicates clearly his own uprootedness from his family, both physically and religiously: "Where you come from is gone, where you thought you were going to never was there, and where you are is no good unless you can get away from it. Where is there a place for you to be? No place" (*WB* 165). He further insists that nothing other than oneself can provide a place to be; for him, the car symbolizes the independence of the willfully enclosed self, an enclosure that will eventually become stifling and coffin-like:

> Nothing outside you can give you any place. . . . You needn't to look at the sky because it's not going to open up and show no place behind it. You needn't to search for any hole in the ground to look through into somewhere else. You can't go neither forwards nor backwards into your daddy's time nor your children's if you have them. In yourself right now is all the place you've got. (*WB* 165–66)

Hazel's search for a car depicts his desire for freedom and for a place that is completely under his own control.

The only problem for Motes when he finds a car is that while he wants to assert his independent control, he lacks the ability to drive well. He is seeking freedom but he does not know how to use it or what it costs. When he asks the young boy at the car lot for the price of the car, the boy replies, "Jesus on the cross. . . . Christ nailed" (*WB* 70). The force of these words hit Motes with a sense of cost to himself, but he can think of them only in the context of his familial religiosity and his rejection of that context. The boy's words imply that the car, symbolic of the soul's movement and freedom, has some connection to the redemptive action of Christ's crucifixion. Motes's understanding, however, is that he is free from any accountability to the divine, and the car represents his independence as the only place to be. These episodes involving the car suggest that, in spite of Motes's growing desire to escape his religious background, he continues to find himself enmeshed in it, not because of others' comments but because of his own confusions. More significantly, Motes's difficulties with the car signify his inability to act on what he says. Although the car has the potential to provide freedom, Hazel is stuck. He lacks experience: he tries to drive away with the brake on, and when it is released the car shoots backward (*WB* 74).

One of the first places Hazel Motes goes with his car is to see Enoch Emery in the park, but what he experiences there becomes the catalyst for his second church. The "Church of Truth without Jesus Christ Crucified" was born of Hazel's attempt to rid human beings of the idea that they are unclean and in need of atonement. But his truth is still measured in relation to Christ's crucifixion, albeit negatively, and so when Hazel is in the Frosty Bottle with Enoch, the seeds for a new formulation of his church are sown. When the two enter, the waitress begins to talk obsessively about cleanliness and compares Hazel to Enoch, who has been pestering her daily, by emphasizing what a clean boy Hazel is. She strikes a chord, however, with her connection of cleanliness to God; even though it may only have been an expression, Hazel Motes recognizes its significance. She says, "Yes sir, there ain't anything sweeter than a clean boy. God for my witness. And I know a clean one when I see him" (*WB* 91).

Hazel is silent, but then finally leans across the counter to the woman in a gesture of self-revelation and says, "I AM clean" (*WB* 91). By using the divine "I AM," reminiscent of God's revelation to Moses in the book of Exodus (3:14), O'Connor portrays how Hazel's declaration of his own cleanliness must be independent of any divine source. The waitress, invoking God as the measure of cleanliness, forces Hazel Motes into a position of assuming that divine measure himself. He concludes his point by acknowledging, "If Jesus existed, I wouldn't be clean" (*WB* 91). Hazel realizes that he is clean only insofar as there is no measure, and to preach a church without Christ crucified is simply to deny the redemptive purpose of Christ according to God's own measure of truth. The realization prompts a change in Hazel, and he now must preach a modified version of his church that will invalidate Christ as the measure by making the measure the absence of Christ. He asks a boy outside the picture show what church he belongs to, and the boy replies, "Church of Christ," to which Hazel answers "Well, I preach the Church without Christ" (*WB* 105). Hazel conceives the name of his church in negative terms, but he also removes the words "truth" and "crucifixion" from it. Since Hazel would not be clean if Jesus existed, he must now insist that "nothing matters but that Jesus was a liar" (*WB* 105). To assert that God is falsehood rather than truth is the only way for Hazel to establish his church and himself as true.

The Church without Christ

In addition to separating truth from God, Hazel must also eliminate mystery and vision. His first sermon of the second church preaches a church that does not challenge the facts: "I'm a member and preacher to that church where the blind don't see and the lame don't walk and what's dead stays that way. Ask me about that church and I'll tell you it's the church that the blood of Jesus don't foul with redemption" (*WB* 105). Hazel's reasoning must go further back than his earlier logic, which posited that the avoidance of Jesus was to be found in the avoidance of sin. He argues instead against the reality of any divine measure, whether for redemption or for sin. Hazel is trying to free himself by rejecting any notion of accountability to anything or anyone but himself. His church has no faith in what O'Connor stipulates as the theological truths of the universe for the Catholic fiction writer—namely the Fall, Redemption, and Judgment (*MM* 185). His argument denies them all in logical progression: "I'm going to preach there was no Fall because there was nothing to fall from and no Redemption because there was no Fall and no Judgment because there wasn't the first two" (*WB* 105). For O'Connor, when these doctrines are rejected by the modern secular world, what is actually being denied is the reality of "sin, or . . . the value that suffering can have, or . . . eternal responsibility" (*MM* 185). Hazel's rebellion is rooted in the desire to dispose of eternal responsibility, and the only way he can preach his way out of that responsibility is to deny the reality of any kind of transcendent order, either external to himself or within himself. The major drawback to his preaching, however, is that his negative appropriation of Christian teaching becomes tedious in the repetition of its doctrines in reverse. Motes never says anything new. He only repeats the same brief, negative message: "He began over and said the same thing again. They left and some more came and he said it a third time" (*WB* 105). Hazel Motes realizes that his preaching lacks power and notices that he is not attracting disciples: "He had spent every evening preaching, but the membership of the Church without Christ was still only one person: *himself*" (*WB* 146; italics mine). He takes his car in to be repaired.

Motes tells the man at the garage that "he wanted the horn made to blow and the leaks taken out of the gas tank, the starter made to work smoother and the windshield wipers tightened" (*WB* 114). Each of these mechanical problems parallels something in Hazel. The silent horn signals his inability to speak the truth no matter how much he preaches his version of truth; the leaks in the gas tank suggest his incontinence of conviction; the sputtering starter exposes his failure to start his church; and the faulty windshield wipers cannot clear his vision. Despite these minor problems, Motes believes that the car is in good condition, and when he asks the mechanic how soon it will be "put in the best order," the mechanic replies "It can't be done" (*WB* 114). Hazel Motes refuses to see the very bad state of his car, and rather than accept the mechanic's truthful appraisal he takes it to another, who speaks falsely about the car's superior condition. Hazel leaves the car with him, "certain that it was in honest hands" (*WB* 115). Mistaken about his own car, he persists in the hope that it will take him where he wants to go. His hope is sustained, however, by accepting lies concerning its condition. When he drives it again with Lily Hawks, he notices that "there were two instruments on the dashboard with needles that pointed dizzily in first one direction and then another, but they worked on a private system, independent of the whole car" (*WB* 124).

The difficulty over the car that Motes experiences reflects the disorder in his soul, which, increasingly, he wants to dissociate entirely from divine reality. The effect is a division within himself, like the car instruments going in different directions, indicating their apparent unruly independence. Hazel senses the conflict and determines that the Church without Christ is deficient because it does not offer anything but a negation of Christ, and his message shifts again to compensate for this lack. Even though Hazel removes the word *truth* from the name of his second church, attempting to negate

Christ as the source of divine truth by calling him a liar (*WB* 105), he is left with the realization that he nevertheless wants his negation to be true. Hazel Motes does not desire the complete abolition of truth; what he desires is a dedivinization of truth. He wants the source of truth to be human, not divine, and yet so long as he seeks to establish the church without Christ, it can only be a derivative, negative appropriation of truth. Hazel Motes wants to overcome his own negation, but the only way he can accomplish this is to create an alternative savior figure. Hazel admits that he "believes in a new kind of jesus," one who is "all man and ain't got any God in him" (*WB* 121), because he can find no other means for preaching his truth without some model of what that truth entails.

The most consistent aspect of Motes's rejection of Christ is rooted in the idea that the Incarnation does not change human beings, nor does the blood of Christ have anything to do with what will save human beings. For Hazel Motes, the religious teaching of his mother has instilled the impression that the only thing connecting human beings to God is human sin. Since there is no positive connection between the human and divine beyond the human need for redemption, and since human beings are in need of God only on account of their sinfulness, Hazel Motes argues that, without sin, divine redemption is irrelevant: "If you had been redeemed, . . . you would care about redemption but you don't. Look inside yourselves and see if you hadn't rather it wasn't if it was. There's no peace for the redeemed. . . . The truth don't matter to you. If Jesus had redeemed you, what difference would it make to you? You wouldn't do nothing about it" (*WB* 140). These comments reveal his belief that there is no positive spiritual connection to God in human beings that would significantly affect the meaning of human existence. There is not even enough to make them desire redemption. But rather than preaching that each individual simply finds his or her own meaning or redemption, Hazel Motes wants to provide it for everyone himself.

The "Holy" Church of Christ without Christ

Motes becomes entangled in his own confusions because he cannot escape two impulses: the desire to preach the truth despite his rejection of it, and the need for a model "savior" to take the place of Jesus. These two impulses come to a head with the advent of Onnie Jay Holy, who gives a third and final name to Hazel's church: the Church of Christ without Christ. Hazel Motes objects to Holy's addition even though it is the most accurate representation of what he preaches. Hazel is ignorant of the contradiction in his thinking that Onnie Jay Holy captures intuitively in this new name; essentially, Hazel preaches a truth without the Truth and a savior without the Savior. As a preacher, Hazel wants to preach a message that he considers true for everyone, even if it is an individualistic truth, but the only "truth" he has to offer is that there is none: "I preach there are all kinds of truth, your truth and somebody else's, but behind all of them, there's only one truth and that is that there's no truth" (*WB* 165). And Hazel's negative appropriation of Christ is apparent in his call for a "new jesus": "What you need is something to take the place of Jesus, something that would speak plain. The Church without Christ don't have a Jesus but It needs one! It needs a new jesus! It needs one that's all man, without blood to waste, and it needs one that don't look like any other man so you'll look at him" (*WB* 140–41).[25] Motes is presented with two potential saviors. Enoch Emery gives him the shrunken mummified man for his "new jesus,"[26] and Onnie Jay Holy gives him Solace Layfield (*WB* 167). The mummy is all man, with no God in him, and the pseudo-prophet Solace Layfield is a consumptive image of Hazel himself. Each reveals the measure of Hazel Motes's rebellion, and he destroys them both.

Although Onnie Jay Holy is a charlatan like Asa Hawks, he too is able to understand Motes's struggle in ways that Hazel himself cannot. Onnie Jay Holy preaches Hazel Motes's own predicament, using Hazel as his prophet in order to make a profit. His first assessment of Hazel's church and, coincidentally, of Hazel's life, is the lack of a congregation or friends. Onnie Jay Holy preaches the loneliness and alienation without friends, which not only describes Hazel's current situation, but suggests the only kind of communal life possible when one despairs of the redemption of human beings: "Not to have a friend in the world is just about the most miserable and lonesome thing that can happen to a man or woman! And that's the way it was with me. I was ready to hang myself or to despair completely" (*WB* 150). Holy understands that sweetness sells, and to counter Hazel's soured disposition and general lack of faith in human beings, he preaches the reality of innocence lost, but with the potential to be recovered in the human heart. More specifically, and in almost direct contradiction to Motes's experience, Holy refers to his own mother, suggesting that sweetness is inherent in human beings, only sometimes forgotten—a position at odds with everything Hazel has understood his Christian religion to be: "Not even my own dear old mother loved me, and it wasn't because I wasn't sweet inside, it was because I never known how to make the natural sweetness inside me show. . . . Every person that comes onto this earth . . . is born sweet and full of love" (*WB* 150).

The final contentious action of Onnie Jay Holy is to change the name of Hazel's church by adding a "Christ." Why does he do this? Because it describes more accurately the nature of the negative church that Hazel preaches. Onnie Jay Holy has obviously heard Hazel preaching about a "new jesus," and so for this reason alone he is right to add a "Christ" to the "Church without Christ"; but the other reason that Holy's addition is relevant stems from the fact that Hazel Motes's church, preached as a negative version of Christian redemption, can only ever be a church of Christ *without* Christ. Hazel's rebellion is in essence parasitic: it is entirely in response to Christ; therefore, all of his attempts to be rid of Christ necessarily fail. Nonetheless, Hazel reacts violently to Onnie Jay Holy's appropriation of his church, who later even refers to it as Onnie J. *Holy's* "*Holy*" Church of Christ without Christ" (*WB* 151).

However, what finally divides the two men is Hazel's claim of spiritual superiority. He sees that Holy wants to "sell" the Church of Christ without Christ, and Hazel knows that the truth cannot be had for money, which was never his interest, unlike both Hawks and Holy: "Listen! . . . It don't cost you any money to know the truth! You can't know it for money!" (*WB* 154). But Hazel cannot escape Holy, since his car has developed a "tic" making it "go forward about six inches and then back about four" and it does this "a succession of times rapidly" (*WB* 154). Holy has caught Hazel in his contradictory state of soul, the car imitating the confusion, as Hazel moves forward and is then set back. Holy tries to give Hazel advice about the car: Perhaps he has flooded the engine? Or he needs to pull out the choke? The discussion of the car is paralleled by the advice Holy gives Hazel about preaching, and when Hazel rejects Holy's addition of "Christ" to his church, Holy argues: "It don't make any difference how many Christs you add to the name if you don't add none to the meaning, friend" (*WB* 157).

Hazel Motes goes to sleep in his car after Holy departs and dreams that "he was not dead but only buried. He was not waiting on the Judgment because there was no Judgment, he was waiting on nothing" (*WB* 160). While it might be true that he is waiting on nothing, Hazel Motes is definitely waiting. Part of the dream includes various eyes looking into the car window at him, and Hazel expects Asa Hawks to come (*WB* 161). By contrast to Onnie Jay Holy, Hawks seems to Hazel more genuine: Holy just sees dollar signs, whereas Hawks might have some insight into truth because of the cost to himself with his self-blinding. Hawks does not come, and instead Hazel goes to his apartment, picks the lock and enters, and strikes a match to look into Hawks's eyes while he is sleeping. Hazel wants to know the truth, and thinking that Hawks may have seen it, he peers into his opened eyes. Hazel experiences the final revelation for his preaching: "The two sets of eyes looked at each other as long as the match lasted; Haze's expression seemed to open onto a deeper blankness and reflect something then close again" (*WB* 162). Asa Hawks is not blind, and Hazel must refigure his church's message. He now has proof that the blind man is not blind, and thus cannot see anything beyond what Hazel can see.

Truth, as Motes has been seeking it, is challenged by Asa Hawks and Onnie Jay Holy: the truth they preach is merely the sham servant of their own interests and is motivated by their desire for money. Hazel Motes, in his negative rebellion, wants to establish a truth in opposition to that taught in his family. He does not want merely to oppose this Christian teaching; he wants to supplant it with his own church. The difficulty of his undertaking is intensified by his confrontation with others who preach their own church alongside his. Rather than accept the relativity of truth, Hazel cannot resist claiming a truth that supersedes the rest: "There's only one truth and that is that there's no truth" (*WB* 165). O'Connor mentions this kind of response in her essay "Catholic Novelists and Their Readers," where she reveals the nature of Hazel's predicament: "Those who have no absolute values cannot let the relative remain merely relative; they are always raising it to the level of the absolute" (*MM* 178). Hazel Motes cannot tolerate the idea that the truth he preaches is on the same level as Onnie Jay Holy's or anyone else's, as this would reduce his truth to individual opinion. Asa Hawks's initial challenge, that "Jesus is a fact," impelled Hazel Motes to confirm the negation of that fact. Where Motes ends up, however, is merely asserting his absolute claim of no truth in order to reject any other possible claim to truth; this is all that Hazel, in his primarily parasitic relation to truth, can maintain.

Conscience

The deficiency in Hazel Motes's rebellion becomes obvious in the conflict within himself. The car's backward and forward movements suggest this inner conflict symbolically, but the most revealing event is Hazel's physical confrontation with the mirror image of himself in the form of Solace Layfield. While Hazel would limit reality to what you can "hold in your hands or test with your teeth" (*WB* 206), he is also conscious of the importance of acting out that belief. He does not simply want to believe that there is no redemption; he wants to *live* as if there is no redemption. The idea of human independence from Christ has ethical implications: to live as though one is completely free and responsible for no one makes for a selfish existence. However, despite Hazel's belief in individual freedom he cannot resist criticizing Onnie Jay Holy and Solace Layfield because they are not "true" (*WB* 152, 203). Again, Hazel is caught in the midst of his truth claims: he cannot live as if there were no truth because he repeatedly wants to measure himself as true.

Ironically, it is as he is preaching about the falsity of conscience—understood as the moral faculty of self-awareness in relation to a larger measure of truth—that Hazel meets "himself" when he looks over at Solace Layfield. Hazel is arguing against the experience of conscience in his efforts to remove the possibility of spiritual insight from human existence: "Your conscience is a trick. . . . It don't exist though you may think it does, and if you think it does, you had best get it out in the open and hunt it down and kill it, because it's no more than your face in the mirror is or your shadow behind you" (*WB* 166). What Hazel lacks more than anything is an adequate spiritual perception of himself. During his sermon on conscience, Solace Layfield joins the scene and provides Motes with an image of his own spiritual condition. Someone in the crowd immediately perceives the external similarity: "Him and you twins?" The appearance of Solace Layfield as Hazel's twin and the idea of conscience are soon intertwined. Hazel answers the question oddly: "If you don't hunt it down and kill it, it'll hunt you down and kill you" (*WB* 168). Hazel is talking about destroying one's conscience, but the implication is that he must also destroy something of himself that is represented by Layfield, a consumptive, hollow-chested man, who is "not true" in his negative response to Christ.[27] Hazel, though moved by the sight of Solace, is unable to see what the image reveals about himself. His own vision is so distorted that he only sees it as an illusion: "He was so struck with how gaunt and thin *he* looked in the illusion that he stopped preaching. He had never pictured himself that way before" (*WB* 167; italics mine). He does not hesitate to identify the illusion as himself, but he does not accept it as real. He decides that this illusion is one of those tricks of the conscience—which does not really exist and therefore must be destroyed—and so he acts on his preaching by killing Solace.

When Hazel hunts Solace down the next night he does not simply kill him; he also condemns the dying man. But the judgment on his "twin" reveals the truth about who Hazel Motes is: "a man that ain't true and one that mocks what is" (*WB* 204). Significantly, Hazel kills Solace with his car, a symbolic expression of a disordered soul that cannot discern the falsehood or division within himself. When Solace is lying face down on the ground, naked and dying, Hazel is satisfied: "The man didn't look so much like Haze" (WB 204). Determining the resemblance to be purely external, and not perceiving his own internal conflict thus mirrored, Hazel is free to reject Solace Layfield's existence as meaningless to him. Yet the death of Solace is not only a symbolic death of Hazel; it is also a murder motivated by Hazel's refusal to acknowledge—indeed his will to destroy—anything that transcends his understanding,[28] in this case, the experience of conscience. In the words of Onnie Jay Holy, the one who presents Hazel with himself, "If you don't understand it, it ain't true, and that's all there is to it" (WB 152). Hazel's truth is self-defined. Hazel is only able to measure others in relation to himself as the locus of truth; he falls short in understanding himself according to any other measure. When Solace tries to speak as he is dying he is addressing Jesus, but it is Hazel who "squat[s] down by his face to listen." Hazel is contemptuous of Solace's weakness in making his confession; yet at the same time he desires to be the one to whom it is addressed: "'You shut up,' Haze said, leaning his head closer to hear the confession" (WB 204–5). Hazel's confusion is revealed in his criticism of Solace Layfield as one who is "not true" and "mocks what is," thereby intimating the possibility of untruth within the self, measured in relation to something which transcends the self. Hazel cannot see his judgment of Solace as a self-judgment because his inner conflict is rooted in wanting both to deny that transcendent measure and to appropriate it for himself.

Self-Blinding Rebellion

After Hazel destroys Solace Layfield, a patrolman destroys Hazel's car by sending it over an embankment with a slight push from his own vehicle. He reminds Hazel, "Them that don't have a car, don't need a license" (WB 209). Bereft of his vehicle for spiritual freedom and physical escape, Hazel is forced to contend with the empty place in which he finds himself. The patrolman suggests his condition: without the acknowledgment of a transcendent measure (a "license"), there is no need for moral justification and no place from which to argue for truth (a "car"). Although Hazel is now actually looking up, he only sees the "blank gray sky that went on, depth after depth, into space" (WB 209). In spite of the suggestion of depth to the sky, Hazel sees only a blank grayness because he does not really know how to see. Does his self-blinding, the response to the state in which he finds himself, help him to see more clearly? O'Connor says that "Haze does not come into his absolute integrity until he blinds himself," but she qualifies this by explaining that Haze's wise blood "gets him further and further inside himself where one may be supposed to find the answer" (*CW* 920). Her comment indicates that Hazel enters into a state of wholeness (integrity) when he is blinded, and yet she withholds judgment about whether he can or does "find the answer." The implication is that the shift of Hazel's vision away from physical sight is required for him to see what and who he is as a spiritual human being, but whether this inward turn is enough remains uncertain.

John Desmond considers the destruction of Hazel's car the impetus for a renewed vision: "Haze turns inward to act out his own integrity and commitment to personal truth by mortification of the body." His extreme penance, according to Desmond, reveals the recognition that he has "to pay" for his acts. Desmond concludes that this mortification "implies his acceptance of an identity within a spiritual order that extends beyond the self, an identity to which he is accountable."[29] Yet while Hazel Motes's acknowledgment of "payment" suggests accountability, it does not appear to overcome the narrow religious vision of his childhood. Hazel's self-blinding reveals his continued misperception of spiritual reality as well as his assumption that the eyes must be detached from spiritual vision, or that the physical has no part in the spiritual, and, finally, that the human relation to the divine must be measured in terms of moral debt. Hazel spends the final days before his death adding to his "payment" by wrapping his chest with barbed wire and walking with stones and broken glass in his shoes, the repetition of the latter penance presumably indicating a return to his mother's religious ideas.

Interpretations of the meaning and outcome of Hazel's self-blinding and penance vary widely. Several commentators have used this blinding to accuse O'Connor of a Manichean separation of spirit and matter, maintaining that she was not, in fact, sacramental in her vision because she thought that the physical world was grotesque.[30] These interpreters claim that O'Connor believed it was necessary for Hazel to destroy his eyes so that he could see the spiritual world beyond this one. They also conclude that O'Connor considered the abnegation of the flesh necessary for spiritual vision. But what is the substance of this spiritual vision? The ability to interpret spiritual renewal inevitably becomes more difficult at this point, because there is no indication in the story that Hazel Motes has any deeper experience of spiritual reality other than a loose notion of "payment," which is no different from his family's religious views. Even subtle and compelling interpretations of Hazel's transformation through his blinding leave the reader with serious doubts about his attainment of vision or insight.[31] Desmond compares the ending of *Wise Blood* to other stories of transformation where there is a "revelation of the numinous." He concludes that "no such revelation occurs in *Wise Blood*."[32]

O'Connor's work is especially prey to the assumption that her Christian view will determine the outcome of her characters' spiritual transformations. As she says in a letter: "I am afraid that one of the great disadvantages of being known as a Catholic writer is that no one thinks you can lift the pen without trying to show somebody redeemed" (*HB* 434). While this in itself is not a refutation of the possibility that Hazel's blinding is redemptive, it does suggest that there might be a deeper judgment found within the story. All of the churches that Hazel preaches are described in relation to Christ, yet how does Christ relate to Hazel's blinding? For some insight into this question, it is worth considering two parallel examples of blinding referred to within the story, namely, those of Asa Hawks and of Paul the apostle, where Christ plays a central role in each blinding.

It seems appropriate to return to a final discussion of Asa Hawks and the nature of his career as a blind preacher because he is a key role model for Hazel Motes. It is Hawks who first perceives the confusion in Hazel and who consequently removes the mark of one preacher and gives him another, as he offers to do during their first encounter (*WB* 51). What is the meaning of and impetus for Hawks's attempted blinding? Asa Hawks provides Hazel with the most compelling instance of someone who apparently lives a life of self-sacrifice, including the significant cost of his eyesight, out of devotion to God. This sacrifice, in addition to the mystery of a blind man who *sees,* challenges the positivistic message that Hazel preaches. When Hazel asks him about his blindness—"If Jesus cured blind men, howcome you don't get Him to cure you?"—Hawks responds by saying: "He blinded Paul" (*WB* 111). Hazel's question seems legitimate and biblically astute; curing blindness seems more typical of Jesus' ministry than causing blindness. But Asa Hawks's identification with Paul's temporary blinding is meant to bolster his reputation: he wants to share in the same experiences as an apostle.

The newspaper clipping saved by Hawks suggests, however, that ten years ago at a revival he promised to blind himself with lime in order "to justify his belief that Christ Jesus has redeemed him" (*WB* 112). The second newspaper article, which Hazel does not see, says that Hawks lost his nerve, but his own recollection of the incident is more revealing as to the religious significance of his experience:

He had preached for an hour on the blindness of Paul, working himself up until he saw himself struck blind by a Divine flash of lightning and, with courage enough then, he had thrust his hands into the bucket of wet lime and streaked them down his face; but he hadn't been able to let any of it get in his eyes. He had been possessed of as many devils as were necessary to do it, but at that instant, they disappeared, and he saw himself standing there as he was. He fancied Jesus, Who had expelled them, was standing there too, beckoning to him; and he had fled out of the tent into the alley and disappeared. (*WB* 114)

In this account we witness the false preacher's confrontation with the truth about himself and his flight from that truth. Hawks is trying to conjure up his own vision, and the spectacle of his faith is worked up for the glory of notoriety.

Hawks speaks of the blinding of Paul as his impetus and inspiration; he, Asa Hawks, is going to justify Christ's redemption. But Paul did not blind himself. His blinding accompanied a vision of Jesus, and his blindness was temporary, for when the scales fell from his eyes they were opened, both physically and spiritually, to a clearer vision of his experience of Christ. Asa's blinding, by contrast, needs the possession of many demons, and it is Christ who turns them aside and stops the deliberate blinding. Asa runs away. He prefers the darkness of the alley into which he runs to acknowledging Christ as the one who gives him his sight.[33] He lives posing as a blind preacher in order to signify his refusal and rejection of the sight offered by Jesus in the tent—a kind of self-inflicted blindness. Asa Hawks chooses the lie of blindness over the truth of sight. He pretends to be blinded by Jesus when it was Jesus who preserved his sight, chasing away the demons required to go through with the act.

How does the account of Hawks's blinding help us to understand Hazel Motes's blinding at the end of *Wise Blood*? Motes is already spiritually blind: he does not "believe anything you couldn't see or hold in your hands or test with your teeth" (*WB* 206). To blind himself physically brings him into accord with his spiritual blindness, and could be interpreted as his rebellion against a spiritual order of reality that he will not accept. One could speculate further about what motivates Hazel Motes. Before killing Solace Layfield he says that he can't stand "a man that ain't true" (*WB* 204), and so Motes might have been trying to be a "true" blind preacher by following through where Hawks had faltered. After killing Solace Layfield, Motes sees a vision of blankness in the sky; the scene concludes with his purchase of a tin bucket and a sack of quicklime to blind himself. Does the emptiness of vision when he looks at the "blank gray sky" make him lose interest in seeing anything else? Or does the idea that the sky "went on, depth after depth, into space" (*WB* 209) remind him that no matter how much he tries to limit his spiritual vision, there is more to see? Each of these possibilities suggests reactions that might have led Motes to blind himself; they do not necessarily explain what the blinding means or reveals. That the self-blinding is a form of atonement—interpreted in light of Motes's references to "paying"—does not make his blinding any easier to understand. If Motes's words and actions suggest repentance, he does not clarify his intentions beyond these vague hints.

Although O'Connor explains that when "Haze blinds himself he turns entirely to an inner vision," the substance of that vision is not made apparent to the reader (*CW* 921). One of the most perplexing aspects of Motes's self-blinding is that there is no obvious indication of an inner revelation or insight on his part after he loses his physical sight. He is silent. In fact, what we learn about Motes's state of mind after his blinding comes with the narrative of his landlady, Mrs. Flood. Blind and without his car at the end of *Wise Blood,* Hazel Motes becomes increasingly ill and completely dependent on Mrs. Flood. There is a noticeable shift in focus in the final chapter: Hazel's vociferous proclamations of his freedom from the spiritual burdens of redemption and sin turn into his vague and muttering sense of obligation and debt while being fed and cared for by Mrs. Flood. In this dramatic change of circumstances, Hazel is confronted by the reality of human interdependence. Although he is not capable of taking responsibility for anyone, his dependence brings home the obligation of responsibility to Mrs. Flood.

The shift in perspective gives the reader a different view of Hazel Motes. Although he does not say much, his character is very present to the reader, especially because his actions elicit such disquiet from Mrs. Flood. However, the drama of the narrative is now carried by her responses to Motes. When she finds money in his wastebasket she becomes incensed by the mishandling of his extra cash, and her concern is expressed in moral terms: "The poor and the needy. Don't you ever think about the poor and needy? If you don't want that money somebody else might" (*WB* 220). Mrs. Flood's reference to charity is significant: O'Connor states directly that Hazel Motes's self-blinding "left him in no state to practice charity" (*HB* 335).

In her letter to Betty Hester, O'Connor describes how St. Thomas says that an act can be derived from charity in one of two ways: "The first way the act is elicited by charity and requires no other virtue—as in the case of loving the Good, rejoicing in it, etc. In the second way, an act proceeds from Charity in the sense of being commanded by it." She explains her point by using the example of St. Catherine of Genoa, who performed strenuous penitential practices for four years, after which she abandoned them to "simple acts of charity" for her remaining twenty-one years. O'Connor reports that these latter years were said to have been the fullest and most "costing" of her life (*HB* 335). The cost of charity in St. Catherine's case was her immersion into a life of responsibility for others. Contrary to this example, Motes seems to act without a clear direction for his painful penances, and he is not at all interested in charity. He lines his shoes with rocks and glass to pay, but when he is asked by Mrs. Flood, "For what?" he claims, "It don't make any difference for what. . . . I'm paying" (*WB* 222). He appears driven by an idea (possibly a command) but lacking a sense of purpose. When Mrs. Flood finds Motes sleeping with barbed wire wrapped around his chest, he explains that he does it because he is not "clean" (*WB* 224). He speaks about his payment as though responding to a command; the mortification of his body seems to be in response to his recognition of his perverse spiritual condition.

In *Wise Blood,* Hazel's self-mortification has the effect of isolating him from others, although in doing so, he becomes Mrs. Flood's responsibility. Through his blindness he puts Mrs. Flood in a position to learn about charity. Hazel's vision and self-understanding are not clear, but his actions and few words have a startling effect on Mrs. Flood. Instead of our focusing on the individual redemption or redeeming vision of the character of Hazel Motes, it might be more appropriate to consider how O'Connor brings the whole drama together with this ending. Is the moral vision meant to come to Hazel Motes alone? Or does the story illustrate where Motes ends up and others begin in relation to a clearer understanding of reality and human responsibility?

Mrs. Flood becomes an interpreter of what spiritual knowledge Motes might possess. Before her encounter with Motes, Mrs. Flood considers blindness to be worse than death, but the blind man's life suggests to her a deeper mystery, a spiritual world where the mind is "big enough to include the sky and planets and whatever was or had been or would be" (*WB* 218). The entrance of this cosmic notion into Mrs. Flood's imagination represents a change in perception: she moves from a conception of human thought as "a switch-box where she controlled from" to the possibility of a transcendent, eternal order spiritually present in Hazel's blind head. She attempts to engage him in guiding her to the spiritual mysteries he appears to see in his blindness, imagining the spiritual experience of eternity as "walking in a tunnel and all you could see was a pin point of light. She had to imagine the pin point of light; she couldn't think of it at all without that" (*WB* 218–19). Mrs. Flood describes the pinpoint of light as a star, reminiscent of the "thousands of stars" moving slowly and unnoticed on Hazel's first night in Taulkinham (*WB* 37).

Mrs. Flood comes to the truer understanding of responsibility as she develops a sense of spiritual insight, sparked by the mystery of Hazel Motes. The cosmic images of eternity, and her notion that "seeing" can extend beyond physical sight, mark her developing view of human spiritual existence. Although she initially thinks that blindness is worse than death, she is nonetheless moved to care for Hazel Motes, accepting him into her life. When she proposes marriage her words attest to a feeling of moral accountability that is heightened by Hazel's dependent state: "I wouldn't do it under any ordinary condition but I would do it for a blind man and a sick one. If we don't help each other, Mr. Motes, there's nobody to help us" (*WB* 227). Mrs. Flood feels responsible for providing a place for others. In her view, "nobody ought to be without a place of their own to be . . . and I'm willing to give you a home here with me, a place where you can always stay, Mr. Motes" (*WB* 227). Her offer is a corrective to Motes's understanding of responsibility: he has spent his time in Taulkinham preaching the opposite view, understanding place as entirely self-contained. Motes believes in complete independence, having argued that "nothing outside you can give you any place" (*WB* 165).

Two policemen find Motes, just before he dies in their patrol car, "lying in a drainage ditch near an abandoned construction project" (*WB* 229). By contrast, the transcendent order of reality, which is represented at the beginning of the novel as some vast construction work that is infinitely underway, both measures and encompasses him. Hazel Motes is forced to abandon his own individualistic construction of meaning, which denies any moral order of reality. His murder of Solace Layfield is consistent with his belief in absolute moral independence, the consequence of his spiritual position. In his blinded state, he is forced to reenter the realm of interdependent human relations: even after his death, he is lying on Mrs. Flood's bed, where she exclaims to his dead body, "I see you've come home!" (*WB* 231). According to O'Connor's positioning of Hazel Motes, and the real outcome of his limited spiritual vision, one could conclude that the human construction project cannot be completed unless it participates in the eternal work of creation "that involve[s] the whole order of the universe and would take all time to complete" (*WB* 37).

This process of creation is not carried out alone, and in the story it continues with Mrs. Flood. The final scene of her seated at the bedside of a dead Hazel Motes suggests her willingness to enter into the mystery of spiritual sight; she stares into his dead eyes with her own eyes shut. The experience is one of limited revelation, but at least a beginning: she "felt as if she had finally got to the beginning of something she couldn't begin, and she saw him moving farther and farther away, farther and farther into the darkness until he was the pin point of light" (*WB* 232). Mrs. Flood's revelation is the acknowledgment of Hazel Motes as the one who extends her vision to a spiritual understanding of reality. He helps her see her responsibility under the aspect of eternity.

CHAPTER THREE

The Violence of Love

The Violent Bear It Away

Self-torture is abnormal, asceticism is not.

—Flannery O'Connor, *The Habit of Being*

Freedom and Control

If the acts of self-inflicted violence and murder done by the preacher Hazel Motes in *Wise Blood* were not grotesque enough, the murder/baptism by the young prophet Francis Tarwater in *The Violent Bear It Away* is certainly liable to test the boundaries of even O'Connor's most sympathetic readers' sensibilities. Hazel Motes's parasitic religiosity can take him no further than preaching the Church without Christ, and his violence is ultimately rooted in a narrow religious vision learned from his family and encouraged by several religious frauds. For all his self-inflicted torture, Motes cannot come to a redeeming vision of God: his violence is the outcome of his single-minded attempt to reconstruct reality in his own image, and this blinds him, spiritually and physically, to a more comprehensive vision of human beings in their relation to the divine. The *Violent Bear It Away* presents the experience of violence differently, in terms of a more complex series of influences and motivations impinging upon the main character. In Francis Tarwater we see a multilayered character whose internal struggle to follow his own will and to choose his own path is complicated by the two major external influences in his life: his great-uncle Mason Tarwater and his uncle Rayber. Tarwater is deeply affected by his two uncles, but this influence gives rise to a compelling dialectic in which his own will to act is both fueled and obstructed. While Hazel Motes reacts primarily against his family's rigid religious mentality, applying its narrow vision to his own "religion," Francis Tarwater is raised by a dynamic religious prophet and then challenged by his atheist uncle: the struggle of their opposing visions is mirrored in Francis's soul.[1] Hazel Motes's violence is the outward expression of his rejection of God: he kills his conscience and blinds himself to spiritual reality. Tarwater's violence is ultimately rooted in his divided self that seeks order and resolution but only by means within his control.

Francis Tarwater has to reconcile two opposed visions of reality vying for his allegiance, both in relation to his uncles and in his experience of self-reflection. There is an explicit recognition in Tarwater that *he* must test what his uncles offer him as truth: "My great-uncle learnt me everything but first I have to find out how much of it is true" (*VBA* 79). Hazel Motes's automatic rejection of everything spiritual in human beings shuts down dialogue—while Tarwater's attitude affords the opportunity for a more dialectical engagement with spiritual reality and, consequently, for diverse levels of conflict. Tarwater does not resist the reality of spiritual experience; he resists the idea of any spiritual claims being imposed upon him. Tarwater is certain of his spiritual freedom; his self-reflective dialogue with his "friend" proves his ability to choose and to act on his own will. However, Tarwater resists any limitations to this freedom; he might want to be a prophet, but only on his own terms and without relinquishing his own control. Certainly the potential for myriad forms of violence is evident in these various struggles, none of which assume simply that violence is to be equated with rebellion or with God's punishment of human beings.[2]

In *The Violent Bear It Away*, the central violent act appears destined to accompany the sacrament of baptism. The other violent actions also appear to be inherently connected to religious experiences rather than the result of rejecting a particular religious idea. All of the violent acts described—whether the old prophet's burning vision of God, the drowning of Bishop, or the violation of Francis Tarwater in the woods—suggest a direct connection to the characters' revelatory insights, perhaps indicating O'Connor's more explicit attempt to draw word and act together sacramentally. Whereas it appears that Hazel Motes tries violently to self-appropriate his vision through penitential acts, the violence comes unsolicited in *The Violent Bear It Away*. The violent actions in the two novels could be further distinguished by O'Connor's comment, "Self-torture is abnormal, asceticism is not" (*HB* 458): one leads only to blindness, the other, perhaps, to a clearer vision of God. Self-torture inflicts bodily violence to no purpose, while asceticism (from *ascesis*, meaning training, or discipline) arises from some intention of aligning the physical and spiritual in human beings. Ascetic practices can nonetheless be experienced as somewhat violent.

In *The Violent Bear It Away* we can witness at least four possible sources of violence: (1) Tarwater's desire to assert control over his vocation and his actions, against what others have determined for him; (2) several different interpretations of asceticism, whether the spiritual control and rigor of Mason Tarwater or Rayber's rigidly disciplined ascetic life; (3) the internal conflicts of various characters, including Mason Tarwater's competing desires for destruction and salvation, Rayber's love of Bishop and his systematic refusal to acknowledge that love, and Francis Tarwater's internal arguments with his "friend" over what to believe and do; and finally, (4) the nature of prophecy itself, which, in its biblical roots, is usually associated with the violence of calling forth both the prophet and those whom the prophet addresses. The complexity and ambiguity of the violence in this novel has significant implications for understanding O'Connor's religious and moral vision. To understand the meaning of the violent acts in O'Connor's fiction requires a theological and ethical analysis of how that violence is measured, a problem that is related to our discussion of the grotesque. As I suggested in chapter 2, O'Connor's use of the grotesque needs to be interpreted through a proper account of her knowledge of what is good: the same is true for understanding her use of violence.

The question of whether O'Connor was unnecessarily subjecting her characters to violence stems from what I consider a general reluctance, perceptible in the scholarship, to explore her theological anthropology fully. Interpreting the violence without exploring her vision of human nature, her theological convictions, and her understanding of the human-divine relation often makes O'Connor's God appear entirely vengeful and her human beings utterly corrupt. In a letter O'Connor wrote to Ted Spivey in 1963, she was compelled to correct one such misunderstanding, evident in his commentary on *The Violent Bear It Away*: "On page 1, you sort of leave the impression old T. [Mason Tarwater] is Calvinist and sees people as dammed by

God. He sees them as dammed by themselves" (*HB* 507). O'Connor's clarification is significant, as it reveals her particularly keen attention to the details of the divine-human relation. What O'Connor emphasizes is Mason Tarwater's perception of human nature. In the novel, Mason's desire for the judgment and damnation of the world turns suddenly into that fury being visited upon him rather than the world; however, this experience is not a punishment from God, but a consequence of the violence of his own outward desire for destruction. What he learns is the difference between God's justice and his own attempt to inflict his idea of it on others: "Having learned much by his own mistakes, he was in a position to instruct Tarwater . . . in the hard facts of serving the Lord" (*VBA* 5–6).

O'Connor's anthropological assertion, that Tarwater "sees them [including himself] as dammed by themselves," should not be taken in isolation. The criticisms of O'Connor's anthropology have tended to be just as vociferous as the complaints about her theology; if her vengeful God is not bad enough, her human beings are worse, depraved and useless without God. To interpret O'Connor's appraisal of human beings (her anthropology) independently of her theology, or even vice versa, is to miss the importance of how she understands the divine-human relation. In a letter to Sister Mariella Gable, dated May 4, 1963, O'Connor remarks: "Ideal Christianity doesn't exist, because anything the human being touches, even Christian truth, he deforms slightly in his own image. Even the saints do this. I take it to be the effects of Original Sin, and I notice that Catholics often act as if that doctrine is always perverted and always an indication of Calvinism. They read a little corruption as total corruption" (*HB* 516).

O'Connor's Christian realism is the starting point for what she is able to see and understand of human experience. She does not idealize human beings as perfectly complete, nor does she assume that this incompleteness makes them purely corrupt. Herein lies the essential drama of O'Connor's fiction: the tension of human incompleteness is rooted in the conflict between the desire for completion and the freedom to resist it or the temptation to proclaim its having been achieved as one's own. To resist being completed by God is to resist submission to the fact of one's limitation and need. This is the intersecting point of O'Connor's anthropology and theology, and it is at this intersection that her characters often experience violence. Add to this the violence of an audience's reception when no such intersection is recognized,[3] and we begin to see why violence in her fiction is not a simplistic solution to an ethical problem, but an attempt to explore the implications of freedom and fallenness in human nature and in the human response to God.

When the issue of violence—including physical and spiritual violence, self-inflicted violence, and outward aggression—revolves specifically around the relationship between human beings and God, it becomes apparent that the violence is always a struggle for control, including the attempt to control what cannot be controlled, the struggle to take away another's control, the refusal to be controlled, and the desire to control oneself. Like the issue of violence, the issue of control resists simple moralistic conclusions. It is not simply a matter of determining that violence is bad and nonviolence is good, or that to be in control is good or not to be in control is good. What is required in these instances is some discernment about the type of relation (self-relation, relating to others or to God) and whether violence and control or their absence are appropriate to the relation. O'Connor's novels, and in particular *The Violent Bear It Away,* dramatically illustrate these issues of relation, rather than simply stating ethical claims about the goodness or evil of violence and control. In this way, O'Connor's fiction is superior to a kind of moralizing that tries to determine, in all instances, the moral validity of violence.

As for the issue of suffering violence, O'Connor's approach is specifically Christian: she understands human suffering to be linked in some way to the Incarnation and suffering of Christ. This is not to say that Christ's suffering on the cross eliminates or magically alleviates human suffering, rather that human beings are not alone in their suffering. Human suffering is not meaningless, nor does it indicate divine indifference. Instead, O'Connor would insist that the divine action of Christ's suffering has a share in human suffering, thus connecting Christ's actions to human life. O'Connor does not suggest that human beings deserve to suffer or that suffering is the point; she simply observes how the experience of suffering can be transformative in its Christian orientation. In a letter written to Betty Hester in 1961 she says: "You will have found Christ when you are concerned with other people's sufferings and not your own" (*HB* 453). O'Connor is critical of sentimentality over suffering that focuses on individual feelings of suffering, rather than an active response to suffering; her Christian ethic of love is connected to suffering with and for others. In a subsequent letter to Hester, O'Connor clarifies further her point: "People's suffering tears us up now in a way that in a healthier age it did not. . . . The kind of concern I mean is a doing, not a feeling, and it is the result of a grace which neither you nor I . . . in the remotest sense possesses. . . . I am just trying to isolate this kind of abandonment of self which is the result of sanctifying grace" (*HB* 454–55). For O'Connor, the focus of concern should be directed toward other people's suffering in an imitation of and participation in Christ's suffering. The central

Christian mystery, underlying everything and ultimately more important than violent conversions, prophetic voices, minor graces, and murdered children, is for O'Connor the fact that life "for all its horrors, has been found by God to be worth dying for" (*MM* 146). The active response of God to human suffering is at the heart of O'Connor's Christian understanding of reality.

To pass over "murdered children" in a sentence like the one above might rightly evoke Ivan Karamazov's outrage over the suffering of children,[4] and the fact that it is a child who is murdered in *The Violent Bear It Away* makes this reference to Ivan's rejection of theodicy particularly relevant. O'Connor would no doubt agree that this injustice is intolerable, but her stories and novels tend to focus more explicitly on the meaning of human suffering and its relationship to God's goodness. This problem is crucial for a reflection on violence in O'Connor's fiction because God is usually implicated in our automatic moral recoil from violent acts. How could a good God *let* this happen? O'Connor mentions Ivan Karamazov in her essay, "A Memoir of Mary Ann": "One of the tendencies of our age is to use the suffering of children to discredit the goodness of God, and once you have discredited his goodness, you are done with him. . . . Ivan Karamazov cannot believe, as long as one child is in torment" (*MM* 227).[5]

In O'Connor's view, the indictment of God for human suffering is not only a diversion from the human responsibility for suffering but also an attempt to construct an ethical system by which all justices and injustices can be tabulated and controlled. O'Connor believes that to see human suffering clearly and honestly is to recognize a limit or lack on the part of human beings, one they cannot control or remove from human life. In one of her lectures, she defines one of the strengths of Southern literature as "a distrust of the abstract, a sense of human dependence on the grace of God, and a knowledge that evil is not simply a problem to be solved, but a mystery to be endured" (*MM* 209). Examining Ivan Karamazov's "rebellion" and O'Connor's response to it is significant insofar as it reorients the question of violence away from formulaic solutions according to an ethical system of Catholic belief or unbelief and toward insight. That is, we obtain a clearer vision of the dramatic whole of suffering and need, and of responsibility and dependence, as they are enacted in O'Connor's fiction. O'Connor indicates that a feeling-centered response to suffering also effects a loss of clearsightedness: "In this popular pity, we mark our gain in sensibility and our loss in vision. If other ages felt less, they saw more, even though they saw with the blind, prophetical, unsentimental eye of acceptance, which is to say, of faith" (*MM* 227).

The difference between feeling and seeing is crucial. When O'Connor suggests that her readers should pay less attention to the number of dead bodies and more to the spiritual realities and actions of grace, she is not thereby dismissing the horror of the dead bodies. Instead she is directing the reader's attention to the "lines of spiritual motion," implying that the dead bodies are not gratuitous but have some inherent connection to the spiritual movement of the story: "Now the lines of motion that interest the writer are usually invisible. They are lines of spiritual motion. And in this story you should be on the lookout for such things as the action of grace in the Grandmother's soul, and not for the dead bodies" (*MM* 113). It should be emphasized that O'Connor is not suggesting a division between dead bodies (insignificant matter) and spiritual reality (grace).[6] She wants to insist upon the centrality of seeing what is "invisible," and perhaps not as immediate as the dead bodies, in order to understand the meaning of the violent actions in relation to something more than their effects. When the dead bodies are seen abstractly, and not in relation to the spiritual movements of the story, they can be perceived as insignificant; O'Connor wants to reorder this assumption by emphasizing a clearer vision of the spiritual. The blind, prophetical eye that O'Connor holds up as preferable to an excess of feeling is not a blindness of undiscerning faith, but an apparent blindness recalling the blind seers in Greek tragedy: lacking the obvious means of sight, they depended on the other heightened senses to see spiritual reality more clearly.

Related to this question of sight is the nature of our knowing and its connection to faith. O'Connor suggests that faith can be known both abstractly as a definition and in the midst of real choice, but to limit it to the former will inevitably leave one unprepared in the latter instance: "Our response to life is different if we have been taught only a definition of faith than if we have trembled with Abraham as he held the knife over Isaac. Both of these kinds of knowledge are necessary, but in the last four or five centuries, Catholics have overemphasized the abstract and consequently impoverished their imaginations and their capacity for prophetic insight" (*MM* 203). The relevance of this statement for interpreting *The Violent Bear It Away* is suggested by the juxtaposition of the biblical story of Abraham's faith with an intellectual definition of faith. For O'Connor, both are necessary, but the knowledge that is rooted in a lived response to life and shared through stories has been overshadowed by the predominance of abstract forms of knowing. Religious thought, however, when reduced to definitions, becomes formulaic and static rather than embodied and imaginative.[7] The human imagination is required in the interpretation of biblical stories no less than literature, and one should no more seek to distil formulaic doctrines from the literary works of a religious author like O'Connor than from the biblical stories themselves.

Matthew 11:12, or Bearing Away

> Listen boy . . . even the mercy of the Lord burns.
>
> —Mason Tarwater

One of the main problems that O'Connor sees emerging from the negative response to violent or grotesque literature is the unrealistic demand for "positive" literature.[8] Her comments on the subject reveal an insistent claim to frame her stories in theological and ethical terms. O'Connor does not write for the sake of the reader's satisfaction, and her spiritual insight into human life cannot avoid what is grotesque in order to "tidy up reality" in favor of a more positive view.[9] What is obvious from O'Connor's discussions of her use of violence and the grotesque is that she understands these human experiences theologically. Even the claim that grotesque literature is a typically Southern feature does not detract from O'Connor's theological purpose: "Whenever I'm asked why Southern writers particularly have a penchant for writing about freaks, I say it is because we are still able to recognize one. To be able to recognize a freak, you have to have some conception of the whole man, and in the South the general conception of man is still, in the main, theological" (*MM* 44).

O'Connor had to contend, however, with the notion that if the story has a moral, it should be an uplifting or inspiring one.[10] O'Connor's aversion to this kind of sentimentality is a matter of critical judgment that should not be misunderstood simply as harshness. Her view of human beings as "fallen" must be understood in relation to what they have fallen away from: God. What O'Connor rejects is the less discriminating human measure of compassion for all human action: "Compassion is a word that sounds good in anybody's mouth and which no book jacket can do without. It is a quality which no one can put his finger on in any exact critical sense, so it is always safe for anybody to use. Usually I think what is meant by it is that the writer excuses all human weakness because human weakness is human" (*MM* 43). O'Connor's appraisal of human nature, and particularly human limitation, is central to her theological and ethical discernment not only of violence but also of sentimentality and an excess of "feeling-centered" judgments: "The kind of hazy compassion demanded of the writer now makes it difficult for him to be anti-anything. Certainly when the grotesque is used in a legitimate way, the intellectual and moral judgments implicit in it will have the ascendancy over feeling" (*MM* 43).

One of the ways in which O'Connor counters this emphasis on human nature as its own standard of moral conduct is by looking at the phenomenon of human nature struggling against itself, in the experience of the "unnatural." In her study of the unnatural, O'Connor not only locates the deficiencies inherent in fallen human nature but also reveals the positive desire to overcome them. The unnatural here is the ascetic impulse, a violent (or so it appears) quelling of the "natural" drives and impulses. O'Connor's comments on violence usually include both its external and internal orientations and indeed suggest her preference for dramatizing the experience of violence within the self. The internal violence of the ascetic is not necessarily a solitary struggle, however, because the ascetic contends with a larger order of meaning. O'Connor understands the interior struggle of asceticism as an unnatural violence—meaning that it struggles against the "natural" instincts of self-preservation and protection—but one that is also capable of nobility and integrity. Writes O'Connor: "I am much more interested in the nobility of unnaturalness than in the nobility of naturalness. . . . The violent are not natural" (*HB* 343). For this reason, she is particularly interested in the relationship between the unnaturalness of the ascetic drive and its theological purpose.[11] As Richard Giannone's study demonstrates, O'Connor was profoundly influenced by the spirituality of the desert fathers and the habit of ascetic discipline directed toward the internal struggle of the will.

O'Connor sees the violence of love in the ascetics' language of spiritual warfare, which is not about external violence but about the internal struggle against the powers of anger, hostility, violence, cruelty, lust, and so on. That this inward focus for O'Connor's ideas about violence is key, and tied to her reading of Scripture, consider John Desmond's comment:

> She cautioned readers not to become mesmerized by the physical manifestations of violence in her stories. Putting it simply, she warned them not to "count the number of bodies" at the side of the road or the ditch, but rather to concentrate on what those explicit acts of violence signified in the interior world. That is, she focused attention on the spiritual violence of inner thought and attitude engraved in the heart and from which acts of murder, deception, rivalry and stigmatizing erupt.[12]

The epigraph to *The Violent Bear It Away,* Matthew 11:12, is a rather enigmatic passage, and while O'Connor wondered whether the book expressed successfully the meaning of the biblical passage, she did feel that the title and the epigraph were the best part of the novel.[13] My intention is not to assess O'Connor's success in fictionalizing the epigraph but to explain how O'Connor understands it, particularly in relation to the question of violence and the moral order of creation.[14] This should aid our understanding of the violent manifestations of Tarwater's rebellion, both externally and internally, and determine the theological relevance of this violence. The biblical text provides the narrative context for the violence since the days of John the Baptist's introduction of Christ, and O'Connor dramatizes the struggle of Tarwater in his response to Christ and the Kingdom.[15] Thus, the violent acts of Francis Tarwater need to be understood with O'Connor's account of the biblical epigraph in mind.

According to O'Connor, the understanding of violence that is expressed by Christ in the Gospels suggests a pattern of self-sacrifice that the followers of Christ are called to imitate, but unlike Christ, the responsibility for others is not rooted in human innocence, nor is it rooted in guilt for that matter. The responsibility for others entails self-sacrifice because the only way to stop violence is to bear it away. In Matthew 11:12, Christ's words constitute the framework for O'Connor's interpretation of violence as it relates to the Kingdom of Heaven: "From the days of John the Baptist until now, the Kingdom of Heaven suffereth violence, and the violent bear it away."[16] For O'Connor, the violence expressed by Christ in this passage describes the violence of love, which involves the experience of self-sacrifice. In a letter, O'Connor refers explicitly to the nature of Christ's words in Matthew 11:12, suggesting that they reveal the "violence of love" (*HB* 382). She is less concerned with the violence of the persecutors and more interested in the violence directed toward the self, borne internally in order to *avoid* becoming a persecutor: "Even when they read the quotation [Matthew 11:12], the fact that these are Christ's words makes no great impression. That this is the violence of love, of giving more than the law demands, of an asceticism like John the Baptist's, but in the face of which even John is less than the least in the Kingdom—all this is overlooked" (*HB* 382). The violence of love is a sacrifice borne by the self, and thus O'Connor equates the violence of love with asceticism (like that practiced by John the Baptist): it is an inward orientation of discipline and restraint done for the love of God and the Kingdom. The epigraph suggests that, in the face of violence, there is sometimes a "violence" required against the self, stemming from the effort to overcome the impulse to more violence.

The Matthew epigraph has two parts, one that refers to the violence suffered by the Kingdom, and one that refers to "the violent" who bear it away. O'Connor refers to "the violent" in one of her letters as "the ascetics," directly linked to John the Baptist, that ascetic of the desert who announces the coming of the Messiah. She defers to Aquinas: "St. Thomas's gloss on this verse is that the violent Christ is talking about represent those ascetics who strain against mere nature. St. Augustine concurs" (*HB* 343). And, in another letter, she makes her interpretation more explicit: "This is surely what it means to bear away the kingdom of heaven with violence: the violence is directed inward" (*HB* 486). The violence is against the self, not for selfish purposes but for something greater, described in this verse as the Kingdom. The Kingdom, among other things, signifies the divine ordering of goodness in the world, and while it suffers violence, it is nonetheless the impetus and source of the human ability to "bear away" violence for its sake. The first half of the Matthew passage provides the necessary context for the asceticism: the inward direction of violence is intended to counter the external violence that is already present and aimed at the goodness of creation. The Kingdom is, in Matthew's Gospel and in O'Connor's interpretation of it, pivotal to the understanding of the direction and order of violence.

Now let us return to the first half of Matthew 11:12. "The Kingdom of Heaven suffereth violence," according to Matthew, and this delineates the violence that is directed toward the divine order of reality. It does not say that the Kingdom is violent, or that violence is required to enter it, but it does say that it suffers violence. Jesus does not make this statement as a matter of discussion or debate, nor does he seem interested in the origins of violence; he describes instead a human response of violent resistance to God's order in creation. In the passages surrounding Matthew 11:12, the resistance to both Jesus and John reveals an unwillingness to hear what they are saying and doing. John the Baptist is too much of an ascetic, and his extremity breeds contempt; Jesus is too familiar with the crowds, and his eating and drinking is perceived as gluttony (Matthew 11:18–20).[17] Jesus certainly is not advocating a preference for gluttony or for extreme asceticism; rather, he is undermining that claim to knowledge of what is good that is measured in terms of human preference. He uses the people's fickle response to himself and John as an example of their desire to bend or to change God's will: "But to what shall I compare this generation? It is like children sitting in the market places and calling to their playmates, 'We piped to you and you did not dance; we wailed, and you did not mourn'" (Matthew 11:16). The Kingdom suffers violence from the desire of human beings to manipulate it according to their own will, and the prophetic call to justice and repentance further engenders violence when it is resisted. Jesus is aware of this proud resistance, and so his words, "Blessed is he who takes no offence at me," in Matthew 11:6 are all the more pressing. Offence is what bars the way to the Kingdom unless the offence is borne away in repentance, through the destruction and mastery of pride.

The second half of the passage can now be seen in light of what it means to bear away internally the human violence against God's goodness. The ascetic impulse is an attempt to absorb, or to take responsibility for, the violence inflicted on the Kingdom of Heaven.[18] Understood in this way, the violence is not directed inward as a negative force, nor is it commanded out of divine sadistic delight. It is, rather, a bearing of responsibility and a quelling of natural pride. The ascetic way is not pursued out of a love of violence or a hatred of the self; on the contrary, it expresses a hatred of violence and the suffering it inflicts, as well as a love of the true self and what is good in it. The sustaining measure is the Kingdom, and it is for the sake of the Kingdom that the choice is made.

In "A Good Man Is Hard to Find," O'Connor has her character, the Misfit, express the tension perfectly. The Misfit knows that it is Jesus who rejects the cycle of violence, and he explains this to the Grandmother, who has just witnessed his hitmen murder her entire family:

> Jesus was the only one who ever raised the dead, and he shouldn't have done it. He thrown everything off balance. If He did what He said, then its nothing for you to do but throw away everything and follow him, and if He didn't, then its nothing for you to do but enjoy the few minutes you got left the best you can—by killing somebody or burning down his house or doing some other meanness to him. (*CW* 151)

The choice the Misfit describes accounts for the different kinds of bearing away: either it is the cross, and the sacrifice of the self that is borne for the greater good, or bearing the weight of the rejection of that goodness by inflicting as much outward violence as possible to sustain it. The outward violence is a sign of the refusal to accept a divinely ordered world; the inward violence is a consequence of the acceptance of that order, bearing away that violence which seeks to destroy it, provided it is done for the love of God.[19] Desmond describes this double movement in the violence of love: "first, the violence of self-denial, the turning of violence inward against the 'natural' self to transform that inner self through asceticism; and, second, the movement outward in acts of love and charity toward the human community."[20]

O'Connor is careful to make distinctions that preserve the violence—both inward and outward—from being gratuitous, which is why the first half of the epigraph, the suffering of the Kingdom, is crucial for perceiving the gravity of the asceticism denoted in the second half. It is the love of God that motivates the action, not asceticism for its own sake. She makes this difference plain in a letter when she mentions Jansenism, the doctrine that denies any possible goodness to the human will: "Jansenism doesn't seem to breed so much a love of God as a love of asceticism" (*HB* 304). This contrast between the desire for violence against the self and the bearing of that violence for the love of God is indeed a central theme of *The Violent Bear It Away*. The old prophet Mason Tarwater comes to learn in time about this difference: "He had known what he was saving the boy from and it was saving and not destruction he was seeking. He had learned enough to hate the destruction that had to come and not all that was going to be destroyed" (*VBA* 6). The prophet learns to know what saves, and he does not pursue what saves by seeking destruction on its behalf or by hating the world or things perishable, including human beings. Rayber, Tarwater's schoolteacher uncle, however, seeks to save himself and others by sheer willpower, and in doing so he ends by destroying the very saving thing he needs—love.

The violence of love can manifest itself in different ways, and so also, correlatively, can the nature of asceticism. Rayber's habits of life can be described as ascetic, but he is espousing an inward violence that wants to control and reject love; whereas the old prophet's love of the world is violent with a vision of the world transfigured. Between these two is Francis Tarwater, who has to choose which vision of love will ground his life and, consequently, the direction of the violence. At the end of the novel, as young Tarwater is on his way to the city and his future, O'Connor suggests that there must be a sacrifice borne, an inward reorientation, and she uses the religious language of life and death: "He must of course not live to realize his mission, but die to realize it" (*HB* 342). This conception of love is tied to the image of love that the child evangelist expresses in her sermon, which is overheard by Rayber and is seemingly directed at him; it also recalls Mason Tarwater's impressions of burning love. She says that the word of God is love, but then asks if anyone present knows what this word is: "The Word of God is a burning Word to burn you clean!" (*VBA* 130–34). The images of life and death are not physical, but symbolic of a movement of the spirit toward what is truly life-giving, perceived when the self is no longer the center of one's existence. It is not a modern or popular conception of love—commonly tied to the gratification of one's desires rather than the disciplined ordering of them—but it is at the heart of O'Connor's ethical vision.

The Gospel epigraph to *The Violent Bear It Away* and the violence in O'Connor's work need to be interpreted as the dramatization of the inward struggle of the soul that is not simply understood in terms of the soul striving against the body, but as an embodied spiritual struggle. As Peter Hawkins says about O'Connor: "The warfare she wages is not, in fact, spirit against flesh, but, rather, spirit *in* flesh."[21] The tendency to construe O'Connor as writing primarily against the unbelief of the modern period is related to the accusation that she was held by a Manichean hatred of secular culture and the human body. The effect of these combined assumptions—that her fiction aimed to shock and thus convert unbelievers to faith and that she considered the physical world to be devoid of goodness[22]—has been to make her God an employer of vicious means and the practice of asceticism a form of self-torture. Such effects are themselves more dualistic or Manichean in attitude than what can possibly be attributed to O'Connor. This distortion is the inevitable outcome of understanding asceticism in solely physical terms, wherein the necessary mortification of evil matter (the body) gives freedom to the spirit. For O'Connor, ascetic training must be understood as a spiritual discipline that subdues the selfish will in the interests of others.

In this sense, the epigraph becomes central to the relation between violence and a sacramental understanding of the Kingdom. The violence and its direction, as stated above by the Misfit in "A Good Man Is Hard to Find," are determined entirely by the response to Christ and the Kingdom. The Misfit does not occupy himself with proving the truth or untruth of Christ, he simply outlines the possible human responses to Christ's model of non-violence. The rejection of Christ will mean outward violence, motivated and spurred by the idea that there is no divine ordering of goodness in the world. The acceptance of Christ entails the willingness, for the sake of the Kingdom and the goodness of the divine order, to suffer violence rather than perpetuate it. The presence of this divine order is affirmed in Francis Tarwater's sacramental vision. His final vision of the multitude eating the bread and fish represents the Kingdom on earth. For Tarwater, the vision reveals the connection between the living and the dead and affirms both the physical and spiritual experience of human responsibility. In this way, the human acceptance of suffering and sacrifice participates in Christ's sacrifice.

John Desmond's work on violence also locates its meaning within the Christian biblical tradition. He notes two common perceptions of O'Connor's violence: either she has a particularly hostile view of life, or she is reflecting the violent world in which we live. Desmond finds both these explanations lacking. In his argument, he attempts to link the use of violence in O'Connor's novels to the Gospel message of nonviolence. Desmond recognizes the fundamentally spiritual character of the meaning and direction of the violence; even in O'Connor's use of external violations, "she focused attention on the spiritual violence of inner thought and attitude engraved in the heart and from which acts of murder, deception, rivalry, and stigmatizing erupt. . . . O'Connor knew well that what must be emphasized and exposed is the interior disposition to violence which creates and directs outward actions."[23] Further, Desmond argues, with reference to her letters and comments, that O'Connor did not participate in "a wholesale rejection of violence, but rather a transformed sense of its aim and meaning."[24] This point is crucial because O'Connor's Christianity tends to make readers assume that she must take an either/or position on violence, when she is in fact identifying the important connection between the ascetic discipline of the individual and the outward action of charity. Desmond understands O'Connor's moral vision as one rooted in the real-life actions of human beings living in community, a state that necessitates the curtailment of the aggressive claims of the selfish individual.

Freedom and Eternal Responsibility

O'Connor's insistence that the "religious" nature of the epigraph's violence is ascetic offers sufficient reason for exploring the meaning of violence in the novel in terms of the soul's struggle with itself in relation to God. The protagonist, Francis Tarwater, embodies this struggle, and, in contrast to Hazel Motes, his resistance is expressed as resistance to external control. The response is a natural one for young Tarwater, since all of the adults he encounters seek to persuade him of their true authority. In particular, Tarwater's great-uncle Mason Tarwater and his uncle Rayber—both formidable influences who feel convinced of the authoritative veracity of their experiences and knowledge—want to impress upon young Tarwater their vision of reality. They seek to "free" Tarwater through their direction and, ultimately, their control. While it may appear on the surface that Francis Tarwater must decide between a religious and nonreligious vision of the world and that the choice to become a prophet is to accept the religious view, Francis's actions and words do not seem to indicate such a struggle. Even if Mason and Rayber can indeed be categorized as religious and nonreligious, respectively, O'Connor's interest in the inner struggle of the soul of Francis Tarwater is what takes the conflict in the direction of consequences and, ultimately, to a place where the ideological categories of "religious" and "nonreligious" are secondary to the primary questions of existential meaning. I argue that the opposition between Mason Tarwater's theism and Rayber's atheism is only the second-level expression of the conflict that really concerns O'Connor; what torments young Tarwater is not so much whether to believe in God's existence, but who he is in relation to God and how that knowledge will affect his life and action.

The theme of control is central in *The Violent Bear It Away*—not only to Francis Tarwater but also to Mason and Rayber. In fact, Francis learns adamant resistance to control under both men's influence, and especially old Mason's. Through a series of flashbacks and stories told by Mason, Francis learns the history of the struggle for control between the two older men. Earlier, Mason returned to live with Rayber, suggesting he might be dying. Rayber, then, took the opportunity to run psychological tests on Mason, with a specific interest in his "archaic" religious beliefs. Mason, not realizing at first that he was being studied by Rayber, rebelled when he discovered Rayber's manipulation. But what Mason rejected and violently resisted was not so much Rayber's deception as his attempt to control, or to consider himself in control of, Mason's thoughts and ideas. For Mason, no one can control one's thoughts or one's spirit: "Where he wanted me was inside that schoolteacher magazine. He thought once he got me in there, I'd be as good as inside his head. . . . Well that wasn't the end of it! Here I sit. And there you sit. In freedom. Not inside anybody's head!" (*VBA* 20).

Rayber is equally resentful of Mason Tarwater's effect on him. When Rayber was seven years old, Mason kidnapped him and, according to Rayber's account, "indoctrinated" him with his religious ideas. Rayber resists Tarwater's charismatic religious control, something he experienced and knows to be especially effective on young minds. This resistance has led Rayber to impose his own ascetic discipline on himself in order to avoid losing control. Rayber suggests to Mason Tarwater that Mason "ruined [his] life," and in the present situation of the novel Rayber transfers his concern to the old man's influence on Francis Tarwater. Rayber says to Mason: "A child can't defend himself. Children are cursed with believing. . . . You infected me with your idiot hopes, your foolish violence. I'm not always myself" (*VBA* 73). Rayber does not want to admit to the vestiges of control that Mason still exerts over him; he insists instead that "I've straightened the tangle you made. . . . I've made myself straight" (*VBA* 73). For Rayber, freedom from Mason Tarwater's control comes with education—one that eradicates the irrational religious notions that Mason espouses.[25] Freedom comes through knowing, especially knowing what is rational and factual. Rayber intends to offer this escape route to Francis, to free young Tarwater from Mason's control: "That's why I want you to learn all you can. I want you to be educated so that you can take your place as an intelligent man in the world" (*VBA* 110). Ironically, Rayber notices a kind of freedom already present in Francis, an "independence," which he clearly sees is owing to Mason's influence. While this independence would otherwise be a good thing, Rayber qualifies the sort that the younger Tarwater has learned: it was "not a constructive independence but one that was irrational, backwoods, and ignorant" (*VBA* 100).

In light of this fight for control between Mason Tarwater and Rayber, we can observe that the corresponding struggle is replayed in Francis Tarwater's soul. Mason does not accept the control of being inside "anybody's head," and Rayber does not accept the religious control of belief and action. Francis Tarwater is trained to be suspicious of control, but in differing directions, especially from listening to Mason Tarwater tell his stories of the conflict with Rayber. The conflict in Francis Tarwater presents itself most clearly when he is with Rayber, and he must simultaneously resist appearing controlled by either of them. When Rayber tries to make Francis do the same tests he did on Mason, Francis is wise to his trick and insists, like Mason, that his mind and spirit cannot be controlled by Rayber: "'I'm free,' he hissed. 'I'm outside your head. I ain't in it. I ain't in it and I ain't about to be'" (*VBA* 111). And yet, when Rayber worries that Francis has been corrupted entirely by Mason's fanatic religiosity, Francis argues that "he [Mason] ain't had no effect on me" (*VBA* 100). Added to the difficulty of Francis Tarwater's effort to resist both his uncles' control, however, is the compelling and onerous claim on his life exerted by his vocation: the call to be a prophet. The call to prophecy is something that Mason has claimed for Francis, and indeed expects of him, but it is also a call for which Francis awaits further, divine confirmation.

This resistance to any control is therefore provoked most forcibly in Francis by God's expectation of him as a prophet, which is voiced through another prophet, Mason Tarwater. Francis does not like the idea of being called to be a prophet, not because he is opposed to being a prophet, but because he resents any claim of control over his life, either when he must listen to Mason's exhortations of his mission or when he is waiting for a sign from God to determine his actions. He likes the fact that Mason Tarwater insists on his spiritual freedom, but hesitates at the thought that the freedom is not absolute: "The child would feel a sullenness creeping over him, a slow warm rising resentment that this freedom had to be connected with Jesus and that Jesus had to be the Lord" (*VBA* 20–21). If Francis has to be a prophet he prefers to be an Old Testament prophet, like Mason sometimes seems to be, rather than one connected to Jesus: "Had the bush flamed for Moses, the sun stood still for Joshua, the lions turned aside before Daniel only to prophesy the bread of life? Jesus? He felt a terrible disappointment in that conclusion" (*VBA* 21). Not only does Francis resist the claim on his life to be a prophet who baptizes in the name of Jesus, he also resists the particular mission to which he is called: to baptize an idiot-child. To this challenge Francis Tarwater is uncommonly resistant, and he voices his resistance to Rayber, although the "silent adversary" is not actually Rayber: "'I won't get used to [Bishop]! I won't have anything to do with him!' . . . He shouted and the words were clear and positive and defiant like a challenge hurled in the face of his silent adversary" (*VBA* 93).

Francis Tarwater's resistance to God's claim on him as a prophet is played out in his internal debate between the ideas of Mason and Rayber, especially on the subjects of freedom and responsibility. The issue of control is linked to how one understands freedom and responsibility, and Tarwater, in order to negotiate this internal dialogue, must come up with his own response to the competing visions of Mason and Rayber. The ultimate focus for this debate is the child Bishop, to whom Tarwater must respond if he is to follow his prophetic mission. But the issue of responsibility to himself and to others first appears when Tarwater has to face the burial of his great-uncle Mason. An internal discussion is mediated through the invisible stranger's voice,[26] which converses with Francis and responds to the internal dialogue that continues in Francis's mind between Rayber and Mason after Mason's death. With Mason gone, the stranger's voice keeps Francis company, but his response to Francis's remembrances of the episodes or arguments between his two uncles is intended to dissuade Francis from being controlled by either of them. The voice argues this, suggesting that Francis understands things *better* than both Mason and Rayber: "The truth is that you're just as smart, if you ain't actually smarter, than the schoolteacher. . . . He had somebody to tell him the old man was crazy, whereas you ain't had anybody and yet you've figured it out for yourself" (*VBA* 38). With this flattery, the voice suggests that Francis cannot continue to abide by either of his uncles' ideas and suggests instead that "nobody can do both of two things without straining themselves. You can do one thing or you can do the opposite." Tarwater automatically assumes—still influenced by the tenor of his uncles' debates—that the choice is between "Jesus and the devil," but the stranger corrects him. "It ain't Jesus or the devil. It's Jesus or *you*" (*VBA* 39). It is thus that Francis Tarwater confronts the nature of the resistance in his soul. "Jesus or you" names the conflict: a struggle for control over his life between himself and God. Francis's internal dialogue voices his ultimate resistance to God for making human beings accountable or responsible in their freedom. He cannot take care of his own interests as well as God's, according to the voice; that would be straining himself. The problem the stranger warns Francis about is reminiscent of Jesus' claim that "no one can serve two masters; for either he will hate the one and love the other, or he will be devoted to the one and despise the other" (Matthew 6:24). As the stranger encourages Francis to believe, "Now I can do anything I want to" (*VBA* 25). But the unresolved issue of the call to prophecy continues to propel the entire drama of the novel and, in a certain sense, determines the nature of Francis's actions and response. This issue of control remains unresolved.

Education

The claim that Francis Tarwater will be a prophet begins to take effect when Mason Tarwater kidnaps him from Rayber in the city and brings him back to Powderhead to educate him. Mason wants to instruct young Tarwater not only in the ways of prophecy, but also in self-knowledge, something Mason considers crucial for the prophetic life. Rayber, of course, vehemently rejects the idea that Mason can educate Francis better than he can. But Mason Tarwater is concerned about the inadequate knowledge Rayber has, especially the absence of true self-knowledge as a human being. What Mason wants for Francis Tarwater is not a religious education in a typical or doctrinal sense, but a lived sense of who he is, in the world, in relation to both God and others. The schoolteacher Rayber will raise Francis Tarwater to think and live according to "facts" alone; that is, according to the scientific method by which he lives his own life. He rejects any religious account of life or its meaning as unprovable nonsense. Instead he governs his life within the boundaries of what can be calculated or rationally understood. For Rayber this is a life that denies the reality of anything larger than himself or beyond his ability to understand, including experiences of love and transcendence.

The old prophet, Mason, inhabits a different spiritual and intellectual world. He senses that Rayber's reductive understanding of the nature of reality is deficient for educating a young boy like Francis, and so he brings the boy to live with him. Concerning his great-uncle's approach to education,

Francis Tarwater states: "His uncle had taught him Figures, Reading, Writing and History beginning with Adam expelled from the Garden and going on down through the presidents to Herbert Hoover and on in speculation toward the Second Coming and the Day of Judgment" (*VBA* 4). The education offered by Mason Tarwater is incorporated within the mythical framework of a religious interpretation of history that situates his present learning in relation to primordial origins and the eschatological future.

Of course, it is often the case that readers find Old Tarwater's approach to education fanatical and ridiculous—certainly outdated—and consider Rayber's approach to be more sensible. The events of the novel, however, are not bound by sensible facts, and O'Connor's purpose is to dramatize the different *visions* of Mason Tarwater and Rayber and the consequences of these visions for human relations. Rayber himself is not reducible to his secular, scientific ideology, and Mason is not only his thundering religious zeal. They should not be caricatured simply as stereotypes battling it out in Francis's soul. The reality of their existence as human beings, complicated by circumstances and actions that run counter to their ideas, makes the interpretive task for Francis Tarwater all the more difficult. For this reason alone, the facts of their teachings do not ultimately reveal who they are; this is obvious enough in the scenes where their ideas are bantered about, whether in the disputes between Mason and Rayber, Mason and Francis, Francis and the stranger, or Francis and Rayber.

Their visions of the world, beyond the words that they offer, evoke inherently moral claims and not simply differing systems of thought. Francis Tarwater has to learn to distinguish the implications of the ethical view in what each says and teaches. The common tendency of the novel's characters (and some interpreters) is to freeze other characters to fit into their ideas. Old Tarwater does not account for, or perhaps even know about, Rayber's gripping experiences of love for Bishop. And Rayber does not know of Mason's doubts and trials by fire. At a very young age, Francis Tarwater is left to struggle with the choice of imitation, either of what his prophet uncle has taught him or what Rayber is trying to teach him. In addition, he is all too aware of, and perhaps unduly biased by, what each thinks of the other. What does emerge slowly in Tarwater's struggle to understand is that the old prophet's account of human life, filled as it is with stories intertwining the lives of the living and the dead, and his mythic conception of spiritual reality as it manifests itself in human decision, render Rayber's rationalistic, ultimately reductive account of reality empty of meaning by comparison. Rayber cannot act, and significantly young Tarwater sees this.[27] What ensues is Francis

Tarwater's insistent and single-minded desire to act in response to Rayber's inaction, but Francis inadvertently rejects Mason's sacramental understanding of the connection between word and act. As John Desmond notes, "Mason Tarwater has both the word of divine truth and the power to 'act.'"[28] Francis acts by drowning Bishop, but as Desmond suggests: "In the act of drowning Bishop he is not freed from the Word—the words of baptism mysteriously pour forth from him. Hoping to redeem himself by this act and 'keep himself inviolate,' Tarwater has in fact steeped himself in guilt and further separation from his true identity."[29]

Baptism

What Mason's death entails for Francis is the burden of having to act, and this realization sparks the internal dialogue, as Francis struggles to choose the orientation of his actions. It is often assumed that Francis's dilemma at this point is concerned primarily with the prophetic vocation in a formal sense,[30] and that therefore the main issue in Francis Tarwater's response is his struggle between acceptance of the old prophet's command that he baptize Bishop and fulfill his role as a prophet and of Rayber's lessons in secular self-salvation. But does Francis's internal dialogue indicate that he is simply deciding which view to accept, or does his own will assert itself in the face of impinging attempts to control him? This is not the choice of a career path so much as it is the choice of the inner orientation of his whole life. Moreover, understanding the moral dimension of prophecy requires us to focus on the object of the prophetic call—Bishop, the idiot-child of Rayber. Mason has commanded Francis Tarwater to baptize and to recognize Bishop in the face of Rayber's denial of the child's inherent human worth. If we are to consider Bishop's tragic baptism in light of the novel's biblical epigraph, we need to examine the religious symbolism of violent acts in Francis Tarwater's quest—those outwardly committed and those inwardly accepted. The epigraph, as I have argued, relates the direction of violence to human responsibility: the choice between bearing away selfish impulses for the sake of others and a larger order of goodness, on the one hand, and asserting one's responsibility only to oneself, inevitably at the expense of others. Francis Tarwater is given two charges of responsibility over Bishop: one comes from his great uncle Mason Tarwater, who urges him to baptize the boy; the other comes from Rayber when he allows Tarwater to take Bishop out in the boat (*VBA* 198).

The motivations of both men for bestowing this responsibility upon Francis reveal their differing accounts of the meaning of responsibility.

Mason Tarwater wants Francis to baptize Bishop because this sacramental acknowledgment of his spiritual worth will be denied the child by Rayber, who has reduced Bishop's existence to a rationally incomplete, and hence less than fully human, being.[31] Rather than interpreting Mason Tarwater's urge to baptize as a ritualized act intended to save Bishop, a necessary act for Bishop to be known by God—as Rayber might argue—it seems instead that his call for Bishop's baptism actually declares this spiritual recognition in the first place. Old Tarwater does not see Bishop as damned and in need of this rite to save him—in fact, he sees him as already saved from Rayber because his limited rational capabilities protect him from Rayber's narrowly rationalistic view of the world. The rite is the recognition and proclamation of Bishop's spiritual worth and dignity before and by God, a recognition not forthcoming from Rayber. Mason confronts Rayber in an early effort to baptize Bishop with the plea that affirms his importance: "Precious in the sight of the Lord even an idiot!" to which Rayber can only respond by questioning that worth, a question that already implies a different measure of worth: "Ask the Lord why He made him an idiot in the first place uncle. Tell him I want to know why!" (*VBA* 33–34). This argument between Mason and Rayber (and in fact the debate of the whole novel) is about the meaning of the baptismal rite in relation to the two understandings of Bishop's life. For Mason Tarwater, Bishop's limited mental capacities make him all the more dependent, which only serves to increase the responsibility of Rayber, Francis, and himself for the child's care and protection.

In Rayber's mind, baptism would be efficacious only if it could magically restore Bishop's mental faculties; his understanding of baptism as a meaningless rite rests on the assumption that it cannot actually change Bishop's intellectual condition. He says to Mason: "You could slosh water on him for the rest of his life and he'd still be an idiot. Five years old for all eternity, useless forever." This perpetual condition of uselessness, Rayber concludes, warrants his refusal of a baptism. And as a matter of principle and for the sake of what he calls "human dignity," he swears to Mason that Bishop will never be baptized (*VBA* 34). Human dignity as Rayber conceives it, however, has serious limitations, and when he describes his decision not to baptize Bishop "as a gesture of human dignity," it becomes apparent that dignity and usefulness reside solely in rational activity.

Rayber's elevated speech might sound noble, cloaking itself in protective concern for Bishop, who would otherwise be mocked by a baptism. But

Rayber reveals himself in a later discussion with Francis (and of course, when he tries to drown Bishop) indicating thereby whose human dignity he is protecting: *his own*. Rayber reiterates his view that "baptism is only an empty act," and then he outlines his own preference for intellectual rejuvenation: "If there's any way to be born again, it's a way that you accomplish yourself, an understanding about yourself that you reach after a long time, perhaps a long effort. It's nothing you get from above by spilling a little water and a few words" (*VBA* 194). Conversely, he suggests to Francis, baptism is not only meaningless and "from above," it is an easy way compared with the self-saving actions of the human will and intellect, which offer a much more difficult, yet goal oriented route. Rayber's path, however, is fraught with limitations, especially for someone like Bishop: "It's the way you take as a result of being born again the natural way—through your own efforts. Your intelligence" (*VBA* 195). Obviously, Bishop is denied this kind of rebirth, and so as to compensate for his lack, Rayber tries to adopt Francis, offering him the salvation that cannot apply to Bishop: "All the things that I would do for him—if it were any use—I'll do for you" (*VBA* 92). There is no "use" in saving Bishop, since what is salvific in Rayber's terms is reduced to intellectual pursuits and education in the "facts" of the "real world."

The conversation between Rayber and Francis on baptism ties directly into the meaning of Francis's mission to baptize Bishop. Rayber, in an effort to prove his conviction about the meaninglessness of the act, suggests that Tarwater baptize him right there in the lodge and get the compulsion out of his system (*VBA* 193). The confrontation is revealing because, so far as Rayber understands it, the issue is simply about Francis's religious indoctrination by Mason, which has compelled him to come and baptize Bishop. Rayber's confusion in this regard brings out Francis's resistance, since Francis understands the difference between Rayber's interpretation of baptism and the real meaning of Mason Tarwater's actions. Rayber confesses that his view of baptism is rooted in the same estimation of Bishop as Mason's. But Rayber is mistaken about why Mason wants to baptize Bishop; he assumes that they both consider Bishop useless. But while Mason prefers a magical act to save him, Rayber simply tolerates Bishop's existence. He argues that, fundamentally, he and Mason were in agreement: "I don't have a compulsion to baptize him. . . . My own is more complicated, but the principle is the same. The way we have to fight is the same" (*VBA* 196). Francis Tarwater knows that what Rayber says is wrong. He knows his great-uncle Mason better than Rayber does, and while he may not yet fully realize the meaning of baptism as Mason understands it, rooted in his desire to *act* more than anything else, he knows (and possibly this is all he knows) that it is different from how Rayber understands things. What this conversation at the lodge reveals to Francis is that Rayber cannot act. Rayber has already tried to "act out" the implications of his view of Bishop by drowning him, but he could not follow through (*VBA* 169). Rayber only talks of his salvation, whereas Tarwater is willing to act and knows the difference; on this point Francis aligns himself most closely with Mason Tarwater: "It ain't the same. . . . I ain't like you. All you can do is think what you would have done if you had done it. Not me. I can do it. I can act" (*VBA* 196). Francis's drowning and baptism of Bishop are active responses to Bishop as a human being, and he knows, however unconsciously, that drowning Bishop is more real than Rayber's attempts to ignore Bishop's existence. Where Francis's action is limited, however, is in his resistance to the connection between word and act. As Desmond suggests, Francis's desire finally to act out his rejection, to put an end to his indecision, is "to act as a means of escaping the threatened burden of the mystery of the Word *in* Act, the Past *in* the Present." Desmond argues that "in denying the 'word' of his great-uncle and his true conscience, Tarwater falls to the opposite extreme of trying to silence conscience and his link with the 'word' of the past through decisive action."[32] We can link this experience to Tarwater's moment of choice as he faces his uncle's claim for his burial.

Burial

From the beginning of the novel, Tarwater is faced with his first major responsibility—burying his great-uncle. Mason's request for a proper burial, and Tarwater's self-conscious rebellion against it and its deeper meaning, is the beginning and the paradigm of Tarwater's confrontation with the call to take responsibility for others. Francis's rejection of his great-uncle's request for a proper burial is the precursor of his struggles over his responsibility for the idiot-child Bishop. Like the burial, the baptism requires him to penetrate the purely external appearance of the rite and to acknowledge the deeper meaning of its significance for Bishop, for himself, and for human life in general. The experience is striking, as Tarwater is confronted with a responsibility for the most dependent human beings: a dead man and an idiot-child. Furthermore, the responsibility includes particular religious rites—namely, burial and baptism—which are intended to honor the inherent worth and dignity of human beings as more than just bodies (even in death and even in the absence of reason). The struggle for Tarwater is to move beyond the view of these rites as empty acts that are rooted in externally determined cause-and-effect rituals required for salvation; he must come to see them as meaningful in both word and action, not separable from each other.

After his great-uncle Mason dies, Francis Tarwater has to contend with the views of "the stranger," of Meeks, and of Rayber concerning one's obligations to the dead, and more broadly, their insistence that there is no spiritual communion between human beings, whether living or dead. Given their comments, it is obvious that each of these characters considers death to be final, but more significantly, in their view, responsibility or accountability ends with the moment of death, as if the embodied human being simply ceases to be an issue once no longer animated. The stranger says the dead are the most impoverished—"The dead are poor. . . . You can't be any poorer than dead." But his remark is not offered to inspire Francis's responsibility to his dead uncle; it is meant to separate the living and the dead by insisting that the dead have no rights. Therefore, about the great-uncle's burial he reminds Francis: "He'll have to take what he gets" (*VBA* 24). The stranger tells Francis that his schoolteacher uncle Rayber "wouldn't consider for a minute that on the last day all the bodies marked by crosses will be gathered" (*VBA* 25). Indeed, when Francis tells Rayber what has happened to Mason—namely, that whatever remains of his burnt body will be rejected by the buzzards and the dogs will carry off his bones—Rayber says, "He got what he deserved" (*VBA* 89–90).

The traveling salesman Meeks, although he has no personal knowledge of Mason Tarwater, speaks with Francis about the dead and the relations between the dead and the living, as they apply to his business policy. As a matter of personal attention to his customers, to give the appearance of caring about their lives, Meeks always asks after a man's wife and children before he sells him a copper flue. The burden of this level of attention, however, is relieved when someone dies; as Meeks says, "Thank God when they're dead. . . . That's one less to remember." Francis Tarwater echoes Meeks's sentiment: "You don't owe the dead anything" (*VBA* 51), to which the stranger's voice adds, as though identifying the real substance of the conversation: "That's the way it ought to be in this world—nobody owing nobody nothing" (*VBA* 51).

We can see the way in which responsibility is resisted in the face of everything that Mason Tarwater has taught Francis, by considering Francis's reluctance to bury his great-uncle according to his wishes. It is not the act of burying Mason that rankles Francis so much as it is the religious details of the burial. These details suggest a larger framework of meaning and purpose in death, including an implicit connection between and obligation for human beings, always owed by the living to the dead. As with the baptism, Francis does not want to have to acknowledge word and act as joined, thus giving meaning to the act beyond himself. Mason Tarwater's death makes Francis suddenly and solely accountable for the proper care of the dead body. The responsibility is burdensome, and what Francis must contend with are the possible reasons why he must do this thing. Mason's desire that his nephew take care of his body when he dies, including the details of the depth of the grave and the erection of a cross, suggests his understanding of the worth and meaning of the individual human being, the physical and spiritual relation of human beings to God, and the family connection they shared during life. Francis is the one Mason trusts to ensure a respectful burial: "All I'm asking you is to get me in the ground and set up a cross" (*VBA* 15). Mason wants to make the connection explicit to Francis, implying that their interdependent relation in life means that Mason will be Francis's responsibility when dead. But he also wants Francis to understand that the manner of treating a dead body reflects something of how one understands a whole human being and that being's relation to the divine. He says of Rayber: "He'd burn me. . . . He'd be willing to pay the undertaker to burn me to be able to scatter my ashes. . . . He don't believe in the Resurrection. He don't believe in the Last Day. He don't believe in the bread of life" (*VBA* 16). Francis wants to dismiss the cross as superfluous: "I'll be too wore out to set up any cross. I ain't bothering with trifles." This reduction of the meaning of the cross to a trifle infuriates Mason, but his concern is not for himself but for Francis, who, Mason perceives, has not understood the meaning of the cross beyond the level of an external symbol. Mason returns Francis to the idea of human responsibility: doing what is right for the dead as an obligation to others and to oneself. The need for these actions is rooted in an understanding of human beings as connected in their physical and spiritual existence through responsibility, communion, and love. He says to Francis: "Burying the dead right may be the only honor you do yourself" (*VBA* 15).

The stranger's voice urges against this responsibility, not only by inverting the relation of responsibility—that is, what Francis is owed by his great-uncle and others—but also by mocking the religious faith of Mason Tarwater as unenlightened and superstitious. The voice of the stranger ridicules the meaning of the religious details of the burial in order to diminish Francis Tarwater's responsibility to Mason. When Tarwater starts to dig his great-uncle's grave, the stranger's voice taunts him, suggesting he burn the body instead. His goal is to convince Francis that his great-uncle's body is now meaningless matter, separated from his soul: "His soul is off this mortal earth now and his body is not going to feel the pinch, of fire or anything else" (*VBA* 36). This creates a conflict for Tarwater, because the separation of the physical and the spiritual does not fit with Mason's embodied religious teachings or Francis's abiding consideration for his great-uncle, and the body that once lived and raised him.

The stranger mocks Francis Tarwater's attention to the details of his responsibility. What Francis once mocked in Mason, he is now defending to the stranger. The debate between Francis and the stranger, or Francis and himself, is the same one he carried on with Mason, except that now it falls to Francis to voice his dead great-uncle's concerns. In this way, Tarwater's internal dialogue embodies the connection between himself and Mason; it also keeps the spiritual presence and words of Mason alive. Francis feels compelled to acknowledge his great-uncle's religious life by burying him with the mark of what ordered that life (the cross); but the stranger tries to reduce the meaning of the gesture by limiting it to a physical object, arguing, "Don't you think any cross you set up in the year 1952 would be rotted out by the year the Day of Judgment comes in?" (*VBA* 36). The stranger's technique is to insist on the termination by death of the spiritual connection between the boy and his great uncle, not to mention between the uncle and his body. While Mason had always instructed young Tarwater about the connection between the living and the dead through spiritual and communal ties, the stranger separates them radically.

Francis had tried dismissing the needs of the dead once in a conversation with Mason, suggesting that "the dead don't bother with particulars," but Mason Tarwater set him straight: "'The world was *made* for the dead. Think of all the dead there are,' he said, and then as if he had conceived the answer for all the insolence in the world, he said, 'There's a million times more dead than living and the dead are dead a million times longer than the living are alive,' and he released him [Tarwater] with a laugh" (*VBA* 16). Francis is shaken by the truth of this statement, although he reveals his shock with only a slight quiver. The effects of Mason's understanding permeate Francis's mind and soul, and he argues with the stranger because he is so indelibly marked by Mason's words. The stranger knows this, and so his mockery turns from Mason to Francis himself, identifying Francis with the ridiculous superstitions of his great-uncle. The stranger wants to root out the idea of responsibility to others altogether: Francis is not burying Mason out of any obligation to him or to the dead; he acts because he is afraid of the moral consequences for himself. He tries to reduce Mason Tarwater's sacramental understanding of human obligation and responsibility to a moralistic fear of an unknown God. The stranger insinuates that, for the sake of religious consistency, the condition of the dead body cannot make any difference to God: "What about people that get burned up naturally in house fires? Burnt up one way or another or lost in machines until they're pulp?" Francis's reply focuses on the relevance of his own action: "If I burnt him. . . . it wouldn't be natural, it would be deliberate" (*VBA* 36). Francis objects to burning his uncle, recalling Mason's horror at the thought of how Rayber might "dispose" of his body (*VBA* 15), but also because Francis senses that what he knows relates to what he does. Again, the stranger rebukes the possibility of responsibility and characterizes Francis's actions as superstitious, but nonetheless self-serving, concerns: "It ain't the Day of Judgment for him you're worried about. It's the Day of Judgment for you" (*VBA* 36).

The idea of responsibility that O'Connor expresses through Francis's experience of his great-uncle's death is one not limited by immediate needs and ends; it is owed not only to the living but to the dead who were once alive, since time and death do not alter its claim. The stranger wants to remove this notion of accountability in kinship, first by arguing that the great-uncle's death is a final break in the communion of Mason and Francis, the body now dead and insignificant, and then by emphasizing (and certainly encouraging) Tarwater's isolation: "You're left by yourself in this empty place. . . . You don't mean a thing to a soul as far as I can see"—to which Tarwater mutters "redeemed" (*VBA* 37), lamely hinting at the possibility of reality going further than what is seen, especially by the stranger. Significantly, this invoking of isolation is also how the stranger discredits Tarwater's prophetic vocation. He points out that Tarwater does not have anyone to whom he can prophesy: "Anybody that's a prophet has got to have somebody to prophesy to. Unless you're just going to prophesy to yourself" (*VBA* 38). Later, at the Cherokee Lodge, the stranger, now identified as a "friend," warns Tarwater against thinking that God is somehow present and waiting to confer prophetic powers upon him. The friend has to emphasize Tarwater's isolation in order to foster the idea of Tarwater's independence from God or any larger order of meaning: "The Lord is not studying about you, don't know you exist, and wouldn't do a thing about it if He did. You're alone in the world, with only yourself to ask or thank or judge; with only yourself" (*VBA* 166–67). The isolation the friend describes becomes more pointed; it is not about a lack of human presence, but of divine transcendence, spiritual community, and the consequent futility of prayer, praise, and judgment.

The conflict engendered by the friend's prompting is between the understanding of oneself as part of a spiritual community that includes the living and the dead or as completely alone, both physically and spiritually. The meaning of moral choice in the novel rests upon this distinction, because it ultimately determines the view of responsibility one holds. Tarwater understands this much—surprisingly, since he has lived most of his life in the backwoods alone with his great-uncle. Yet, his great-uncle has taught him the meaning of community, without an obvious, or necessarily living one in which to participate. The perception of the spiritual difference between community and isolation—the first still possible in physical solitude, the second possible in the midst of hundreds of people—is noted by Tarwater both in the backwoods and in the city. At Powderhead, he counts himself free "for the pursuit of wisdom, the companions of his spirit Abel and Enoch and Noah and Job, Abraham and Moses, King David and Solomon, and all the prophets, from Elijah who escaped death, to John whose severed head struck terror from a dish" (*VBA* 17). And in the city, when he accompanies his great-uncle Mason, he is struck profoundly by the absence of human relations along the streets: "His head jerked backwards after each passing figure until they began to pass too thickly and he observed that their eyes didn't grab at you like the eyes of country people" (*VBA* 26–27). He decides instinctively that the city is evil, not on any formally religious grounds, but because he feels that these human beings are not responding to one another in any real or engaged way. The stranger wants to break down these intuitive experiences as a means of eliminating Francis's connection to Mason Tarwater and, as a consequence, his feeling of responsibility.

Bishop

While the initial encounter with the stranger's voice in Francis Tarwater's internal dialogue begins over a dead body, his return to the city takes him toward an apparently dead mind in a living body—Bishop, whom Tarwater must choose either to acknowledge or reject, both in terms of his prophetic call to the ritual of baptism and in terms of his human responsibility. How Francis responds to the stranger's urgings in relation to Mason Tarwater is directly related to his subsequent experiences, and these affect his response to Bishop. I suggest that as the immediate focus of Tarwater's prophetic call, Bishop anchors the entire novel as the focal point for human responsibility, but more important, for what it means to be a human being. O'Connor intends this dramatic convergence on the character of Bishop, as she notes in a letter including other such innocent types: "Sarah Ham ["The Comforts of Home"] is like Enoch [*Wise Blood*] and Bishop—the innocent character, always unpredictable and for whom the intelligent characters are in some measure responsible" (*HB* 434). The issue of responsibility is best understood in relation to why one is responsible and to whom. The stranger considers Tarwater responsible only to himself, not to Mason, because the latter is dead and exists no more. Bishop is likewise dismissed by the stranger because he is already mentally dead. In the boat, the stranger counsels: "No finaler act than this. . . . In dealing with the dead you have to act. . . . It's only one dimwit you have to drown" (*VBA* 215). The stranger defines life and death rather narrowly and exclusively, and yet the striking effect of the novel, which, ironically, is revealed through this internal dialogue of Francis with the stranger, is that Mason Tarwater is still very much alive to Francis, and that Bishop's powerful affection—compared with Rayber's monotonous logic—makes him appear full of life, despite his intellectual deficiency.

The symbolic convergences between the characters of Mason and Bishop for Francis Tarwater suggest the continuing effects of Mason's prophetic charge, a request second only to that concerning his proper burial. Such convergences also represent the embodied spiritual communion of Mason's sacramental vision of reality. When Francis first sees the child, Bishop, the kinship with Mason is obvious: "He stood there, dim and ancient, like a child who had been a child for centuries," and the connection between Mason and Bishop is felt by Francis, who senses that "the child *recognized* him, that the old man himself had primed him from on high. . . . The little boy was sticking out his hand to touch him" (*VBA* 93). Francis finds the demanding presence of the child as difficult as Mason's presence. In this, Francis is like Rayber, and in fact he shares Rayber's distress at Bishop's presence. Francis's struggle is very much concerned with this issue of the conjunction between the physical and the spiritual (whether denied by the stranger and Rayber or affirmed by Mason). What impresses Tarwater most about his great-uncle's profession as prophet is the very physical and frenzied nature of the old man's battles with God: after a few days in the woods Mason looked "as if he had been wrestling a wildcat, as if his head were still full of the visions he had seen in its eyes, wheels of light and strange beasts with giant wings of fire and four heads turned to the four points of the universe" (*VBA* 8). By contrast, Mason's sermons about Jesus seem overly spiritual; they are less engaging and visually arresting to Francis Tarwater than the fiery visions. If Tarwater is going to be a prophet he wants to be an Old Testament type, not a spiritual follower of Jesus.

Francis is not prepared, however, for the fact that Bishop, despite his inability to speak or reason, exerts an insistent and undeniable presence. Rayber advises Tarwater to ignore him: "Just forget Bishop exists. . . . He's just a mistake of nature. Try not even to be aware of him" (*VBA* 117). But neither Rayber nor Francis can do this. The living, meaningfully silent presence of Bishop poses a challenge to Tarwater. At the most obvious level, Bishop is the one whom Mason has named for Tarwater to baptize, initiating his prophetic future; but Bishop is more than the fulfillment of Francis's prophetic role. Despite his lack of verbal communication, Bishop is a presence to contend with here and now. Apparently in contrast to Francis's preference for Mason's more physical prophetic expressions, Francis abhors Bishop's very physical nature. Bishop is always grabbing at Francis, trying to touch him; he breathes heavily and with gurgling noises; he eats loudly, "like a hog" according to Francis, and perhaps because "he don't think no more than a hog" (*VBA* 116). Although Bishop is verbally silent, he is nonetheless a very noisy child. Francis has a vivid material imagination of his prophetic role from his observation of Mason Tarwater, but this is altered by his experience of Bishop. Francis repudiates the immediate physical pull of his presence, thereby excessively spiritualizing the prophetic call. This spiritualized calling is evident in his desire for a momentous sign to inaugurate his prophetic role: "When the Lord's call came, he wished it to be a voice from out of a clear and empty sky, the trumpet of the Lord God Almighty, untouched by any fleshly hand or breath. He expected to see wheels of fire in the eyes of unearthly beasts" (*VBA* 22). With Mason Tarwater, Francis wants his wild prophetic actions without words, especially not sermons on the bread of life and Jesus; with Bishop, Francis wants a clear, disembodied voice, without the physical proximity of this idiot-child.

The wordless communication of Bishop seems intended by O'Connor as a symbolic corrective to Francis's presumptions about his prophetic calling, but perhaps it could also be said that she is addressing her own prophetic art. In a letter to Andrew Lytle, she remarks that, while her stories are usually aggressive in their portrayal of grace and love, she feels compelled to write about these experiences differently, not simply in terms of technique but, as her biblical allusion suggests, in terms of other forms of witness: "I keep seeing Elias in that cave, waiting to hear the voice of the Lord in thunder and lightning and wind, and only hearing it finally in the gentle breeze, and I feel I'll have to be able to do that sooner or later" (*HB* 373). Her comment elucidates the same experience facing Tarwater: instead of an unembodied, clear, and wild vision, he confronts Bishop, an idiot-child, incarnating the call of his prophetic life and silently, gently demanding him to make a choice. All of Tarwater's experiences of Bishop are associated with verbal silence and water. The water symbolizes the life-giving waters of baptism, of cleansing, of drowning; the silence defies Tarwater's expectations of his call, but it is also what comes when he drowns Bishop.

From his very first telephone call to Rayber's house, Tarwater has the premonition of an encounter. The strangeness of the new phone instrument leaves him "holding the earpiece tight against his head, his face rigid as if he were afraid that the Lord might be about to speak to him over the machine. All at once he heard what sounded like heavy breathing in his ear." He does not immediately realize the person on the other end is Bishop, and notices that "there was a silence over the telephone but it was not a silence that seemed to be empty" (*VBA* 82). When Tarwater does realize who it is, he gets angry and insists that he does not want to speak with Bishop, to which, "the heavy breathing began again as if in answer. It was a kind of bubbling noise, the kind of noise someone would make who was struggling to breathe in water" (*VBA* 83). This foreshadowing of the drowning of Bishop also illustrates the lack of control that Tarwater feels in the face of this silent witness to his prophetic role. Like Rayber, Tarwater despises Bishop's ability to undermine his control, and his presence constantly reminds him of the prosaic, quiet revelation of his calling. This threat to their control elicits violence from both Rayber and Francis, violence that is directed toward Bishop, and in turn, themselves. Because Rayber cannot control the violence of love that he feels for Bishop,[33] he must somehow reduce his capacity for it in himself, by anesthetizing himself to its effects (*VBA* 182). Francis's experience is different; his violence is enacted upon Bishop when he drowns him, thereby defeating Bishop's control. But simultaneously his experience of control is mingled with the loss of control as he utters the words of baptism.

What is at stake for both Rayber and Tarwater, reflected in their responses to Bishop, is the threat of the "intimacy of creation," or engagement with the world in a spiritually embodied way, which finally is tied to their images of God. Bishop, symbolic of the mediating presence of incarnate divine love, threatens their control of themselves; for Rayber this presence evokes overwhelming love that is "powerful enough to throw him to the ground in an act of idiot praise" (*VBA* 113), and for Tarwater it evokes the prophetic urge to baptize and acknowledge Bishop's life. Both respond to Bishop in a way that expresses their rebellion against a transcendent order of meaning that threatens their ability to control their own experiences. While Mason Tarwater sees Bishop's intellectual lack as fortuitous, revealing God's justice—"The Lord . . . had preserved the one child he had got out of her from being corrupted by such parents. He had preserved the child in the only possible way: the child was dim-witted" (*VBA* 9)—Rayber regards Bishop's life as reflective of God's injustice. His response is one of anger and resentment: "His normal way of looking on Bishop was as an *x* signifying the general hideousness of fate. He did not believe that he himself was formed in the image and likeness of God but that Bishop was he had no doubt" (*VBA* 113). In his own rationalistic way, Rayber, like both Tarwaters, has expectations of what God and love should be like, and for him it comes down to usefulness. The overwhelming love that he feels in relation to Bishop is troublesome because it does not make sense, nor does it appear useful to love someone like Bishop. Love could be used generally or as a means to improve his sister's life, for instance (*VBA* 113).

But Rayber fears any love that is out of his control: "It was love without reason, love for something futureless, love that appeared to exist only to be itself, imperious and all demanding, the kind that would cause him to make a fool of himself in an instant. And it only began with Bishop" (*VBA* 113–14). Rayber tries to stifle this love definitively by drowning Bishop, assuming that the child's death would end the gripping love he feels, but he loses his nerve. To compensate for this failure, Rayber chooses to live a highly controlled existence, described in fact, as "rigid ascetic discipline" (*VBA* 114). Yet, in this case, the ascetic impulse is directed inward, not in order to bury the selfish will, but in an effort to control any real engagement through love with the world and other human beings. Rayber resists the physicality of life, preferring instead a detached, intellectual existence. His asceticism, in effect, is a denial of life; it is like Francis Tarwater's repulsion for the bread of life (*VBA* 21) and sacramental participation in the world: "He did not look at anything too long, he denied his senses unnecessary satisfactions. . . . He was not deceived that this was a whole or a full life, he only knew that it was the way his life had to be lived" (*VBA* 114). The major hindrance to this style of life for Rayber, however, is Bishop, which Tarwater perceives when he arrives at the schoolteacher's house: "The child might have been a deformed part of himself [Rayber] that had been accidentally revealed" (*VBA* 93).

The loss of control that Francis Tarwater resists is also threatened by Bishop's presence, but for different reasons. With the death of Mason, Francis feels suddenly free of the old prophet's control over his life, except for the continuance of that control in the form of his prophetic mission. Bishop stands in the way as an obstacle between Tarwater and his freedom. Francis can baptize the boy and initiate his life as a prophet, or drown him in order to gain his freedom. He senses that to baptize Bishop will have more limiting consequences for him than drowning him, and he concludes that the violent action of drowning Bishop will most effectively prove himself in control, without being accountable to the added witnesses of Mason or God at the event of a baptism. Further, the choice implies Tarwater's ascetic detachment (like Rayber) from the world, which he resists by averting his gaze in order

> to keep his vision located on an even level, to see no more than what was in front of his face and to let his eyes stop at the surface of that. It was as if he was afraid that if he let his eye rest for an instant longer than was needed to place something—a spade, a hoe, the mule's hind quarters before his plow, the red furrow under him—that the thing would suddenly stand before him, strange and terrifying, demanding that he name it and name it justly and be judged for the name he gave it. He did all he could to avoid this threatened intimacy of creation. (*VBA* 21–22)

What this account suggests is that the call to name the human experience of the world is missing from Francis Tarwater's actions. He avoids the incarnate world or the intimacy of creation by not speaking or responding to it. Francis Tarwater's interior battle is not finally the same as Rayber's intellectual ascetic discipline, because Francis is more heavily influenced by Mason Tarwater. The struggle Francis faces concerning his prophetic vocation and Bishop's relation to it is more a matter of spiritual wrestling between the self and God concerning control. Mason Tarwater's own struggle as a prophet is revealing in this regard, because he had once dissociated himself from the world in his desire that the Lord destroy it. Instead, Mason is called to face the judgment of his naming of the world, which inevitably includes himself. When Mason Tarwater is first called on by God to be a prophet, he, like Francis, has very grand visions of himself and what being a prophet means:

> He had been called in his early youth and had set out for the city to proclaim the destruction awaiting a world that had abandoned its Savior. He proclaimed from the midst of his fury that the world would see the sun burst in blood and fire and while he raged and waited, it rose every morning, calm and contained in itself, as if not only the world, but the Lord Himself had failed to hear the prophet's message. It rose and set, rose and set on a world that turned from green to white and green to white and green to white again. It rose and set and he despaired of the Lord's listening. Then one morning he saw to his joy a

finger of fire coming out of it and before he could turn, before he could shout, the finger had touched him and the destruction he had been waiting for had fallen in his own brain and his own body. His own blood had been burned dry and not the blood of the world. (*VBA* 5–6)

Mason's experience is one of human limitation and judgment of the human pretension to see and define all of reality according to this limited capacity. Mason's prophetic proclaiming (in its damning view of the rest of creation) had revealed his expectations of God, what he desired, rather than what was expected of him. His judgment was ill-conceived because it did not account for his participation in the creation he judged.

What is important about the old man's burning vision is that precisely this experience—the movement from an outward judgment/naming of creation to an inward experience of the demand for the justification of that judgment—is the form of Francis Tarwater's experience in the novel as a whole. This transformative lesson of self-knowledge and accountability is the only thing that can save Francis from himself, though Francis will only really come to understand that fact when he sees the connection between his words and his actions and the need to understand them in relation. This is how Mason educates: he tells a story of himself in order to articulate the drama of how Francis will come to know himself. This tale of Mason's prophetic call hints at O'Connor's account of the movement and direction of violence: the violence is first directed outward, toward the world (apparently devoid of God), as the prophet judges the world from what he thinks is a divine perspective. The movement of the violence is reversed, however, and turns back on Mason himself—not to destroy him, but only to remove the illusion of who he is, as a prophet and as a human being, and to show him the discontinuity between what he says and what he does.

Francis Tarwater does not want to bring on the destruction of a sinful world so much as he wants to resist an embodied spiritual existence that demands his participation, and so he acts to reject that kind of world by drowning Bishop. For Francis, to participate in that existence is to lose control of himself by losing his freedom to the responsibility that communal life entails. To murder Bishop is to reject the spiritual and physical communion of human beings, who are all responsible for all. Rayber rejects intellectually the penetration of this sacramental order into his consciousness, but Francis, who acts his rebellion rather than thinking it, must violate it externally. It is not a clearly decided choice, however, and Rayber's coldness both fuels

Tarwater's rebellion and quells it. When Rayber, speaking of Bishop and others like him, says that "in a hundred years people may have learned enough to put them to sleep when they're born," Tarwater's expression suggests a double response to Rayber's attitude: "Something appeared to be working on the boy's face, struggling there, some war between agreement and outrage"(*VBA* 168–69).

Although the war between agreement and outrage is the struggle that remains undecided even at the moment of drowning (and baptism), the stranger's voice pushes Francis toward agreement because this encourages freedom from responsibility. Tarwater is warned that if he baptizes Bishop he will be doing it forever, and as he reflects on this eternal constraint and responsibility, he meets up with a man in the park who echoes the voice and the temptation to serve no one: "Be like me, young fellow. . . . Don't let no jackasses tell you what to do" (*VBA* 166). The voice counseling Tarwater preys upon his pride, suggesting that not even a divine call should affect his decisions. The stranger proposes that Tarwater take the matter of his divine election into his own hands by drowning Bishop as an act of defiance; the suggestion comes from the voice, but the idea, along with the devaluation of Bishop's worth is Rayber's (*VBA* 165).

Resistance

The tension that mounts in Francis's soul during the days preceding the drowning/baptism, is caused by his desire for, and yet his resistance to, a sign from God concerning his prophetic call. Francis Tarwater wants a physical manifestation of his calling and mission, and the stranger feeds his pride by suggesting he should accept nothing less than an "unmistakable sign," such as "water bursting forth from a rock . . . [or] fire sweeping down at his command and destroying some site he would point to, such as the tabernacle he had gone to spit on" (*VBA* 162). Yet, although the stranger's voice insists on something momentous, Francis wonders if the hunger he feels— "Since the breakfast he had finished sitting in the presence of his uncle's corpse, he had not been satisfied by food, and his hunger had become like an insistent silent force inside him"—might be a sign of his desire for the bread of life. The voice is "adamant that he refuse to entertain hunger as a sign" (*VBA* 162). After Francis's experience of listening to the charismatic child preach, he felt even more justified in desiring some obvious sign of his mission; he returned to Rayber's house, sat up in bed, and "raising his folded hat as if he were *threatening the silence,* he . . . demanded an unmistakable sign of the Lord" (*VBA* 163; italics mine).

This demand for a sign betrays the real issue for Francis: his desire to choose his own destiny. He desires a sign that he feels is appropriate, while he resists the silent claims of Bishop and the now-dead Mason. When the sun falls on Bishop's head at the pool in the park, Francis is drawn toward him. The permeating silence signals something to him: "He felt a distinct tension in the quiet. The old man might have been lurking near, holding his breath, waiting for the baptism. His friend was silent as if in the felt presence, he dared not raise his voice. At each step the boy exerted a force backward but he continued nevertheless to move toward the pool" (*VBA* 165). Rayber, sensing Francis's intentions, snatches Bishop away, and Tarwater sees his own image in the pool. He chooses: "I wasn't going to baptize him . . . flinging the silent words at the silent face. I'd drown him first. . . . Drown him then, the face appeared to say" (*VBA* 165). Francis finally refuses this sign of baptism in the park, because, as his "friendly" voice counsels him, the acceptance of any sign will oblige him to further missions and to accountability to the Lord from whom the sign came. The only way to be in control of your life, cautions the voice, is to do it yourself without waiting for a sign from anyone else: "You have to take hold and put temptation behind you. . . . If it's an idiot this time, the next time it's liable to be a nigger. Save yourself while the hour of salvation is at hand" (*VBA* 166).

Francis Tarwater has to overcome the command to baptize Bishop by making his own choice. Instead of baptizing, he will drown, thereby ending the prophetic claim upon his life and the responsibility that it entails. Tarwater violently acts out his rebellion by killing Bishop, but he lacks sufficient control to avoid baptizing him at the same time. The baptism, while troubling to Tarwater, does not make him feel as though his refusal loses its weight. He reduces the baptism to empty words: "'They were just some words that run out of my mouth and spilled in the water.' He shook his head violently as if to scatter his thoughts" (*VBA* 209). He says to the truck driver on his way back to Powderhead: "I'm in full charge there. No voice will be uplifted. I shouldn't never have left it except to prove I wasn't no prophet and I've proved it. . . . I proved it by drowning him. Even if I did baptize him that was only an accident. Now all I have to do is mind my own bidnis until I die" (*VBA* 210). Francis Tarwater's mission is done; he has turned the violence outward against the order that he felt impinging upon his freedom, refusing its call, and now his choice is to remain in his isolated but free existence at Powderhead. His desire to "mind [his] own bidnis" until he dies portrays his absolute claim for independence and a life without responsibility. As O'Connor explains in a letter to Ted Spivey, "the whole action of the novel is Tarwater's selfish will against all that the little lake (the baptismal font) and the bread stand for" (*HB* 387). This is the height of his rejection, and as he leaves the trucker and begins marching back toward Powderhead, he vows to "live his life *as he had elected it,* and where, for the rest of his days, he would make good his refusal" (*VBA* 218; italics mine). In the midst of this march he meets another who has said no, namely, the stranger with the lavender shirt and panama hat.

Judgment and Vision

Just before Tarwater is picked up, he meets the woman at the filling station, where he wants to buy a drink. This is Francis's first encounter with someone from his community who knows his uncle as a man and not simply as a textbook case of mad religious fanaticism. This episode is critical for our grasp of the theme of judgment in the novel, as well as its relation to violence, because it recalls us to the fact that Francis has done wrong by his great-uncle Mason, in the same moment we are recoiling from his violence against Bishop. The starkest mention of judgment after his killing of Bishop comes when Tarwater approaches the black-eyed woman: "There was all knowledge in her stony face and the fold of her arms indicated a judgment fixed from the foundations of time" (*VBA* 225). The force of her judgment is not physical, nor are there words of damnation. She simply knows what Tarwater has done and awaits his response, her judgment contingent upon his ability to answer for his actions:

> The boy pulled himself together to speak. He was conscious that no sass would do, that he was called upon by some force outside them both to answer for his freedom and make bold his acts. A tremor went through him. His soul plunged deep within itself to hear the voice of his mentor at its most profound depths. He opened his mouth to overwhelm the woman and to his horror what rushed from his lips, like the shriek of a bat, was an obscenity he had overheard once at a fair. Shocked, he saw the moment lost. (*VBA* 225)

Tarwater's soul is empty of an answer but for some ugly words, a judgment and shame worse than anything else he could experience. The voice and counsel of his "mentor," his internal friend, is, at its most profound depths, obscene. He leaves her, shamed and disappointed with himself, yet longing for companionship to atone for his failure "to make good his refusal." He "wanted to explain to someone what he had failed to explain to the woman and with the right words to wipe out the obscenity that had stained his thought" (*VBA* 226). The obscenity feels like a failure to Francis: "The boy's mind was too fierce to brook impurities of such a nature. He was intolerant of unspiritual evils and with those of the flesh he had never truckled. He felt his victory sullied by the remark that had come from his mouth" (*VBA* 226). The obscenity is too fleshly, too unspiritual, and Francis, considering that this sullies his spiritual defiance, perhaps begins to recognize the intrinsic connection between his obscenity and the defiance, as well as the need to justify in words, his actions. Just as Francis once sought spiritual signs "untouched by any fleshly hand or breath" (*VBA* 22), he now desires to make his rebellion pure and free of any physicality or ugliness. As he moves to drown Bishop he is described thus: "He felt *bodiless* as if he were nothing but a head full of air, about to *tackle all the dead*" (*VBA* 215; italics mine). Even before Francis is raped by the stranger in the lavender shirt, he is forced to acknowledge the obscenity in himself, to acknowledge that his violence against Bishop was not simply a disembodied act of will. It was an ugly, fleshly, obscene act of violation rooted in a spiritually defiant will, and this is made explicit when Francis is at the receiving end of such an act. When he is raped he can no longer admit that "making good one's refusal" is a disembodied act.[34]

There are two exchanges early in the novel that foreshadow Tarwater's rape: one involves Mason Tarwater and the other Rayber. The question remains whether these foreshadowings confirm that Tarwater's rape is the only way he can be saved—generally assumed to be the judgmental religious view—or whether they reveal Mason's and Rayber's different perceptions of judgment and justice. The first comes from Mason Tarwater concerning, notably, the prophetic life, a difficult vocation not fully determined by the prophet. He warns that if he dies before baptizing Bishop, then Francis will have to take over. Francis is unimpressed by this task, displeased with the idea of such a minor first mission: "'[The Lord] don't mean for me to finish up your leavings. He has other things in mind for me.' And he thought of Moses who struck water from a rock, of Joshua who made the sun stand still, of Daniel who stared down lions in the pit" (*VBA* 9–10).

Recalling his own lessons learned after dictating the fantastic destruction of the city to God and mistaking his prophetic role for that of a divine judge, Mason directs Tarwater: "It's no part of your job to think for the Lord. . . . Judgment may rack your bones" (*VBA* 9–10). Is it the case, then, that because Tarwater's bones are literally "racked," the rape is the judgment that Mason predicted? And would Mason condone such a judgment as an affirmative answer would seem to assume? Or is Mason's prediction fulfilled in the "tremor" that goes through Francis as the black-eyed woman judges his shameful treatment of his great-uncle (*VBA* 225), a judgment not immediately retributive and physical, but eternal and related to Francis's responsibility to the dead? This kind of judgment requires a reorientation in vision—of the world, and others, but predominantly of oneself. Old Tarwater warns Francis that the prophetic calling makes one more prone to assumptions about God's judgments and that, given his own experiences, the judgment is often turned back on oneself. To defy one's human limitations is invariably its own punishment, and Francis's excessively spiritualized notion of his prophetic calling is finally exposed by his own obscenity and by the obscene act of the stranger in the lavender shirt.

The second reference, a comment offered by Rayber when Mason Tarwater has just baptized Francis Tarwater as a baby, is even more suggestive of the rape. After Mason tells Rayber that he has baptized Francis, Rayber takes the water bottle and pours it over Tarwater's bottom, repeating the words of baptism, saying "now Jesus has a claim on both ends" (*VBA* 73). While Rayber's pronouncement might insinuate that the claim of Jesus is again, literally enacted with the rape, it is necessary to consider Rayber's religious sensibilities in order to assess clearly his conception of judgment. The second baptism is Rayber's attempt to be provocatively irreverent. He derides Mason's assumption of Francis's spiritual dignity by parodying the sacredness of the act. Rayber finds the act meaningless. His gesture does not predict the necessity of Tarwater's rape as judgment, but it is a foreshadowing of the rape itself. This distinction is crucial: Rayber's action portends the cruel consequences of such irreverence to human dignity, when human worth and sanctity are not acknowledged as divinely given and revealed, when words are enacted, and when actions require an answer.

Neither Mason nor Rayber are able to prepare Francis Tarwater, however, for the violation that he experiences at the hands of the stranger, whose name suggests the incarnation of the voice. Francis becomes the victim of his own rebellion, not divine retribution (or divine grace). And because his suffering is experienced as a violation of both his body and soul, Francis comes to a realization of their connection. Is the rape a divine judgment on Francis's rebellion, either as a punishment or as the means for Francis's spiritual enlightenment? To suggest that the rape is an act of divine grace is perverse and completely foreign to O'Connor's view of God. Finally, it seems that whether the divine judgment is intended to punish or to enlighten, such a view is too simplistic in its portrayal of divine justice and the struggle of the human will. It represents divine justice as retributive and argues a view of human nature that is determined and not free in its choice either to do evil or to do good. O'Connor's concern with Francis's actions is not centered on judgment, but on responsibility. As he lies naked in the woods, "propped up against a log that lay across a small open space between two very tall trees" (*VBA* 232), on his cross of suffering, Francis is drawn beyond himself and what has happened, to a "final revelation." Francis's eyes are burned clean, and they "looked as if, touched with a coal like the lips of the prophet, they would never be used for ordinary sights again" (*VBA* 233). Implicit in this description is the idea that Francis has yet to experience his revelatory insight: the pain and horror of his encounter with the stranger has served to "burn his eyes clean," but the rape is not the revelation. His vision has cleared, and what he will see as a prophet who has suffered and come to understand the implications for his irresponsible behavior is a community that draws him beyond his own self-interest.

What Francis is compelled to seek is at Powderhead, the home from which he ran and which, after murdering Bishop, is his destination. For all of Francis's previous isolation and his desire to flee the constraints of human community and responsibility, he is now confronted with a multitude:

> Everywhere, he saw dim figures seated on the slope and as he gazed he saw that from a single basket the throng was being fed. His eyes searched the crowd for a long time as if he could not find the one he was looking for. Then he saw him. The old man was lowering himself to the ground. When he was down and his bulk had settled, he leaned forward, his face turned toward the basket, impatiently following its progress toward him. The boy too leaned forward, aware at last of the object of his hunger, aware that it was the same as the old man's and that nothing on earth would fill him. His hunger was so great that he could have eaten all the loaves and fishes after they were multiplied. (*VBA* 241)

Tarwater's vision of the multitude sharing in the food of life conveys O'Connor's understanding of the mystical community "composed of all the living and the dead, who are bonded together by one central act—the Incarnation and Resurrection of Christ."³⁵ The vision of the multitude is Francis's revelation of grace. In this final eucharistic vision, Francis Tarwater's ideas of spiritual freedom find substance and deeper meaning in the obligations of love. While the rape leaves Tarwater alone with the illusion of freedom, the mystical community shows him the object of his hunger and welcomes him into the reality of human dependence and responsibility.

The question of judgment, therefore, is understood by O'Connor within the context of responsibility—particularly eternal responsibility, which is conjured up by the vision of the dead, "living" congregation at Powderhead. Understood in this way, the brief experience with the woman at the filling station and the encounter with the lavender-eyed stranger both become part of a complex process of self-revelation in Francis Tarwater. It is a revelation that opens his eyes, not only through the shock and pain in the woods, but also through the penetrating gaze of the black-eyed woman when he is unable to account for his actions. When faced with the challenge of justifying himself to her—which is not an issue for the stranger in the car, who simply flatters and encourages Tarwater's insolence for his own perverse ends—Tarwater is only able to utter an obscenity. More than the revelation of the stranger's perversity and evil, Tarwater is shaken first by his own. But perversion and evil are two things over which he has no control. Francis learns something about the evil he has committed, and then he learns something about the life of freedom without responsibility. He sees these two things as the same.

In the final lines of *The Violent Bear It Away,* Francis recognizes himself as joined with those "who would wander in the world, strangers from that violent country where the silence is never broken except to shout the truth. He felt it building from the blood of Abel to his own, rising and engulfing him. It seemed in one instant to lift and turn him" (*VBA* 242). But surely Tarwater is not Abel. He is not the one who suffered death at the hands of his brother; he is the one who has committed the crime against his cousin Bishop. Yet in this moment of being lifted and turned, Tarwater experiences, with this redirected vision, the blood of Abel and Bishop crying out for justice (Genesis 4:10); he comes to know Abel's suffering and takes it inwardly upon himself. He knows in this felt cry for justice that he is responsible for Bishop and his great-uncle. In this sense, Tarwater is also Cain,³⁶ a murderer marked and left to wander (Genesis 4:12–17), who must begin to live out anew this responsibility to others. This inward responsibility that Francis carries with him is not dedicated to a violent judgment of the city toward which he turns. Francis is bearing away the violence of himself and others, with the new sights he has seen, in order to confront the children of God. Some might assume, like the old prophet Mason Tarwater once did, that the city is damned and worthy of destruction, but Francis's quest has nothing to do with destruction, other than the destruction of the false idols of human self-sufficiency and autonomy. He sets out to warn the children of God who lie sleeping of the "terrible speed of God's mercy." But the warning comes from an experience of that burning mercy, through which Tarwater has begun to understand his limits and his responsibility for others.

CHAPTER FOUR

Purgatorial Visions

"Revelation"

The Burning Up of Virtue

In the story "Revelation," Ruby Turpin has a revelatory experience that O'Connor, in a letter to Betty Hester, describes as a "purgatorial vision" (*HB* 577). Few scholars have followed up on the significance of that description in direct relation to the story's meaning.[1] I would argue that this crucial comment provides an interpretative clue, not only for the final "vision" of the story but for understanding Ruby Turpin's spiritual development. There is, in fact a series of spiritual experiences that lead Ruby to her final vision; she is able to make sense of its ethical implications because the purgatorial experience has already begun. The dramatic vision at the story's end is only the final culmination of Ruby's visionary experience, richly detailed by O'-Connor's subtle use of biblical symbols. What is necessary for such an interpretation, however, is some attention to O'Connor's source for the idea of a purgatorial vision and the attending purgatorial images. O'Connor's reading of the mystics is often alluded to in her writing collected in *The Habit of Being*, and there is one mystic in particular, St. Catherine of Genoa (1447–1510), whose treatise on purgatory we know O'Connor read.

   Through a careful examination of St. Catherine's text one can recognize certain important elements of purgatory also present in "Revelation."

O'Connor describes St. Catherine's notion of purgatory as "realization," thus emphasizing the revelation of self-knowledge as integral to the purgatorial vision (*HB* 118). The purgatorial experience is not one of fear, or of reward or punishment, and it is obvious that in both St. Catherine's treatise and O'Connor's story that the importance of virtue is secondary to love and self-knowledge. The purgatorial vision purifies human beings of their mistaken notions about themselves in relation to God. Moreover, the vision has its meaning in the midst of this life, not the afterlife, and Ruby is indeed transformed by it according to O'Connor: "She [Ruby Turpin] gets the vision. Wouldn't have been any point in that story if she hadn't. . . . And that vision is purgatorial" (*HB* 577). But O'Connor's comment is not the only evidence of the role of purgatory; the story itself provides clues as to the nature of the vision and in what ways Ruby understands its meaning in relation to herself.

The story chronicles the spiritual movement of Ruby Turpin's soul from being judged a "wart hog" through her purgatorial ascent to a proper vision and understanding of herself in relation to God. Although she insists she is not a "wart hog from hell" (*CW* 647), Ruby must descend into herself and grapple with the meaning of the judgment. The struggle is fierce as she seeks alongside Job and other biblical characters to find a response that will justify *herself* to God. However, what she discovers in the process, which has its culmination in her final vision, is that it is precisely her self-justification that hinders her ascent. Ruby needs to be purged of the idea of her own righteousness so that she can seek the source of righteousness outside the shallow category of a "good disposition."

While it is the vision in "Revelation" that O'Connor explicitly names as purgatorial, there are significant images of purgatorial themes in both *Wise Blood* and *The Violent Bear It Away* that connect them to the story of "Revelation" and form an interesting progression for our discussion. The motifs of burning in the two novels and in "Revelation" all signify purgatorial experience. In these stories, the burning, always accompanied by water (another medium of purification) symbolizes the purging that is required in order to purify oneself before God or to be purified by God.[2] In *Wise Blood,* in spite of his lack of vision, Hazel Motes realizes that he is not "true." Hazel intuits that the truth in human beings comes from an encompassing, divine measure of truth and that to reject the measure that "is" by setting up one's own measure is a mockery of truth. His response is to end his untrue vision of the world and of God by bringing on the purging/purifying lime and water and burning his eyes to clean his vision (*WB* 210). His form of purgation fails, however; his attempt to burn clean his own vision shows that he is unable to differentiate between purgation and destruction. What Hazel Motes needs is a transformation of vision, not its elimination.

In *The Violent Bear It Away,* the purgatorial symbols of fire and water abound. These symbols, understood in relation to the experience of purgation, reflect Francis Tarwater's desire to be free from divine control, particularly its requirement of responsibility for others. Tarwater drowns Bishop in an effort to reject the constraint on his freedom, but in the process also "baptizes" him. This baptism challenges Tarwater's attempt to purge his existence of responsibility. His being raped in the woods by the stranger prompts another purgation by Tarwater, this time with fire "eating greedily at the evil ground, burning every spot the stranger could have touched" (*VBA* 232). The uniqueness of the purgatorial images of fire and water in *The Violent Bear It Away* rests in their duality. Tarwater is caught in the middle of his growing apprehension that water both drowns and baptizes and that violation and purgation both burn. While Hazel Motes only understands purgation as destruction, Tarwater learns the tension of being in the middle, faced with the choice of action and its direction. In this way, the symbolism of purgatory expands from the first novel to the second; in one of O'Connor's final stories, "Revelation," the purgatorial vision shapes the whole story.

Ruby Turpin's experience is markedly different from that of Hazel Motes or of Francis Tarwater: she is already convinced of her divine election and salvation. She does not want to save herself or to deny God. Ruby Turpin takes it for granted that her religious beliefs keep her in right relation to God, but she lacks a proper relation to herself. In a sense, Ruby needs to be confronted with herself from a perspective different than her own. Her self-love distorts her vision of others: religious self-satisfaction makes her a harsh critic. As the story unfolds, Ruby's self-righteous attitude is revealed to be irresponsible and harmful to others: her love of her Christian virtue is a disordered form of love. Instead of loving God and others, she loves herself more, priding herself on her goodness. The point of the purgatorial experience is not to punish the rebel or the hypocrite, but to bring the purged to a realization of the order of love.

In the foreword to an edition combining St. Catherine's two major writings, the translator, Serge Hughes, describes her work on purgatory: "*Purgation and Purgatory* is an account of Catherine's understanding, through revelation and meditation, of the transformation of the self through the love of God."[3] The focus of the meditation is not the afterlife. St. Catherine's meditations on purgatory are about this life, "witnessed while still in the flesh" (71), and the relationship between self-love and the love of God. The marching souls that Ruby Turpin sees are part of such a witnessing vision, not a visual depiction of the afterlife or a final judgment on her soul. The purgatorial vision and the experiences that precede it allow for a transformation of Ruby's self-understanding while "still in the flesh." This point is significant since Ruby's vision could be viewed as a final judgment, with God meting out his just rewards and punishments. The final scene could also be interpreted as an indictment of human judgments, whether classist, economic, or racist.

However, neither direction of inquiry develops the theological question of who the self is before God (a question central to O'Connor's thought) and the ethical implications for this in Ruby Turpin's experience. This is *the* question of the story, shouted out to God, then returned and asked of Ruby also: "Who do you think you are?" (*CW* 653). Purgatory, or a purgatorial vision as Ruby experiences it and St. Catherine describes it, is the cleansing of the soul from self-love in order to know the self more truly in relation to God.[4] In Ruby's case, self-love inflates her image of herself and her Christian virtue; this lack of perspective in turn makes her love her own goodness more than she loves God. What she learns from her purgatorial vision is that, when divorced from the love of God and others, her virtue is only a false moral superiority. It takes her virtues being "burned away" for Ruby to begin to see how love is the ordering force of morality in her vision.

St. Catherine of Genoa and Purgatory

St. Catherine of Genoa's *Purgation and Purgatory* displays her vision of purgatory and its meaning in life as the soul moves toward perfection in God. It speaks to a spiritual experience combining suffering, joy, and love as human beings stand in the divine presence; St. Catherine often admits that her words and expressions never fully communicate this experience. Not intended as a literal account of purgatory, her testimony is a spiritual revelation of God's love and how it is experienced in the human soul. The order of love in the human soul determines the nature of the purgatorial experience as the soul nears God, which might explain why characters like Tarwater and Ruby Turpin can have such differing experiences of purgation. For St. Catherine, what is central to the experience is the reordering of human love, usually directed toward the self, through the presence of divine love. Whatever bars the way to the love of God and the reception of that love in human life is purged. This divine-human love orders all of St. Catherine's meditations: "All that I have said is as nothing compared to what I feel within, the witnessed correspondence of love between God and the Soul" (78). St. Catherine's treatise begins with the account of her vision "while still in the flesh" of "the fiery love of God, a love that consumed her, cleansing and purifying all" (71). God's love is imaged as fiery in its power both to consume and to purify; this power is necessary to cleanse the imperfect loves of human beings, which impede the soul's experience of God. The purgation is desired by St. Catherine more than feared, and it is her joy to experience "union with God in this loving purgatory" (71). The purgatorial experience is centered on the realization of the soul's connection to and desire for God through love, and, at the same time, the realization of the human, sinful impediments to God's love. St. Catherine notes both the suffering and joy that accompany these two types of realization bound to this experience, and yet her vision suggests that the joy "increases day by day because of the way in which the love of God corresponds to that of the soul" (72).

According to St. Catherine, there is no movement of the soul toward God that is not impelled by the soul's intrinsic, divinely instilled desire for God. St. Catherine insists that "in its creation the soul was endowed with all the means necessary for coming to its perfection" (80). The purgatorial experience of being in-between human imperfection and God's perfection is the reason for suffering. The soul is aware that something blocks it from God, and "the more the soul is aware of that impediment, the greater its suffering" (73). This is not inflicted by God as punishment; this suffering comes from the soul's recognition of what it is and what it lacks in relation to God. The reasoning of moral cause and effect is absent in the soul's experience of purgatory, according to St. Catherine, as the soul does not calculate its measure in terms of reward or punishment, especially in the presence of God:

> These souls cannot think, "I am here, and justly so because of my sins," or "I wish I never had committed such sins for now I would be in paradise," or "That person there is leaving before me," or "I will leave before that other one." They cannot remember the good and evil in their past or that of others. Such is their joy in God's will, in His pleasure, that they have no concern for themselves. . . . Should they be aware of other good or evil, theirs would not be perfect charity. (71)

The perfection of love is achieved by overcoming human notions of justice, fueled by human interests and self-love. St. Catherine says that the suffering of purgatory is the purging of the individual's concern for the self in the presence of God: "The greatest suffering of the souls in purgatory, it seems to me, is their awareness that something in them displeases God, that they have deliberately gone against His great goodness. In a state of grace, these souls fully grasp the meaning of what blocks them on their way to God." In this condition, according to St. Catherine, "all words, sentiments, images, the very idea of justice or truth, seem completely false" (78).

What this realization offers is the awareness of the distinction between human ideas of what is just or good and what truly measures that justice or goodness. The effect is purifying in the sense that human beings are made aware of their self-defined measure of justice and how this is not only lacking, but is in fact an impediment to knowing God's justice and goodness, since "all goodness is a participation in God and His love for His creatures" (73). St. Catherine explains her purgatorial vision as one in which the human being strives for perfection and yet finds mostly imperfection, causing suffering. This is the heart of the vision, because it suggests that the experience of purgatory is the experience of God's graciousness and mercy toward human beings in their state of being "in-between" the poles of perfection and imperfection. What must be purged is the idea of perfection and goodness as human possessions so that the true source of perfection and goodness can be seen. This is the purification of purgatory:

> Things man considers perfect leave much to be desired in the eyes of God, for all the things of man that are perfect in appearance—what he seeks, feels, knows—contaminate him. If we are to become perfect, the change must be brought about in us and without us; that is, the change is to be the work not of man but of God. This, the last stage of love, is the pure and intense love of God alone. (81)

Ultimately, the experience is both human and divine. As St. Catherine says, the change is both "in us and without us," and part of her treatise takes up this mystery through her analogical account of the human search for perfection. For O'Connor, this process of turning away from the self and toward God is the experience of conversion, conversion not as a singular event with a miraculous or permanent change of heart, but as a series of turns. O'Connor describes it in one of her letters: "I think once the process is begun and continues that you are continually turning inward toward God and away from your own egocentricity and that you have to see this selfish side of yourself in order to turn away from it" (*HB* 430). These movements are not external. They are inward spiritual movements that are manifest in the way human beings love God, others, and themselves. The turn is not away from the self and outward toward an external God; the turn that both O'Connor and St. Catherine describe is an inward movement toward knowledge of God and the purified self.

St. Catherine notes the difficulty of describing the desire for perfection in the human soul, especially when perfection is present but not complete. She uses the image of hunger, which is in us and yet is a desire that can only be satisfied by something beyond us: "Joy in God, oneness with Him, is the end of these souls, an instinct implanted in them at their creation. No image or metaphor can adequately convey this truth. One example, however, comes to mind. Let us imagine that in the whole world there was but one bread and that it could satisfy the hunger of all" (76). St. Catherine discusses different levels of hunger, as well as different levels of willingness to seek that one bread, but for the hungry souls in purgatory she suggests that the experience is one of seeing some of the bread and hoping for more: "This, then, is their suffering, the waiting for the bread that will take away their hunger" (77). Again, the suffering is not inflicted as a form of punishment, nor is it otherworldly; it is present in life, inherent in the experience of desiring the satisfaction of a hunger that cannot be satisfied by human efforts alone.

How does St. Catherine's description of purgatory relate to Flannery O'Connor's fiction? It is quite obvious that St. Catherine's treatise on purgatory includes references that are used almost directly in O'Connor's novels and stories; the influence of this text should not be underestimated in relation to O'Connor's writing. Some further reflection on St. Catherine's text on purgatory—with direct reference to the novels—will help indicate what St. Catherine and O'Connor understand to be essential in the purgatorial experience. It will also shed light on the development of the theme of purgatory within O'Connor's fiction. As I have suggested, the novels *Wise Blood* and *The Violent Bear It Away* both contain significant elements of purgatorial cleansing, not only in the images of burning connected to vision/sight, but also in the central characters' quests for the meaning of their existence (and often their resistance) in relation to the divine. This quest is self-consciously illustrated by the Misfit in the story "A Good Man Is Hard to Find," when he tries to understand his place, or where he "fits," given his actions and the actions of others toward him: "I call myself the Misfit . . . because I can't make what all I done wrong fit what all I gone through in punishment" (*CW* 151).

In different ways, stories such as this one illustrate aspects of St. Catherine's explanation of purgatory, including how the experience should not be understood. The Misfit makes a claim similar to one made by Hazel Motes in *Wise Blood:* they both understand the process of punishment in terms of debt/debtor relations, with the expectation of an eventual even balance between God and human beings. St. Catherine's treatise on purgatory clarifies explicitly why the debt/debtor relation does not work in the human approach to God. Purification through the purgatorial vision is not to be mistaken, according to St. Catherine, with settling a score, paying a debt, or even being punished; it is a movement toward God that brings with it the realization of the self and the necessary purging of self-centeredness. The purging is desired and accepted, but what is purified is the soul's excessive love of itself, replaced by a love of God that is transformative. It is not a debt owed in the sense that human beings are able to "pay" it. She writes:

> If contrition could purge it, the soul would turn to it in an instant and forthwith pay its debt; and it would do so impetuously, since it has a clear appreciation of the meaning of that impediment in its way. (On his part, God does not forgive one spark of the debt due in keeping with his just decree). The soul, for its part, no longer has a choice of its own. It can seek only what God wills, nor would it want otherwise. (82)

In the *Violent Bear It Away*, Francis Tarwater's primary experience is not one of guilt or fear of punishment, but of desiring a clear message from God. While Tarwater wants to insist that he is not searching for a religious life (especially in his protests to Rayber; *VBA* 109), he has trouble denying his strange hunger that food does not remedy: "I feel hungry but I ain't" (*VBA* 213). While the theme of hunger in the novel is tied to O'Connor's sacramental understanding of the world and to the kinship between the living and the dead portrayed in Tarwater's final eucharistic vision at Powderhead, it is also tied to the experience of purgatory. St. Catherine's treatise uses hunger to describe the soul's desire for God, including the recognition of God as both the source and satisfaction of the hunger. It is with this hunger that Tarwater struggles: "His hunger had become like an insistent silent force inside him, a silence inside akin to the silence outside" (*VBA* 162). Given the use of the metaphor in *Purgation and Purgatory*, it is possible to relate O'Connor's emphasis on Tarwater's hunger to her reading of St. Catherine. Tarwater's experience echoes St. Catherine's description of the hungering desire inherent in human nature to be one with God:

> That bread is what a healthy man, with an appetite, would seek; and when he could not find it or eat it, his hunger would increase indefi-

nitely. Aware that that bread alone could assuage his hunger, he would also know that without it his hunger could never abate. Such is the hell of the hungry who, the closer they come to this bread, the more they are aware that they do not as yet have it. Their yearning for that bread increases. (76)

The suffering here is internal, presented as hunger but indicative of a spiritual yearning. The spiritual hunger experienced by Tarwater is in itself reordering, because it hints to him of the deeper truth of who he is, not simply as an individual but in relation to the source and end of his hunger. The soul's hunger is self-revelatory through his desire and ultimately his lack, which must come from something greater than himself. As Tarwater experiences his final vision of the multitude eating from one basket, he becomes "aware at last of the object of his hunger . . . and . . . that nothing on earth would fill him" (*VBA* 241).

With the story of Ruby Turpin in "Revelation," O'Connor provides us with a more compact envisioning of the purgatorial experience than what is available in the novels. In "Revelation," the reordering of Ruby's love frames the whole story, and so it is that Ruby's purgatorial vision, while revealing to her the measure of her soul, also reveals the true ordering of love. If the purgatorial vision in "Revelation" is understood primarily as a judgment scene, the reordering of love that Ruby experiences is neglected. As St. Catherine's treatise suggests, the purgatorial experience is one of being purged of self-love enough to know what human beings are and can be through the purifying love of God. The reordering of vision described by St. Catherine is at the heart of Ruby's transformation: "God revivifies the soul with a special grace of His. In no other way could the soul renounce its self-centeredness or return to the pristine state of its creation; and as the soul makes its way to its first state, its ardor in transforming itself into God is its purgatory, the passionate instinct to overcome its impediments" (81). Clearly this kind of purification still involves a measure of divine judgment, but the story itself, by means of different images and biblical allusions, discloses the particular nature of the judgment. An adequate interpretation requires more than equating the final vision with Ruby's final judgment. I suggest that Ruby's vision itself is purgatorial in the sense described by St. Catherine; but I also believe that the entire story, not just the final vision, reveals the purgatorial cleansing and transformation of Ruby Turpin. This spiritual reordering in O'Connor's story includes several images of the soul's descent and ascent as it discovers its place in the "in-between" of purgatory.

External and Internal Visions: God and the Unconscious

O'Connor scholars tend to diverge in their interpretations of Ruby Turpin's final vision. I believe that these divergences tend to be indicative of a more fundamental division in the assessment of the human-divine encounter. Commenting on Ruby Turpin's redemption, Sura Rath notes that "critical polarity hinges on the *source* of Ruby's epiphany: whether it is internal, the redeeming awareness emerging from the dramatic unfolding of the crisis she confronts; or whether it is external, the vision gratuitously descending upon her as a narrative *coup de grace*."[5] Among the various scholars who argue this question in one direction or the other, Frederick Asals and Marshall Bruce Gentry represent the "external" and the "internal" views, respectively. While Asals recognizes to some extent the inner transformation of vision in O'Connor's characters, he focuses his analysis more on the insistent aspect of the divine action in revelatory encounters.[6] Using Abraham Heschel for his account of the prophetic thrust of O'Connor's fiction, Asals describes O'Connor's prophetic consciousness as being projected onto her characters, causing them to be relentlessly pursued by God while they remain in rebellion or revolt. Asals does note O'Connor's comment in that "our age is an age of searchers and discoverers" (*MM* 159), but he suggests that O'Connor could not actually dramatize this search, especially the conscious search for God, in her fiction. According to Asals, O'Connor's characters are pursued, sought after, and hounded by God, but they are rarely in pursuit of God themselves. He argues that the "dominant cast of the religious event in her fiction is what Heschel calls 'anthropotropic' rather than 'theotropic': the 'turning of a transcendent Being toward man' rather than the 'turning of man toward a transcendent Being.'"[7]

Two things are assumed here without argument: one is that the movements of the human soul are typically patterned or immediately obvious to the reader, reflected primarily in external actions rather than symbolically revealed; the second assumption is that the direction of the pursuit is an either/or possibility, not only in general terms, but as a central feature of O'Connor's fiction. If, as Asals asserts, "reason leads not toward revelation but away from it" in O'Connor's fiction,[8] then her characters are necessarily barred from any ascent or spiritual search that might be revelatory, leaving no alternative but Asals's contention that the fiction is entirely anthropotropic.

What occurs in such an interpretation is an effective narrowing of the meaning of the experienced vision itself; it has no other purpose than to inform Ruby that "the first shall be last and the last shall be first." The purpose of the vision is thus reduced to a radical separation between the human and the divine. Asals interprets the procession through fire in the final vision as a purging without distinction, because it "cleanses everyone not only of his sins, but also of his virtues." Instead of considering why this burning up of virtue is critical for Ruby's self-understanding, Asals assumes too quickly that the entire human moral enterprise is worthless in light of the divine measure, which necessitates its destruction in the purgatorial vision. He determines that Ruby's "virtues" of good order and respectable behavior are no longer useful in eternity: "although these gifts are apparently their *worldly* responsibility, they have no final value in themselves."[9] The purgation, therefore, constitutes a removal of the worldly order of virtues, according to Asals, rather than a transformation of Ruby's *worldly* understanding of the measure of her virtue. In his interpretation, the purgatorial vision ends up being the destruction of all things worldly; although noting O'Connor's comment that "the man in the violent situation reveals those qualities least dispensable in his personality, those qualities which are all he will have to take into eternity with him" (*MM* 114), Asals seems to deny the possibility of such a qualified purgation in "Revelation." He concludes: "All that the visionary procession of 'Revelation' clearly carries into eternity with it is the purifying action of the fire itself."[10]

One of the interesting similarities between Asals's discussion and Gentry's, even though they understand the source of the vision differently, is their focus on the unconscious in their analyses. Asals, while presumably describing O'Connor's Thomistic influences, refers to his dependence on Victor White's book, *God and the Unconscious* for his description of intuition and visionary knowledge.[11] O'Connor read White's book, as well as other Jungian psychoanalysts, but her appreciation of them is marginal,[12] and her language and thought about human nature are more centrally influenced by the biblical and classical Greek traditions. More specifically, O'Connor's understanding of personal religious visions and experiences is grounded primarily in the Christian mystical tradition. She makes this distinction between twentieth-century psychoanalysis and the ancient religious teachings clear in one of her letters: "The kind of 'belief' that Jung offers the modern, sick, unbelieving world is simply belief in the psychic realities that are good for it. This is good medicine and a step in the right direction but it is not religion" (*HB* 382). For O'Connor, what the psychoanalytic tradition offers is the recognition of the *psyche* (soul) as a reality in human experience, which, she says "the great mystics have always faced and that the Church teaches . . . we must face." The ideas of psychoanalysis are not novel to O'Connor, and she further notes that they fail to offer a comprehensive account of psychic realities: "St. Catherine of Genoa said 'God is my best self,' by which she realized probably what Jung means but a great deal more" (*HB* 382). Whatever O'Connor might have thought about the psychoanalytic tradition, it is clear that her understanding of the religious vision is not that it is rooted in the unconscious. In Asals's argument, the emphasis on the unconscious negates the role of reason in the revelatory experience, and hence, the possibility of the soul's noetic movement toward God. His use of Victor White leads Asals to accept an account of reason that is less differentiated than Aquinas's account, because he ends by separating reason from any experience of vision or intuition. Thus while he notes that the imagination, according to Aquinas, is the main receptor of the revelatory experience, he concludes, in contrast to Aquinas, that it is not connected to the activity of the intellect and is therefore forced into the unconscious. The imagination, he says, "seems most open to revelation when it is withdrawn, that is, when it is unconscious. In short, 'it is through the sub-rational that the super-rational is brought to human consciousness.'"[13]

In Gentry's interpretation, the unconscious is the focus of Ruby Turpin's vision, but instead of a withdrawn intellect, which leaves the unconscious open to the divine revelation, Gentry construes an active unconscious, which allows Ruby to make her own revelation to herself. Gentry's interpretation of the final vision comes from a different direction: Ruby is the source, and she projects the vision from her own unconscious. As in Asals's argument, the psychoanalytical language, while at times relevant, is not complete in its assessment of the spiritual experience. Gentry's consideration of religious ideas, especially his focal theme of redemption,[14] is dependent on formal textbook definitions (in this case from the *Catholic Encyclopaedia*), which he often uses as rigid templates for his evaluation of the religious symbols in O'Connor's fiction. The result can be confusing for an analysis of the purgatorial vision in "Revelation," especially since Gentry discusses Turpin's vision in terms of redemption rather than purgation. This point is not mere pedantry; there is a difference between the nature of the experiences, and O'Connor explicitly names this vision as purgatorial. Moreover, even though the human being is a participant in the spiritual experience of purgation in varying degrees, the event itself is primarily an experience of being measured by a transcendent God. But Gentry focuses on Turpin's self-redemption through a conscious/unconscious struggle, making "Mrs. Turpin's unconscious more clearly responsible for her vision of entry into a heavenly community."[15] This explanation has the fantastic effect of construing a vision that emerges from the unknown (other) world of the unconscious only to be projected into the unknown (other) world of the heavenly community, which is equally vague in Gentry's description: "Mrs. Turpin is like a hog from hell, and she is going back where she came from, but her real origin, Mrs. Turpin senses, is heaven, and her residence in hell is a stopover on her way back to heaven."[16] Essentially, Gentry uses the religious language of heaven and hell but leaves the meaning of the words empty, replacing their meaning with what he calls the "strength and wisdom of the unconscious."[17] Where I find these analyses of O'Connor's religious symbolism to be lacking is in their reluctance to engage the images, both explicit and implicit, of O'Connor's religious imagination. As I hope to show in what follows, recognition of O'Connor's dependence on St. Catherine's account of purgatory is necessary for understanding the direction and nature of Ruby Turpin's spiritual experience in "Revelation."

A Country Female Jacob

> If the story is taken to be one designed to make
> fun of Ruby, then it's worse than venal.
>
> —Flannery O'Connor, *Habit of Being*

O'Connor resisted interpretations suggesting that Ruby Turpin is evil or damned in the final vision. Harold Bloom's comment concerning the fire of "Revelation" is that "all are necessarily damned."[18] Yet this common notion ignores the subtle action of purgatory, which is more than destruction and certainly not tantamount to damnation. In O'Connor's letter to Betty Hester, describing Catherine Carver's assessment of "Revelation," O'Connor notes that Carver "found Ruby evil. Found end vision to confirm same . . . [and] suggested I leave it out. I am not going to leave it out. I am going to deepen it so that there'll be no mistaking Ruby is not just an evil Glad Annie. I've really been battling this problem all my writing days" (*HB* 554). By way of suggesting that this is a typical problem in the interpretation of her work, O'Connor notes that the manner in which her own religious thinking is perceived—conflated with the interpretation of her fictional characters—inevitably leads to the assumption that her vision is narrow and judgmental. This is why she wants to deepen the meaning of the vision so that Ruby is not simply dismissed as a bigot who gets what she deserves. While the general assessment of Ruby's vices is limited to her racist or classist attitudes,

O'Connor is looking to reveal the motivations behind these ideological traits. Ruby does not understand who she is as a human being, especially as a religious one, and her self-love is most obviously manifest in her love of her own righteousness. The vision is not used to blame her or to judge her as evil, but to show Ruby her faulty, human measure in the face of a higher one.

Further, to focus exclusively on the final vision as a judgment scene is to ignore the development of the story, including other important biblical allusions. My analysis of the story addresses the question of order and hierarchy and how it is both understood and misunderstood in the story, especially by Ruby Turpin. This discussion will be framed by an interpretation of three biblical references within the story: to Job, to the unintelligible writing on the ceiling (Daniel), and to the reversal of the first and the last (Matthew).[19] The interplay between these biblical passages and Ruby's search to understand who she is in relation to God portrays the breakdown of simplistic hierarchical categories and reveals the significant movement of descent and ascent in the reordering of Ruby's soul. The final purgatorial vision culminates with Ruby Turpin's self-realization, not of her (first or last) place in the afterlife, but her place in the middle of this life and how she loves others and God in this life.

Health and Sickness

The doctor's office is the right place to begin for someone who is ill. Although it is Claud who has the doctor's appointment for his swollen leg, Ruby is also in need of healing, not physically, but spiritually. Ruby's soul is disordered, and her particular symptoms emerge once she is sitting in the waiting room, observing the other people around her, and recollecting her night-time hierarchical imaginings. The disorder is apparent, not only from her classification of human beings according to race, class, and wealth, but more significantly because her vision is lacking in love and in spiritual orientation. The hierarchy is secular, Ruby is the judge, and her concern is limited to external accumulations and physical characteristics: "On the bottom of the heap were most colored people . . . then next to them—not above, just away from— were the white-trash; then above them were the home owners, and above them the home-and-land owners" (*CW* 636). Confusion creeps into her ordering when the external forms of merit cross racial and social lines, leaving her with the problem of colored or common people who have considerable money. Generally, Ruby witnesses the fluidity of material possessions and the consequent instability of her measure: "Some of the people with a lot of money were common and ought to be below she [sic] and Claud and some of the people who had good blood had lost their money and had to rent and then there were colored people who owned their homes" (*CW* 636). With the breakdown of her unreliable classification of human beings according to their possessions, color, and status, Ruby is left dreaming of "all the classes of people . . . moiling and roiling around in her head . . . all crammed together in a box car, being ridden off to be put in a gas oven" (*CW* 636). This horrific ending to her classification is the end product of her disordered soul, caught up as it is in merely human notions of hierarchy and bereft of love. Ruby's dictum that "you had to *have* certain things before you could *know* certain things" (*CW* 639) is the measure of this hierarchical ideal, a measure that is finally challenged at the end of the story, where, as we will note, the biblical verses about the first and the last are preceded by the story of the rich young man who must give up all of his possessions in order to follow Jesus. It is the movement of reversal from Ruby's first vision in the doctor's office to her final vision—from an ordering according to external possessions to an ordering of love—that effects the transformative purging of Ruby's self-love. The hierarchy of Ruby's construction is not meant to be condemned by a reversed hierarchical judgment; it is to be overcome through love.

In the doctor's office, Ruby's self-love takes the form of drawing attention to herself, measuring her good fortune against the others in the room: "We got a little of everything" (*CW* 638); "When you got something . . . you got to look after it" (*CW* 639); "The day has never dawned that I couldn't find something to laugh at" (*CW* 643); and "If its one thing I am . . . it's grateful. When I think who all I could have been besides myself and what all I got, a little of everything, and a good disposition besides" (*CW* 644). Ruby is convinced that the problem with others less fortunate than herself is their laziness: "Help them you must, but help them you couldn't" (*CW* 642). The irony in this is that Ruby is equally lazy about herself in a way that she does not yet understand. Mary Grace's book, pitched at Ruby Turpin's head, puts Ruby in need of the doctor's help and ends her image of wellness. But Mary Grace's words force Ruby also to question herself in relation to some larger order of meaning. Mary Grace is straddled by the doctor on the floor, and Ruby looks *down* at her, this time quite literally, to hear Mary Grace say "Go back to hell where you came from, you old wart hog" (*CW* 646).

This statement has been understood in different ways, depending on whether the experience is interpreted as religious or not. It is always seen as a judgment, but stemming from different sources: the non-religious interpretations see Mary Grace's words as the appropriate response to Ruby Turpin's judgmental attitude, because they redirect the judgment back on herself,[20] whereas many of the religious interpretations focus on the messenger's name, Mary *Grace,* and assume that they are a direct revelation of God's judgment on Ruby.[21] While the name Mary Grace is probably not unintentional, to assume its literal meaning lacks imagination and engagement with other aspects of God's graciousness.[22] Many interpretations characterize Mary Grace's declaration as a kind of final word on Ruby, a judgment that is justified and accurate given her atrocious attitude toward the others in the waiting room. In my view, what Mary Grace says to Ruby is gracious, but not in the sense of a conclusive judgment. Mary Grace's criticism provokes the beginning of Ruby's questioning, and awakens her soul's search for meaning. The divine measure is subtle, and it draws out more questions from Ruby, forcing her, perhaps for the first time, to contend with herself and that which compels her.

Indeed, to be called a wart hog from hell leaves Ruby with more questions than answers, and the questions are essential for the process of reorientation that the declaration triggers. Three questions, in particular, disturb Ruby, and she finally voices them near the end of the story. The first has to do with her identity: "How am I a hog and me both?" (*CW* 652). This question raises the possibility of a division within herself, the possibility that her spiritual orientation has better and worse directions that can in fact coexist. The second question is directed at God's purpose in disturbing Ruby's relatively peaceful faith: "What do you send me a message like that for?" This question has its ultimate expression in her questioning of God—"Who do you think you are?"—as Ruby grapples with her limited ability to understand the meaning of the message. Finally, the last question revolves around her eternal destiny: "How am I saved and from hell too?" (*CW* 652–53). This is the question that implicates Ruby's idea of her own righteousness, and forces her to contend with the possibility that righteousness, let alone salvation, is not measured or created by her own goodwill. It also suggests that perfect salvation or damnation are not realistic human prerogatives, and that their meanings are more ambiguous than the simple dichotomy of "in" or "out."

The questioning sparked by Mary Grace's outburst entails a process of reflection and purification, as the soul moves away from its self-defined measure to see itself in the presence of a transcendent measure. St. Catherine of Genoa writes of God's drawing action, which engenders the purgatorial experience: "He tugs at [the soul] with a glance, draws it and binds it to Himself with a fiery love that by itself could annihilate the immortal soul. In so acting, God so transforms the soul in Him that it knows nothing other than God; and He continues to draw it up into His fiery love until He restores it" (79). From her words we can observe that the purgatorial movement is not a matter of a hierarchy of judged souls, but of the individual soul's orientation in relation to the divine. In Ruby's vision of the people crammed into the boxcar, the suffocating atmosphere of her confused human ordering symbolizes the soul's paralysis. Because Ruby's classification of human beings is limited to external traits without any recognition of their connection to inner reality, she has eliminated the freedom of human life, which is rooted in the soul's free response. The movement and reordering of Ruby's soul, through the process of questioning, is what begins to make this inner freedom apparent to her.

Job

Images of false hierarchies, combined with real movements of ascent and descent, permeate the ensuing reflections that Ruby has when she returns home from the doctor's office. Her first inclination is to lie down, and placed horizontally on her bed she must contend not with her hierarchical classification system but with herself: "The instant she was flat on her back, the image of a razor-backed hog with warts on its face and horns coming out behind its ears snorted into her head. She moaned a low quiet moan" (CW 647). The suffering caused by this image makes Ruby weep and defend herself against the charge, but to no avail. Ruby's situation imitates Job's: with her respectability questioned and tested, she is being urged to examine herself; but instead, she can only direct her examination outward, toward God or whoever has treated her unjustly. Ruby's tears turn rather quickly away from herself when she considers, according to her habitual hierarchical ordering, the others who would have been more deserving of the judgment she received: "She had been singled out for the message, though there was trash in the room to whom it might justly have been applied" (CW 647). This immediate hierarchical comparison, which reveals Ruby's unwillingness to examine herself for any sustained period, establishes her anger instead of regret, and as her tears dry, "her eyes began to burn instead with wrath" (CW 648).[23]

Ruby Turpin thus at first resists any questioning of her "respectability" by instituting her own measure of justice, which would indict anyone who would question her righteousness. The two central questions of the Book of Job, from both the human and divine perspectives, are fittingly applied to

Ruby Turpin's experience. Gerald Janzen notes that the question "'Why do the righteous suffer?' is posed in Job within the context of a prior and (at least for the narrator) deeper question posed by God: 'Why are the righteous pious?'"[24] Ruby does not want to acknowledge this second question, asking only the first: "Occasionally she raised her fist and made a small stabbing motion over her chest as if she was defending her innocence to invisible guests who were like the comforters of Job, reasonable-seeming but wrong" (*CW* 648). Ruby defends her righteousness, like Job, and her invisible guests, like the comforters of Job, insist that she must have done something to offend God and that this suffering is the necessary payment.[25] But what is the significance of the Job analogy for this story? In what sense are the comforters of Job wrong, and in what sense is Ruby like Job? Perhaps the comforters of Job are wrong in that they are interested in divine justice only in order to decipher why Job deserves God's punishment (not unlike, it might be noted, the interpreters of Ruby Turpin, who are convinced that God is judging and consequently punishing her for her self-righteousness). Ruby is like Job in that she is more interested in her question as to why the righteous suffer, than in God's question—Why are the righteous pious?—the most important question for the story, as well as for Ruby. It is only with this question that the reward/punishment mentality is transcended in order to consider the true measure of righteousness and goodness. Ruby desires a reward for being a "respectable, hard-working, church-going woman" (*CW* 648), and she is certain as she sings along with the hymn that "wona these days I know I'll we-eara crown" (635). Furthermore, like Job, whose righteousness is tied to his prosperity, Ruby identifies her level of respectability with what she and Claud own. This is obviously tested for Job when his possessions are taken away. Ruby's test is still to come. Righteousness, when measured by God, is not done for the sake of reward or fear of punishment; it is desired for its own sake. The apparent conversation that Ruby carries on with her invisible guests suggests the beginning of the internal dialogue, between the innocent Ruby and guilty Ruby (How can she be both?), which will be vocalized soon enough in the pig parlor before her vision.

The Writing on the Wall

One of the interesting symbols representing the challenge to Ruby's hierarchical thinking in these scenes of self-reflection is her visual relation to the ceiling as she is lying flat on her back in bed. Although she is looking *up* at the ceiling (indicative of her soul's ascent) she is forced to see things—namely, the comforters of Job and the unintelligible handwriting—on a parallel plane. The second biblical allusion, to the handwriting on the wall (which in this story appears on the ceiling), is the revelation of the true measure of Ruby's righteousness. This reference is virtually ignored in the commentaries on O'Connor's "Revelation," but it makes a significant point about the appropriation by human beings of divine justice. The reference is to the Book of Daniel, where Belshaz'zar insists on using the silver and gold vessels that his father Nebuchadnez'zar had taken out of the temple in Jerusalem (Daniel 5:1–14). At the moment the king and his guests begin drinking their wine from these vessels, "the fingers of a man's hand appeared and wrote on the plaster of the wall of the king's palace" (Daniel 5:5). No one can read or understand the writing on the wall. After none of the king's wise men are able to decipher the message, the queen asks the king to consult Daniel. The king offers Daniel many gifts and rewards to make his interpretation known to him. Daniel refuses the rewards (5:17). He reminds Belshaz'zar of his father's fate, caused by his impiety and excessive pride, and warns him that witnessing this has not humbled his heart (5:22). He chastises him for offering his guests wine from the vessels of God's house "but the God in whose hand is your breath, and whose are all your ways, you have not honored" (5:23). According to Daniel's interpretation, the message inscribed as *Mene, Mene, Tekel, Parsin* (5:25) reveals that God has numbered the days of Belshaz'zar's kingdom, he has been weighed in the balance and found wanting, and his kingdom is divided between the Medes and Persians (5:26–28).

The story of Belshaz'zar, conjured up by Ruby's scrutiny of the ceiling "as if there were unintelligible handwriting" on it (*CW* 648), suggests a spiritual parallel to her story. Belshaz'zar insists on using the purloined temple vessels for his own purposes, praising the gods of "silver and gold, of bronze, iron, wood and stone" to the exclusion of the "God in whose hand is [his] breath." Ruby has become so enamored of her ideas and assumptions of righteousness that she has established herself as the measure of not only her own salvation but also of those around her. Daniel emerges as the interpreter for both stories, who, upon refusing Belshaz'zar's offers, reveals himself to be the one who seeks to know God's word without desiring a reward. His reading of the words speaks politically to Belshaz'zar and spiritually to Ruby: her days are numbered, requiring her attention to the orientation of her soul. Second, she has been measured by God's justice and found wanting in her lack of mercy. Finally, her kingdom, or soul, is divided against itself in her love of her own righteousness over the true source of righteousness.[26] After studying the ceiling, Ruby does what might seem at first strange: she asks Claud to kiss her. Yet if, according to the purgatorial movement of the story, the soul is being drawn toward God through love, then perhaps Ruby is becoming aware of how her self-love is an impediment, causing her inner division ("How am I a hog and me both?"). The kiss could signify a change of direction in the order of her loves. Ruby Turpin is thinking about who she is, what she has been called, and what is being revealed to her: "Her expression of ferocious concentration did not change. . . . She continued to study the ceiling" (*CW* 648). This upward gaze, from which she turns briefly to consider her husband lying prone beside her, suggests Ruby's reorientation of vision: it moves differently now—from herself to God and then back to other human beings.

When Ruby goes out to give water to the workers, we are reminded of one of her comments in the doctor's waiting room: "I sure am tired of buttering up niggers, but you got to love em if you want em to work for you" (*CW* 639). Her offer of water on this particular evening is not only an act of love, however utilitarian Ruby might consider it; it is also an act of confession. Ruby's loving act of giving the workers water is transformed by her willingness to admit to all of them what Mary Grace has called her. The love here demands humility and this effects a change in Ruby. Earlier she was unable to tell Claud, not wishing "to put the image of herself as a wart hog from hell into his mind" (*CW* 648). But in front of her workers, with whom it would have been even more important to maintain an image of superiority, Ruby confesses, thus lowering her self-righteous image. What Ruby realizes is that she must confront the ugly possibility that Mary Grace is right about her, and so she struggles to speak the words. She hesitates several times, indicating the deep spiritual conflict that is forcing her to face the ugly side of herself, to question her love of herself and her own righteousness: "'She said,' Mrs. Turpin began, and stopped, her face very dark and heavy. The sun was getting whiter and whiter, blanching the sky overhead so that the leaves of the hickory tree were black in the face of it. She could not bring forth the words. 'Something real ugly,' she muttered" (*CW* 650). Ruby sees herself as the black hickory leaves in the presence of the whitened sky, purified by the sun. The flattery of the women—"She sho shouldn't said nothin ugly to you. . . . You the sweetest lady I know"—who deny the truth of the charge, only enrages her at this point, since she now knows the lie for what it is. Her recognition of their flattery as she makes her confession indicates the healing and reordering of her soul, and it convinces her of the truth about herself. Slightly humiliated by her confession nonetheless, Ruby growls "idiots!" and intimates that her confession might be better directed: "I got more to do than just stand around and pass the time of day" (*CW* 650). Ruby is not finished, but she is now prepared and ready to complete her ascent. Ruby is now contending with her inordinate self-love, as her previous estimations of herself are stripped away. As St. Catherine puts it: "Quite still and in a state of siege, the me within finds itself gradually stripped of all those things that in spiritual or bodily form gave it some comfort; and once the last of them has been removed the soul, understanding that they were at best supportive, turns its back on them completely" (85).

Stripped of her pride, wounded and humiliated, Ruby heads for the pig parlor, with the look of "a woman going single-handed, weaponless, into battle" (*CW* 651). She climbs up by the fence around the pig parlor and takes the hose away from Claud so that she might be alone for her final appeal. She is trying desperately to wash the hogs clean, desiring to make herself and them clean for her ascent, but her anger interferes with her vision: "Her free fist was knotted and with the other she gripped the hose, blindly pointing the stream of water in and out of the eye of the old sow whose outraged squeal she did not hear" (*CW* 652). She shouts out two demands across the pasture, receiving a different response for each. The first demand addresses the sentence pronounced on her and its inconsistency with her own hierarchical ordering. Ruby insists that the hierarchical order of human worth as she conceives it, and to which she clings, is real, so that no amount of shuffling will change it: "'Go on,' she yelled, 'call me a hog! Call me a hog again. From hell. Call me a wart hog from hell. Put that bottom rail on top. There'll still be a top and bottom!'" To this charge only a "garbled echo returned to her" (*CW* 653). Ruby's confusion here is rooted in her inability to think beyond the human hierarchy of her own construction. By insisting (for the moment) that no matter where she stands, and despite God's manipulations (like putting the bottom rail on top), there will still be a "top and bottom," Ruby fails to transcend her hierarchical mode of thinking. O'Connor's inclusion of this statement reveals Ruby's resistance to the simple substitution of one hierarchy for another. The garbled response implies her confused question.

Her second question, "'Who do you think you are?' . . . carried over the pasture and across the highway and the cotton field and returned to her clearly like an answer from beyond the wood" (*CW* 653). This question returns clearly because it is the right question, it has just been misdirected. Now the question is asked of her. Ruby understands this instantly, as she essays to make an immediate reply: "She opened her mouth but no sound came out of it." At this moment, Ruby realizes that she does not have the answer to the question, and so her impediment—as St. Catherine of Genoa would call it—is that she does not really know who she is before God. All of Ruby's previous self-descriptions fail her in this encounter. In St. Catherine's treatise on purgatory, she clarifies that the souls who realize their impediments do not dwell on their suffering: "They dwell rather on the resistance they feel in themselves against the will of God" (79). The experience leaves her feeling vulnerable, not only for herself but for the one she loves, and as she watches Claud's truck on the highway it appears as a child's toy to her. The magnitude of what she is witnessing in this spiritual dialogue reduces all things in the face of it. Ruby contemplates Claud's toylike truck and realizes that "at any moment a bigger truck might smash into it and scatter Claud's and the niggers' brains all over the road" (*CW* 653), a possibility that freezes her until she sees the truck returning. When she must answer for who she is and is left speechless and vulnerable, her attention to herself is replaced with attention to another. Her self-love is diverted, and her vulnerability is transferred to other human beings, if only momentarily, and it is this that opens her soul to the ensuing visions. Whereas the image of the boxcars carrying their passengers to the gas ovens did not even give Ruby pause, her vision of the tiny vulnerable truck in the distance, with Claud and the workers in it, provokes her concern for them.

Ruby is described as a "monumental statue coming to life" (*CW* 653) once Claud returns safely, and with this action comes the story's concluding descent and ascent of the soul. First, Ruby's vision descends as "she bent her head slowly and gazed, as if through the very heart of mystery, down into the pig parlor at the hogs. They had settled all in one corner around the old sow who was grunting softly. A red glow suffused them. They appeared to pant with a secret life" (*CW* 653). Ruby understands herself connected to the hogs in a real way, on a level deeper than that of status or ideas of hierarchical ordering. She looks at them "as if she were absorbing some abysmal life-giving knowledge" (*CW* 653). Then Ruby ascends to the final vision lifting her head to look at the sky. The answers to Ruby's questions become clearer. She identifies with the hogs panting with their "secret life," which partakes of the divine life that animates all creatures. Ruby is no longer categorizing according to external measures; she sees the mystery of being "a hog and her both" through the spiritual connection of all living beings. By transcending the hierarchical nature of her thinking through the movements of her own soul, Ruby is freed to look at herself, and the question that she had previously directed toward God alone is accepted by Ruby as the question posed to *her*. The other question that concerns Ruby comes from being called a wart hog from hell. Ruby Turpin takes this judgment literally, and ponders the question: "How am I saved and from hell too?" (*CW* 652). Her question is partially answered by the descent and ascent of her soul, revealing to Ruby the human possibility of being oriented in different directions. Her external hierarchical ordering of soul-less beings who are either "in" or "out," "above" or "below," is broken down by her initiation into the life of the soul, which is determined, not by external measures, but by its relations of love to God, to others, and to the self. What Ruby discovers is her place in the middle, or (in St. Catherine's language) the state of being "in-between" the poles of perfection and imperfection. Ruby's final vision, however, is deflating to her pride, and requires her to come to the final purgative experience of *kenosis,* or self-emptying in the imitation of Christ.[27] Her ascent cannot continue with her desire to find "equality with God." Her humility is the only way through this final purgation, where the descent to a recognition of her true self is what will bring her back "up" to God.

First and Last

The final vision of the souls moving along the bridge through the field of living fire is the rest of the answer to Ruby's question of salvation. The purgatorial vision is not meant to continue Ruby's confusion, but to correct it. We could interpret the vision as the literal enactment of the biblical passage in Matthew 19:30: "But many that are first will be last, and the last first" (see also Matthew 20:16, Mark 10:31, and Luke 13:30). But this interpretation ignores what Ruby Turpin is coming to understand about herself and the nature of the purgatorial experience. In Matthew and Mark, the first/last dictum is preceded by the story of the rich young man. In this story, a man comes to Jesus and asks what he has to do to inherit eternal life.[28] After Jesus repeats the commandments to him, the man says that he already observes all of them. In Mark's account, it says "Jesus, looking upon him loved him, and said to him, 'You lack one thing; go, sell what you have and give to the poor, and you will have treasure in heaven; and come, follow me'" (Mark 10:21). He must give up everything he owns—for this is what blocks him—to the poor.

Ruby is presented with the same choice in her witness of the purgatorial vision. To follow Christ she must not give up her money, she must give up her inflated idea of herself. The one thing Ruby lacks is humility, and Christ's command to give that away, by "counting others as better"—like the young man's abdication of wealth in the service of the poor—is the *kenosis* that Ruby must accept. Ruby's self-emptying therefore, will bring her treasure in heaven with the ability to complete her ascent and rise to the God who resists the proud. She is not being divinely judged as one of "the last" through a simplistic reversal of the hierarchy she creates, since this would only echo Ruby's confused ideas shouted across the fields: "Put that bottom rail on top. There'll still be a top and bottom!" The experience is not externally hierarchical, but is rather a movement within the soul, either closer or further from God, depending on one's degree of self-love. The purgatorial experience, as St. Catherine describes it, is the burning away of our excess self-love as we approach God: "The last stage of love is that which comes about and does its work without man's doing" (81). The only way to overcome self-love is with humility rooted in love of God.[29] This is the moment of self-realization because it is Ruby Turpin's love of her own goodness that has kept her from seeing herself and the fact that "no one is good but God alone" (Mark 10:18).

When Ruby sees a fiery vision of souls marching toward heaven in which she is not in the lead—in which none of her expectations of the proper order appear—she is altered by the implications. She does not experience the revelation simply as an antidote to her hypocrisy, nor does she experience it as a biblical reversal of fortune (in which the first shall be last and the last first): she comes to know herself before God. St. Catherine accounts for this purging of the souls who have recognized God: "These insights are not of the soul's own doing. They are seen in God, in whom they are more absorbed than in their own suffering, for the briefest vision of God far surpasses any human joy or suffering. And yet that vision, even when surpassing, does not attenuate in the least their suffering and their joy" (84–85). The spiritual purging Ruby experiences is mirrored by what she observes, namely, the faces "shocked and altered" from "even their virtues . . . being burned away" (*CW* 654). Ruby's vision is purified not by her own efforts but through her witness to the burning away of her self-professed virtues. Here is the ethical power of the story. The image is reflective not of her punishment but of her moral choice. She sees herself on the bottom. She learns that love is the ordering force—*not* moral status according to external measures or even religious belief.

The movements of Ruby Turpin's soul describe the pattern of ascent and descent and the purifying movement toward God, reflecting the *kenotic* patterning of Christ who empties himself in the service of others. The transformative experience of purgation is described by the mystic, St. Catherine of

Genoa, to illumine the connection of the soul to God, including both its rejection of and longing for the divine. O'Connor uses the purgatorial images from St. Catherine in her fiction, and particularly in "Revelation," to suggest that the human soul moves and is ordered by its relation to God and that resistance is as much an experience of that relation as is drawing near. The source of the self is mystery, and while certain modern authors try to locate this mystery in the unconscious, the classical and biblical symbolizations of this mystery call it *God*. O'Connor makes the distinction between God and the unconscious because the experience of God is not an unconscious one, despite the fact that it is mysterious.

The transformation of Ruby Turpin works through her conscious participation in the divine mystery of the soul's ascent. Nonetheless, this participation involves more than her consciousness: Ruby must also act, by choosing the orientation of the will in relation to God. The soul is not just dragged up or thrown down; it seeks and responds actively to the divine that is its source and destination. But in this dialogue, Ruby is being resisted, because her response is too proud in her assumption of righteousness. The questions posed to Ruby, and those that she asks of God in response, are crucial to the reordering of her soul. But they are incomplete without her humiliation and confession, begun in front of her colored workers and continued in her willingness to identify herself with the hogs in her pen. Moreover, Ruby learns that the nature of righteousness is not a human possession that determines one's worth in the presence of God, but an active, embodied relation to others—which is explicitly described in Philippians 2:3–8. The only way for Ruby to be truly righteousness in the presence of God is to humble herself in the service of others. This humbling, says St. Catherine, is the destruction not of the soul but of the egoistic self: "In this purification, what is obliterated and cast out is not the soul, one with God, but the lesser self" (80).

Conclusion

When the moral vision of great artists is incarnated in literature, it can be experienced by the reader, not merely as an ethical metaphor or a series of examples for right living, but as a lived vision. The reader's responsibility is to participate in the stories as one open and willing to experience the artist's evoked vision of reality. Flannery O'Connor advocates a simple approach to interpreting literature: "When anybody asks what a story is about, the only proper thing is to tell him to read the story. The meaning of fiction is not abstract meaning but experienced meaning, and the purpose of making statements about the meaning of a story is only to help you to experience the meaning more fully" (*MM* 96). To seek the meaning of a story independently of the experience of reading it is to evade the existential encounter central to art, which O'Connor considers essential for grasping its meaning. Her advice reveals something true about ethics and points to my intentions for this study. The fact that the meaning of a story cannot be abstracted from experience can also be said of ethics: if "ethics" simply describes the things people do, and if meaning is to be found in experience, then it can be said that every human action is infused with meaning. My suggestion that O'Connor's sacramental view fosters an "ethic of responsibility" in her fiction is a "statement of meaning" that is offered as a new way of experiencing the moral dimension in her art.

O'Connor's presentation of love is prophetic in its challenge to the prevailing modern understanding of love as personal fulfillment rather than as self-sacrifice, as individual preference rather than as communal responsibility.

O'Connor's moral vision, with its focus on the connection between love and responsibility, is akin to another prophetic writer, Fyodor Dostoevsky. Both writers found love to be in some sense a mystery; charity comes to the Christian as an imperative to love others more than the self.[1] When O'Connor explains that "love and understanding are one and the same only in God" (*HB* 543), she signifies the mystery of love as it is experienced in human life. The direction of love reveals an ethical choice, and O'Connor's artistic exploration of this choice in her fictional art is not meant to be didactic but revelatory: "Fiction writing is very seldom a matter of saying things; it is a matter of showing things" (*MM* 93). O'Connor sees ethical issues in light of the biblical prophetic tradition, which does not prescribe legally based moral rules as much as it advocates "love, humility and righteousness of action."[2] This comment of Eric Voegelin's, familiar to O'Connor, identifies love and humility with 'righteousness of action': her ethical vision is centered on righteousness, not as self-glorification, but as love that seeks the good of others over the self.

O'Connor's understanding of love is at the heart of her sacramental theology.[3] In a letter written to Betty Hester, she says that "children know by instinct that hell is an absence of love" (*HB* 244). O'Connor's theological views were more often measured in relation to love than anything else: purgatory as the purging of self-love from the soul as it ascends to God, and hell defined by the degree to which the soul participates in love. The connection is telling. Rather than defining such notions in doctrinal terms, O'Connor uses the experiential and ethical language of love. Sin is a reality, but the truer reality of human life in relation to God is love: "It is what is invisible that God sees and that the Christian must look for. Because he knows the consequences of sin, he knows how deep you have to go to find love" (*HB* 308). Her point does not indicate the separation of spirit and matter; she is not claiming that the invisible world of the spirit is more important than sensed reality. What she means, therefore, is that the ethical responsibility of human beings is rooted in the invisible, eternal ties of spiritual communion among all human beings. Love is the ordering force of reality, and the direction of one's love expresses one's response to that reality.

One can observe a development in the presentation of love through the spiritual struggles lived by O'Connor's characters, as well as a change in tone that suggests a subtle redirection in O'Connor's art and religious thought. There appears to be a progression in O'Connor's treatment of the idea of love in the three stories I have examined in this book. My purpose in placing the three fictional works in the order I have is not simply for the clarity of a chronological analysis, but because I think that this progression reveals a movement of the reordering of love and, ultimately, it reveals how the love of God and others is at the heart of O'Connor's ethic of responsibility. It is important to understand the connection between these loves when interpreting her fiction. Against the idea that O'Connor is concerned only with human-divine relations of love, she describes the moment of grace in "A Good Man Is Hard to Find" to Betty Hester: "You say there is love between man and God in the stories, but never between people—yet the grandmother is not in the least concerned with God but reaches out to touch the Misfit" (*HB* 379). O'Connor's sacramental fiction is not about abstract experiences of the love of God; she reveals a deeper understanding of how the love of human beings, known and lived as responsibility for others, is the way to know and love God.

Love is virtually absent in *Wise Blood*. Hazel Motes wants a "Church *without* Christ," so as to contain any redemptive purpose or spiritual reality solely within himself, effectively eliminating the possibility of anything transcendent or spiritually binding, including love. His one-man show keeps him virtually isolated, and the more driven he is to preach individual autonomy from religious claims, the more he withdraws inside himself. His blindness symbolically completes his isolating vision. Motes's inability to practice charity stems from his preoccupation with penitential acts that are motivated not by love, but by an idea that these self-torturing acts will satisfy his "debt" to God. His understanding develops from a position of absolute spiritual autonomy to a calculative (legalistic) view of human responsibility. The only glimpse of love that is not calculated or owed comes from Mrs. Flood, whose charity springs from her emerging sense of spiritual awareness and connection to other human beings.

In *The Violent Bear It Away*, O'Connor identifies love more directly and clarifies its relation to the ethical realm. In this novel, love appears as a mysterious power that threatens to overcome reasoned opinions, but it also provides a spiritual link between the living and the dead that suggests the idea of responsibility for others. The burden of this responsibility, dramatized in Francis Tarwater's life by the imperative of burying his uncle Mason and baptizing his cousin Bishop, makes him long to escape such obligations. Francis Tarwater resists this embodied, enacted love in favor of an abstract spiritual freedom from accountability and responsibility for others. The aim of his existence is to act, but as a disembodied spiritual will, untainted by the flesh; he resists the incarnate world and consequently he is unable to appreciate the kind of love that Mason Tarwater affirms.

Mason is the only one who does not envision love as a threat; he sees the mystery of love and its connection to God through sacramental communion.

The Eucharistic image at the end of the novel, which becomes the revelatory vision of Francis, reveals the kinship bonds between the living and the dead, through blood and community, with all of the obligations and responsibilities that attend these relations.

Ruby Turpin's experience in "Revelation" evokes the problem of self-love and what is needed, namely confession and humility, to relinquish it. Ruby's problem becomes obvious with every comment she makes about other human beings. Her self-righteousness certainly makes her oblivious to humility, but it is her unsacramental vision of the human-divine relation, evidenced in her external measures (i.e., class and wealth) of spiritual worth that is her primary problem. But what is the dynamic of the movement from self-love to love of others and of God? Ruby's self-love is isolating and abstracted from real human experience because she cannot see beyond herself to loving anyone else. So she must empty herself in order that she might be open to receiving a new vision of who she is in relation to God and others. This pattern of *kenosis* is, for O'Connor, the Christian sacramental view of love. The ethical power of this story comes with the burning up of Ruby's virtues in the final revelation scene. O'Connor shows how love is the true virtue and how undue attention to one's moral virtues has the (decidedly unvirtuous) effect of inflating self-opinion, which ultimately blocks the way to love and responsibility for others. Ruby needs to undergo the purgative experience of having her self-love burned away, an experience of humility, in order to know God and to love others more than herself.

⬚ ⬚ ⬚

When a writer dies as young as O'Connor, one is tempted to reflect on where her thought was moving and what kind of work might have come next. Although this can be no more than speculative, other scholars have also noted that O'Connor was trying to do something different. In a letter dated February 4, 1960, she writes: "I have got to the point now where I keep thinking more and more about the presentation of love and charity, or better call it grace, as love suggests tenderness, whereas grace can be violent or would have to be to compete with the kind of evil I can make concrete. At the same time, I keep seeing Elias in that cave, waiting to hear the voice of the Lord in thunder and lightning and wind, and only hearing it finally in the gentle breeze, and I feel I'll have to be able to do that sooner or later, or anyway keep trying" (*HB* 373). O'Connor describes two experiences in this letter: a desire to write about love, or grace that competes with the concrete evils conjured in her fiction, and yet a desire to write in a way that transcends her usually aggressive style. By the time of her death, her style of the grotesque, especially evident in *Wise Blood* and her first collection of short stories, had given way to the mystical ascent in "Revelation" based on St. Catherine of Genoa's vision of purgatory. I think O'Connor was able to realize both of her desires. The "violence of love" was her response. In *The Violent Bear It Away*, she uses her biblical epigraph to introduce the "violence" of a love that does more than the law commands by competing with violent acts nonviolently. And O'Connor's last few stories do take on gentler, mystical tones. The violence in "Revelation" has a purifying effect; to be free of self love brings Ruby to a truer vision of herself, God, and others.

She writes in another letter in 1963: "I've been writing eighteen years and I've reached a point where I can't do again what I know I can do well, and the larger things that I need to do now, I doubt my capacity for doing" (*HB* 518). O'Connor's last novella in progress at the time of her death—an eponymous expansion of the short story "Why Do the Heathen Rage?"—had as its main character an ascetic monklike figure who carried on a correspondence with a woman living on a commune involved in radical social activism. The manuscript pages of this work in progress seem to suggest that O'Connor was interested in the relation between the love of God as it is expressed in individual religious training and devotion, and a socially oriented activism—or a mutually enriching dialogue between the active and contemplative religious lives. O'Connor's basic interest in writing about love in its relation to God and other human beings was indeed present in her sacramental view of the world, which, as a Catholic, did not fundamentally change in the course of her life.

What can be perceived from this discussion of her work, however, is that her writing developed in this regard, as she mastered and then felt compelled to move beyond her most famously recognized writing form, the grotesque. The fiction of the grotesque serves to remind human beings of what is absent and distorted in human existence; the fiction of love would serve to remind human beings of what is good and worth seeking in human existence. It does not seem surprising that, as O'Connor neared the end of her life, her writing moved toward the contemplation of the soul's ascent into the purifying love of God.

Introduction

1. Although O'Connor does not identify her position in this way, responsibility for others is implicit in her moral vision. In one essay she refers to the idea of "eternal responsibility" as one of the things the secular world does not believe in, but which is central to her Catholic belief in the Fall, Redemption, and Judgment (*MM* 185).

2. My use of "ethics" and "moral vision" interchangeably is intended to suggest that O'Connor's ethic of responsibility is a way of seeing and interpreting reality, which can be experienced and known through the drama of her stories. Ethics—a word that means simply, "what people do"—are rooted, for O'Connor, in an understanding of reality, and they are revealed by what human beings do in response to that reality. O'Connor describes her interest in human conduct using the language of moral vision, but for the purpose of identifying that vision more explicitly, the word *ethic* can help to suggest a patterned response that chooses a particular mode of conduct (in relation to love, e.g.) and comes out of a particular moral vision. To depict O'Connor's moral vision as the "ethic of responsibility" confirms her Christian belief in human responsibility as the true order of love.

3. See Paul Elie's fine biography, *The Life You Save May Be Your Own* (New York: Farrar, Straus and Giroux, 2003), for his comment about O'Connor's affinities with Dostoevsky: "She was no Tolstoyan. . . . She was a Dostoevskian" (192).

4. Fyodor Dostoevsky, *The Brothers Karamazov,* trans. Richard Pevear and Larissa Volokhonsky (New York: Vintage Books, 1990), 320.

5. See Jacques Maritain, *Art and Scholasticism and the Frontiers of Poetry,* trans. Joseph W. Evans (New York: Charles Scribner's Sons, 1962), 36n: "The creature is deserving of compassion, not contempt; it exists only because it is loved."

6. Also known as Augustine's *amor Dei* and *amor sui.*

CHAPTER ONE.   Sacramental Theology and Incarnational Art

1. The correspondent "A," a pseudonym used in *The Habit of Being,* has been posthumously identified as Betty Hester.

2. See Louis D. Rubin, Jr., "Flannery O'Connor's Company of Southerners: or, 'The Artificial Nigger' Read as Fiction Rather Than Theology, *Flannery O'Connor Bulletin* 6 (1977): 47–71. Rubin argues that the emphasis in the scholarship on O'Connor's theological views has interfered with the literary critical interpretations of her fiction. His position, therefore, is to interpret "O'Connor as a Southern writer rather than as a theologian." Rubin suggests that "what we need is criticism that will explore the complexity of the work, and not merely to seek to use it to make theological observations" (71). Although I do not accept Rubin's radical distinction between O'Connor's theological and literary concerns, his argument offers a valid criticism of some of the moralistic, theological interpretations of O'Connor's work that assume a moral or religious meaning can simply be "extracted" from the fiction.

3. John Desmond offers a striking description of this distinction, concluding that the misunderstanding is rooted in how O'Connor's religious thought relates to her work. His summary provides another reason for the need to clarify how the ideas of Maritain and Aquinas, as theological aesthetics, are crucial for interpreting the relation between O'Connor's religious ideas and her fiction. Whereas I focus on how a theological understanding of art yields certain moral implications in the fiction, Desmond's argument focuses on O'Connor's biblical view of history: "to indicate a way of viewing and understanding the specific objects and actions she creates and to see how they are linked to her vision of history considered in its totality." See John Desmond, *Risen Sons: Flannery O'Connor's Vision of History* (Athens: University of Georgia Press, 1987), 7–8.

4. See Frederick Asals, "The Limits of Explanation," in *Critical Essays on Flannery O'Connor,* ed. Melvin Friedman and Beverly Lyon Clark (Boston: G. K. Hall, 1985), 49–53. Asals emphasizes O'Connor's lack of formal theory in these essays to suggest that the inconsistencies in *Mystery and Manners* should not be held against O'Connor, but, what is more important, they should not be used to interpret the fiction. Clearly, there have been interpreters who have used O'Connor's comments and explanations quite unquestioningly and without discrimination, but Asals's near rejection of the significance of O'Connor's theoretical formulations about prose commentaries is overly dismissive. The more general problem here is the separation between theory, as Asals understands it, and the fiction. While O'Connor makes some comments about her lack of training in *literary* theory, her work is not devoid of theoretical insights. Asals limits the usefulness of theory in several ways, but most strikingly by identifying it as an activity of "the pure intellect, wrapped away in abstraction" (49). The equation of the intellect with abstraction will be more fully explored in relation to O'Connor's thought in the section "Reason and Imagination" in this chapter.

5. There are numerous references to Thomas Aquinas in O'Connor's letters, which indicate that she read both him and Maritain. Regarding the *Summa Theologiae,* she wrote: "I read for about twenty minutes every night before I go to bed" (*HB* 93). But it is also clear that she read Thomistic ideas in Maritain: "The novel is an art form and when you use it for anything other than art, you pervert it. I didn't make this up. I got it from St. Thomas (*via Maritain*) who allows that art is wholly concerned with the good of that which is made; it has no utilitarian end" (*HB* 157, italics mine). Her comment parallels directly *Art and Scholasticism,* where Maritain writes: "Art, which rules Making and not Doing, stands therefore outside the human sphere; it has an end, rules, values, which are not those of man, but those of the work to be produced. This work is everything for Art; there is for Art but one law—the exigencies and the good of the work" (9).

6. The separations listed here are described by O'Connor in *Mystery and Manners* (184). She says that they are "separations which we see in our society and which exist in our writing."

7. O'Connor refers to the importance of Maritain's *Art and Scholasticism* quite regularly in her letters: "It's the book I cut my aesthetic teeth on, though I think even some of the things he [Maritain] says get soft at times. He is a philosopher and not an artist but he does have great understanding of the nature of art, which he gets from St. Thomas" (*HB* 216). One can observe, not only from the guiding tone of Maritain, but also from O'Connor's appropriation of his formulations in her own writing, that this work was a formative influence on her Christian aesthetics.

8. Jacques Maritain, *Art and Scholasticism,* 66.

9. Ibid., 39–40.

10. The continuity with Maritain's ideas is evident throughout O'Connor's prose writing. "If you were to make of your aesthetic an article of faith, you would spoil your faith. If you were to make of your devotion a rule of artistic activity, or if you were to turn desire to edify into a method of your art, you would spoil your art." Maritain, *Art and Scholasticism,* 66.

11. O'Connor says further, identifying this approach as specifically Manichean, "He will think that the eyes of the Church or of the Bible or of his particular theology have already done the seeing for him, and that his business is to rearrange this essential vision into satisfying patterns, getting himself as little dirty in the process as possible. His feeling about this may have been made more definite by one of those Manichean-type theologies which sees the natural world as unworthy of penetration" (*MM* 163).

12. Maritain, *Art and Scholasticism,* 47.

13. Desmond, *Risen Sons,* 15.

14. She says further: "When anyone writes about the poor in order merely to reveal their material lack, then he is doing what the sociologist does, not what the artist does. The poverty he writes about is so essential that it needn't have anything at all to do with money" (*MM* 132).

15. See Frederick Asals, *Flannery O'Connor: The Imagination of Extremity* (Athens: University of Georgia Press, 1982), 48–62; Mary Gordon, "Flannery O'Connor: *The Habit of Being*," in *Good Boys and Dead Girls* (New York: Viking Penguin, 1991), 39; Martha Stephens, *The Question of Flannery O'Connor* (Baton Rouge: Louisiana State University Press, 1973), 9.

16. See Asals, *Flannery O'Connor*, 58. Asals argues that O'Connor's early work was Manichean, especially given her negative view of the body and the physical world in *Wise Blood*. This kind of analysis is dependent on equating the protagonist's actions with the author's worldview rather than interpreting the fiction with a measure other than the story itself.

17. "Today's reader, if he believes in grace at all, sees it as something which can be separated from nature and served to him raw as Instant Uplift" (*MM* 165).

18. Note her comment in a letter to John Hawkes: "Grace, to the Catholic way of thinking, can and does use as its medium the imperfect, purely human, and even hypocritical" (*HB* 389).

19. O'Connor comments on the conjunction and shared traits of the novelist and the believer (whether or not they are the same person): "a distrust of the abstract, a respect for boundaries, a desire to penetrate the surface of reality and to find in each thing the spirit which makes it itself and holds the world together" (*MM* 168).

20. Mary Gordon, *Good Boys and Dead Girls*, 39.

21. Lorine Getz, *Nature and Grace in Flannery O'Connor's Fiction* (New York: Edwin Mellen Press, 1982), 4.

22. Ibid., 32–37.

23. For O'Connor's book review of von Hügel, see Flannery O'Connor, *The Presence of Grace, and Other Book Reviews*, comp. Leo J. Zuber, ed. Carter W. Martin (Athens: University of Georgia Press, 1983), 21–22.

24. Gwendolen Greene, ed., *Letters from Baron Friedrich von Hügel to a Niece*, (Chicago: Henry Regnery, 1955), 121. Related to this question are the question of immortality and the preoccupation with what von Hügel calls "survival." See Greene's introduction, 40.

25. Greene, *Letters*, 121.

26. See Marshall Bruce Gentry, *Flannery O'Connor's Religion of the Grotesque*, (Jackson: University Press of Mississippi, 1986), 6–7.

27. Desmond, *Risen Sons*, 9.

28. See, among others, Ralph Wood, *The Comedy of Redemption: Christian Faith and Comic Vision in Four American Novelists* (Notre Dame, Ind.: University of Notre Dame Press, 1988); Rubin, "Flannery O'Connor's Company of Southerners"; Robert H. Brinkmeyer, Jr., "Asceticism and the Imaginative Vision of Flannery O'Connor," in *Flannery O'Connor: New Perspectives*, ed. Sura Rath and Mary Neff Shaw (Athens: University of Georgia Press, 1996), 169–82; Arthur F. Kinney, "Flannery O'Connor and the Art of the Holy," *Virginia Quarterly Review* 64, no. 2 (Spring 1988): 217–30.

29. For a more detailed and thoughtful analysis of these influences in O'Connor, see Marion Montgomery, "Flannery O'Connor's Sacramental Vision," *This World* 4 (1983): 119–28.

30. Sura P. Rath has offered a very clear analysis of the Thomistic influence, including the role of Maritain. See Sura P. Rath, "Ruby Turpin's Redemption: Thomistic Resolution in Flannery O'Connor's 'Revelation,' *Flannery O'Connor Bulletin* 19 (1990): 1–8.

31. Maritain, *Art and Scholasticism,* 10–11.

32. Jacques Maritain, *Creative Intuition in Art and Poetry* (Cleveland: World Publishing, 1953), 3.

33. Ibid., 32.

34. Ibid., 33.

35. It should be mentioned that Maritain uses the terms "intellect" and "reason" interchangeably, and for this discussion I will follow this practice. He says: "I use the words intellect and reason as synonymous, in so far as they designate a single power or faculty in the human soul" (Maritain, *Creative Intuition,* 3).

36. Ibid., 55.

37. Ibid., 4.

38. Ibid., 65.

39. *The Presence of Grace,* comp. Zuber, 124.

40. Maritain, *Creative Intuition,* 123.

41. Ibid., 125.

42. Ibid.

43. Ibid., 127.

44. For this discussion and my analysis of reason in O'Connor's thought, I wish to acknowledge an important source on the ancient/modern distinctions of reason, to which my own understanding is indebted. See Eric Voegelin, "Reason: The Classic Experience," in *The Collected Works of Eric Voegelin,* vol. 12, *Published Essays, 1966–1985,* ed. Ellis Sandoz (Baton Rouge: Louisiana State University Press, 1990), 265–91. The use of Voegelin is relevant for this discussion of O'Connor, especially because O'Connor was familiar with Voegelin's work and in fact reviewed the first three volumes of his philosophy of history series, *Order and History.* These book reviews are found in *The Presence of Grace,* comp. Zuber, 60–61, 67–68, 70–71.

45. See Frederick Asals, *Flannery O'Connor,* 229. Asals describes the intellectuals in O'Connor's work as follows: "Again and again the revolt of her protagonists takes the form of an exaltation of consciousness, of the mind, as the seat of their illusory self-sufficiency," and then he immediately refers to this particular portrayal of her character's illusions as stemming from "the anti-intellectual strain in her work." Asals's identification of the "illusory self-sufficiency" of O'Connor's characters with her "anti-intellectualism" reveals a typical problem in the interpretation of O'Connor's understanding of reason; while the description of the intellectual's autonomy and self-sufficiency rooted in the mind is partly the focus of O'Connor's criticism; it is not an "anti-intellectual" position. However, the apparent connection between

this description of the intellectual's quest for autonomy and O'Connor's so-called anti-intellectualism is inevitable only if we are limited to a reductionistic definition of the intellectual pursuit.

46. Asals opposes these faculties of imagination and reason in his reading of O'Connor's work, and his discussion serves to establish the fact that the range of reason is narrowly defined in the interpretation of O'Connor's writing: "But in her fiction the violence of the opposition between reason and imagination pushes the orthodox distinction between these faculties to its extreme limit. If the visions of her later work are a form of knowledge indeed, they are not only unavailable to but actively opposed by any motion of the discursive intellect. Reason leads not toward revelation but away from it: the rationalistic tendency is one of abstraction from the earth, from the body, from the concrete world altogether. . . . The imagination, on the other hand, feeds on the world of the senses, and her climactic visions present their knowledge as experience, supernatural awareness that comes in the images of the natural world" (Asals, *Flannery O'Connor,* 213–14). Not only does Asals's critique contradict what O'Connor and Maritain say about reason, it has the effect of pairing the experience of natural and the supernatural through the imagination and the senses alone and of cutting off the intellect and the imagination from the spiritual movements of the soul.

47. Desmond, through Gerhart Niemeyer, refers to the similarity between Eric Voegelin's description of the life of reason being "firmly rooted in a revelation" and O'Connor's account of the soul's experience of mystery. See Desmond, *Risen Sons,* 98–99.

48. In a letter to the same student, O'Connor writes: "One result of the stimulation of your intellectual life that takes place in college is usually a shrinking of the imaginative life. This sounds like a paradox, but I have often found it to be true. Students get so bound up with the difficulties such as reconciling the clashing of so many different faiths such as Buddhism, Mohamedanism, etc., that they cease to look for God in other ways" (*HB* 476).

49. Maritain, *Art and Scholasticism,* 182, n. 97. Thanks to Graeme Ward for his help with the Latin translation.

50. Ibid., 47.

51. Paul Elie tends to characterize O'Connor's dependence on Maritain by suggesting that she used "the habit of art" as license to "segregate her art from her everyday life." A close examination of the letters would show that this was not the case. See Elie, *The Life You Save,* 327–28.

52. Maritain, *Art and Scholasticism,* 74.

53. Ibid.

54. Rosemary Magee, *Conversations with Flannery O'Connor* (Jackson: University Press of Mississippi, 1987), 8.

55. O'Connor argues that "sorry" Catholic fiction is more often the result "not of restrictions that the Church has imposed, but of restrictions that [the writer] has failed to impose on himself" (*MM* 153).

56. The essay from which this quotation is taken is titled "The Catholic Novelist in the Protestant South," and so she is emphasizing "Catholic" in this context. It is clear, however, that the word "Christian" would also be applicable here.

57. In a letter concerning the relation between nature and grace O'Connor remarks that "cutting yourself off from Grace is a very decided matter, requiring a real choice, act of will, and affecting the very ground of the soul" (*HB* 389). This issue of the (negative) choice of the will is not a focal point in Maritain's work, whereas it is a recurring theme in O'Connor's fiction.

58. *The New Oxford Annotated Bible with the Apocrypha,* Revised Standard Version, ed. Herbert May and Bruce Metzger (New York: Oxford University Press, 1962). Unless otherwise noted, I use this edition throughout for biblical references.

59. Kathleen Feeley, *Flannery O'Connor: Voice of the Peacock* (New York: Fordham University Press, 1982).

60. In her copy of Buber's *Eclipse of God: Studies in the Relation between Religion and Philosophy,* O'Connor marked the following passage: "I have never in our time encountered on a high philosophical plane such a far-reaching misunderstanding of the prophets of Israel. The prophets of Israel have never announced a God upon whom their hearers' striving for security reckoned. They have always aimed to shatter all security and proclaim in the opened abyss of the final insecurity the unwished-for God who demands that His human creatures become real, they become human, and confounds all who imagine that they can take refuge in the certainty that the temple of God is in their midst. . . . The primal reality of these prophecies does not allow itself to be tossed into the attic of 'religions': it is as living and actual in this historical hour as ever." See Arthur F. Kinney, *Flannery O'Connor's Library: Resources of Being* (Athens: University of Georgia Press, 1985), 26.

61. Karl Martin, in his essay "Flannery O'Connor's Prophetic Imagination," *Religion and Literature* 26, no. 3 (1994): 33–58, analyzes O'Connor's prophetic ideas in the fiction through Walter Brueggemann's *The Prophetic Imagination* (Philadelphia: Fortress Press, 1978).

62. Feeley, *Flannery O'Connor: Voice of the Peacock,* 141. This passage from Voegelin is quoted in Feeley.

63. I will return to a further discussion of the relation between the imaginative and moral vision of the prophet below.

64. Thomas Aquinas, *Summa Theologiae,* trans. Fathers of the English Dominican Province (London: Burns Oates and Washbourne, 1934), II–II, q. 171, art. 1. Subsequent references to this work will be made in the text.

65. She describes this title of being a "realist of distances": "Prophecy is a matter of seeing near things with their extensions of meaning and thus of seeing far things close up" (*MM* 44).

66. F. C. Copleston, *Aquinas* (London: Penguin Books, 1955), 43–44.

67. It is perhaps helpful to outline how arguments are made in the *Summa.* For each subject there is a division of parts, questions, and articles. The topic of "Prophecy" is taken up in the "Second Part of the Second Part" of the *Summa;* it is

divided into four general questions (according to prophecy's "nature," "cause," "manner," and "division") and each question is discussed in a series of articles. The articles are divided further. They begin with a question (e.g., "Whether prophecy pertains to knowledge?") and this question is followed by several, usually two to four, objections written by Aquinas but referring to the arguments of various other authors and texts. Aquinas then offers his own answer to the question, which opposes the arguments of the objections. After stating his answer, he replies to each objection in turn, listed as "Reply Obj. 1, 2" etc., before moving onto the next article, where the process is repeated.

68. Interestingly, immediately following this passage, Aquinas writes "Hence among the heathen nations they were known as *vates, on account of their power of mind*" (II–II, q. 171, art. 1, emphasis in original). I mention this because Jacques Maritain's initial descriptions of poetic knowing in *Creative Intuition in Art and Poetry,* include a definition of the ancient *vates,* who were diviners and thus, for Maritain, had a similar role to the poet, whose spiritual knowledge of things is creatively translated through art and poetry.

69. See Martin Buber's comment in *The Prophetic Faith* (New York: Harper and Row, 1949), 103.

70. She says in her essay "Catholic Novelists and Their Readers" that "every mystery that reaches the human mind, except in the final stages of contemplative prayer, does so by way of the senses" (*MM* 176).

71. Magee, *Conversations with Flannery O'Connor,* 106.

72. Asals suggests that O'Connor appears to be a morally judgmental author and narrator: "Like God Himself, she seems to preside in her fiction as both creator and derisive judge" (Asals, *Flannery O'Connor,* 131).

73. O'Connor's prophetic vision, according to Asals, is determined primarily by her Catholic beliefs, "the general substance of which was transmitted to her through the church" (Asals, *Flannery O'Connor,* 158).

74. Asals also refers to Aquinas's definition of prophetic vision as a quality of the imagination rather than a moral faculty, but he suggests that this means the moral question can be dismissed in favor of a more artistic discussion of imagination. He also indicates that O'Connor's use of this reference reveals her interest in their separation: "In the separation between the imaginative and the moral that she so eagerly seized upon in Aquinas . . . O'Connor articulated a justification for her own kind of fiction" (Asals, *Flannery O'Connor,* 157–58).

75. Maritain, *Art and Scholasticism,* 65.

CHAPTER TWO.   **Moral Vision and the Grotesque**

1. Philip S. Keane, S.S., *Christian Ethics and Imagination* (Ramsey, N.J.: Paulist Press, 1984), 3.

2. O'Connor uses "mythic," or *mythos,* to refer to the stories that human communities share to describe or account for the sacred and spiritual history of their lives. Myths are stories that speak to the aspects of existence that cannot be described literally; rather they suggest evocatively the spiritual dimension of human experience.

3. Rosemary Magee, *Conversations with Flannery O'Connor,* 87.

4. Peter S. Hawkins, *The Language of Grace: Flannery O'Connor, Walker Percy, and Iris Murdoch* (Cambridge, Mass.: Cowley Publications, 1983), 28.

5. John Desmond, *Risen Sons,* 53.

6. Ibid., 57.

7. Flannery O'Connor, unpublished lecture manuscript, Troy State College, file 249b, dated 4/24/63, p. 3.

8. Ibid.

9. Richard Giannone, *Flannery O'Connor and the Mystery of Love* (Urbana: University of Illinois Press, 1989), 9.

10. L. Gregory Jones, *Embodying Forgiveness: A Theological Analysis* (Grand Rapids, Mich.: William B. Eerdmans, 1995), 145.

11. See Romans 13:8: "Owe no one anything, except to love one another." This passage suggests a corrective to Hazel's legalistic understanding of his debt. The only thing that should be considered "owing" to one's neighbor is love, which, instead of procuring individual autonomy, acknowledges and encourages interdependence through bonds of friendship and caring.

12. This reference to lack of hearing and lack of sight is related to the passage in Isaiah 6:9–10 (also quoted by Jesus in Matthew 13:14–15). It is an important image in *Wise Blood,* and it is proclaimed by Asa Hawks to Hazel Motes, as will be discussed presently.

13. Gentry, *Religion of the Grotesque,* 122.

14. This was brought to my attention by Richard Giannone; see *The Mystery of Love,* 7.

15. Ibid., 8.

16. In a letter O'Connor calls Motes a Protestant saint (*CW* 919), recalling her critical remarks concerning the Protestant separation between nature and grace I discussed in chap. 1.

17. Consider Hazel's grandfather's preaching on the apparent lack of vitality and spirit in the soul: "They were like stones! he would shout. But Jesus had died to redeem them! . . . Did they understand that for each *stone soul,* He would have died ten million deaths?" (*WB* 21, italics mine).

18. I will quote the full passage from Isaiah for this discussion: "And he said, 'Go, and say to this people: "Hear and hear, but do not understand; see and see, but do not perceive." Make the heart of this people fat, and their ears heavy, and shut their eyes; lest they see with their eyes, and hear with their ears, and understand with their hearts, and turn and be healed.'" O'Connor herself also likely has Isaiah in

mind in her comment that "to the hard of hearing you shout, and for the almost-blind you draw large and startling figures" (*MM* 34).

19. The language of the "heart" here is used with reference to the passage from Isaiah. It should be noted however, that references to love and to experiences of the heart are virtually nonexistent in *Wise Blood*. It is nonetheless true that O'Connor saw the heart as the source of charity and the human locus for a sacramental under-standing of the world. Part of Hazel Motes's problem is that his expression and inter-pretation of reality is entirely intellectual; he does not acknowledge the perception of the heart. It is for this reason that some interpreters consider his character "thin." O'Connor would say this dimension of experience is superseded by the intellect in Hazel, and this absence of love is intended to be noticed.

20. For instance on the train, Mrs. Hitchcock speculates that Hazel's hat is one that "an elderly country preacher would wear" (*WB* 10); the taxi driver says to Hazel, "You look like a preacher. . . . That hat looks like a preacher's hat," and later, "It ain't only the hat. . . . It's a look in your face somewheres" (*WB* 31). Later Hazel nearly shouts at Leora Watts, "What I mean to have you know is: I'm no goddam preacher," to which she condescendingly replies, "Momma don't mind if you ain't a preacher" (*WB* 34).

21. In "The Life You Save May Be Your Own," Mr. Shiftlet describes the human being as composed of body and soul, using the image of the car for the soul: "But the spirit, lady, is like a automobile: always on the move" (*CW* 179).

22. Desmond, *Risen Sons,* 58.

23. Ibid, 59.

24. When Hazel is in Leora Watts's bedroom he recalls having seen a naked woman at a local carnival as a child. His mother, who "wore black all the time and [whose] dresses were longer than other women's" intuits that Hazel is guilty. She asks, "What you seen?" and without saying anything more provokes Hazel to a peni-tential act of walking with small rocks in his shoes until he thinks Jesus might be satisfied (*WB* 61–64).

25. Hazel says this before he meets Onnie Jay Holy, when the third church is named. The implication in these preceding passages is that the Church without Christ (focused on a divine Jesus) is soon to become the Church of Christ without Christ (through the introduction of a "new jesus" who is "all man").

26. The story line of Enoch Emery is an important and fascinating one, but my analysis of Hazel Motes prevents me from addressing it here in detail. The conver-gence of Hazel's preaching and Enoch's mission is significant, however, as the mummy represents man without the breath of divine spirit, which is the substance of Hazel's "new jesus." As O'Connor says "Enoch, in his wise blood, unerringly lights on what man looks like without God and obligingly brings it for Haze to have a look at" (*CW* 920). To be presented with such a "man" repulses and humiliates Hazel Motes, forcing him to contend with the image of his rebellion. It is well worth reading the full account of the theft and offering (*WB* 173–89). The mummy is also

an interesting symbol of the "family" relations between Hazel Motes and Sabbath Lily Hawks. Sabbath immediately begins to treat the mummy as a child, coddling it in her arms before Hazel destroys it. The "child" appears after an account of the sexual encounter between Hazel and Sabbath, symbolizing the empty, dead issue of their nonprocreative union.

27. After Hazel's first encounter with Solace Layfield he develops a cough that echoes in his chest as though it were hollow (*WB* 184). The text describes Hazel's cough "like a little yell for help at the bottom of a canyon" (*WB* 189).

28. See Martha Stephens, *The Question of Flannery O'Connor,* 77–78. Stephens concludes that because O'Connor recognized the integrity of Hazel's rebellion, she was supportive of this logical conclusion to Hazel's "quest." Stephens states that the murder is intended to illustrate "Hazel's super-integrity for the earnestness of his pursuit." Stephens's comment confirms that O'Connor's use of the word "integrity" in her preface to *Wise Blood* has been interpreted to mean "good" or "moral." Furthermore, Stephens adds the adjective "super" to integrity, thus importing a heightened moral purity to Hazel's actions. The problem with Stephens's analysis is that integrity is narrowly understood as moral purity, without any recognition of its relation to wholeness in the individual. This murder is one of the ugliest revelations of Hazel's distorted vision of truth, displaying Hazel's blindness to his lack of wholeness in his quest to be independent of the divine.

29. Desmond, *Risen Sons,* 57.

30. Ibid., 3. Desmond identifies three main sources arguing for Manichean elements in O'Connor's work: John Hawkes's "Flannery O'Connor's Devil," *Sewanee Review* 70 (Summer 1962); Martha Stephens's *The Question of Flannery O'Connor;* and Frederick Asals's *Flannery O'Connor.*

31. For a thoughtful analysis of this issue of Hazel's transformation, see Richard Giannone, *Flannery O'Connor and the Mystery of Love.* Giannone considers Motes's conversion a foregone conclusion given O'Connor's comment that his integrity is rooted in his *inability* to resist Jesus: "*Wise Blood* shows that one can be driven to *virtue* by what one is not, by a power that is not one's own" (8–9; italics mine). I agree that what makes one virtuous comes from a power that is not one's own. But according to O'Connor, the movement toward virtue is not inevitable—human beings are always free to resist it (*MM* 182). It seems that the issue here is the *degree* to which Hazel resists the divine pull and whether he actually overcomes his resistance in his final actions of the novel. Giannone suggests (with a helpful discussion of the scriptural usage of "sainthood") that Motes becomes virtuous, and he also says that Hazel, despite his resistance, is utterly transformed: "In the end, the would-be nihilist Hazel Motes becomes a saint for our unbelieving age" (9–10).

32. Desmond, *Risen Sons,* 60.

33. Asa Hawks's recollection and subsequent actions are strongly reminiscent of what Søren Kierkegaard describes in *The Sickness unto Death* (trans. Howard V. Hong and Edna H. Hong [Princeton, N.J.: Princeton University Press, 1980]:

"Whether a person is helped miraculously depends essentially upon the passion of the understanding whereby he has understood that help was impossible and depends next on how honest he was toward the power that nevertheless did help him" (39).

CHAPTER THREE.   The Violence of Love

1. The differences in the nature of their rebellion are subtle, based on different religious experiences that should not be confused as the same. Frederick Asals, in *Flannery O'Connor: The Imagination of Extremity,* notes that "in both [*Wise Blood* and *The Violent Bear It Away*] the protagonist is a young fundamentalist in revolt against his religious heritage" (161). To lump Motes's and Tarwater's "religious heritage" together (with the likely assumption that any significant religious heritage is considered "fundamentalism") as though they were raised with similar religious ideas is to ignore the obvious indications to the contrary.

2. The rebellion/punishment theme is a relatively common dichotomy used for interpreting the violence in O'Connor's fiction, often related to the epigraph of the novel. Gilbert Muller states the either/or direction of violence: "Violence . . . illustrates both the pointlessness of a purely secular world and the indispensable need of God to correct the absurdity of man's condition" (see Gilbert H. Muller, *Nightmares and Visions: Flannery O'Connor and the Catholic Grotesque* [Athens: University of Georgia Press, 1972], 96). Such a reduction eliminates the possibility of violence that is neither rebellion nor divine affliction but the internal struggle of the soul in the world and *in relation* to God.

3. On reception, O'Connor remarked, "The Catholic who does not write for a limited circle of fellow Catholics will in all probability consider that, since this is his vision, he is writing for a hostile audience" (*MM* 146).

4. See the chapters entitled "Rebellion" and "The Grand Inquisitor" in Fyodor Dostoevsky's *The Brothers Karamazov* (236–64).

5. Ivan Karamazov's rejection of any higher harmony if it costs one suffering child is compelling, and even Alyosha cannot resist agreeing with the terms as Ivan sets them out. The clear difference, however, appears in their respective responses to the outrage. Despite Ivan's moral indignation, he responds methodically, abstractly (he collects the accounts of his suffering children in newspaper clippings) and thus calculates that the "system" of God's justice is intolerable to him. Alyosha, although honest in his pain over the suffering of children, does not conclude that one can somehow free oneself from the responsibility of it by blaming God. His response is to live with it, truthfully, and to live with the children who do suffer, knowing them as real human beings. The difference lies in their participation in the reality of suffering; Ivan views it from an intellectual distance, while Alyosha is active and engaged.

6. This point is often belaboured in the interpretation of stories like "A Good Man Is Hard to Find," particularly in response to O'Connor's later comments on the story. O'Connor speaks of a moment of grace that occurs with the grandmother's final gesture toward the Misfit, while the old woman is still aware of her murdered children and grandchildren in the woods; the response to O'Connor's remarks is usually one of moral outrage at her apparent "spiritual" insensitivity. Her interpreters quickly and superficially assume an immediate causal relation between violence and grace—owing to O'Connor's alleged devaluing of the body—which is utterly void of subtlety. See, for instance, Claire Kahane, who writes: "Her peculiar insistence on absolute powerlessness as a condition of salvation so that any assertion of autonomy elicits violence with a vengeance, the fact that she locates the means of grace repeatedly in the sexually perverse as in Tarwater's rape, or in the literally murderous rage of characters like the Misfit, suggest that at the centre of her work is a psychological demand which overshadows her religious intent." Clare Kahane, "Flannery O'Connor's Rage of Vision," in *Critical Essays on Flannery O'Connor,* ed. Melvin Friedman and Beverly Lyon Clark (Boston: G. K. Hall, 1985), 121.

7. O'Connor writes, "Frequently, in reading articles about the failure of the Catholic novelist, you will get the idea that he is to raise himself from the stuff of his own imagination by beginning with Christian principles and finding the life that will illustrate them" (*MM* 182).

8. The topic of O'Connor's essay "The Fiction Writer and His Country," written in 1957, is a response to a *Life* editorial that criticized American novelists for not acknowledging and writing positively about the success and prosperity of their country. O'Connor responds to this call for a literature that illustrates the "joy of life itself" as follows: "What these editorial writers fail to realize is that the writer who emphasizes spiritual values is very likely to take the darkest view of all of what he sees in this country today. For him, the fact that we are the most powerful and wealthiest nation in the world doesn't mean a thing in any positive sense. The sharper the light of faith, the more glaring are apt to be the distortions the writer sees in the life around him" (*MM* 26).

9. "Tidy up reality" is a phrase that O'Connor quotes from Baron von Hügel in her essay "Catholic Novelists and Their Readers" (*MM* 177).

10. O'Connor often received letters criticizing her use of violence and the grotesque. In her essay "The Grotesque in Southern Fiction" she says, "I once received a letter from an old lady in California who informed me that when the tired reader comes home at night, he wishes to read something that will lift up his heart. And it seems her heart had not been lifted up by anything of mine she had read. I think that if her heart had been in the right place, it would have been lifted up" (*MM* 47–48).

11. By offering an analysis of the texts and traditions of the desert fathers, an excellent study reveals the importance of ancient ascetic spirituality in O'Connor's

fiction. See Richard Giannone, *Flannery O'Connor, Hermit Novelist* (Urbana: University of Illinois Press, 2000). Giannone's analysis of *The Violent Bear It Away* offers an insightful interpretation of the ascetic, solitary heroes of the novel and how their struggles are representative of desert spirituality (144–73).

12. John Desmond, "Violence and the Christian Mystery: A Way to Read Flannery O'Connor," *Literature and Belief* 17 (1997): 130.

13. In a letter dated March 16, 1960, she writes, "I am speaking of the verse, apart from my book; in the book I fail to make the title's significance clear, but the title is the best thing about the book. I had never paid much attention to that verse either until I read that it was one of the Eastern fathers' favorite passages—St. Basil, I think" (*HB* 382).

14. Virginia Wray claims that a theological interpretation of the epigraph "can elucidate only the verse itself, not the title; it can say nothing about O'Connor's understanding of and adoption of the verse as the title of her second novel" (107). This separation of the meaning of the novel from O'Connor's choice of biblical epigraph, in addition to sidelining all theological analysis of O'Connor's novel, is stated as though it were simply a matter of fact, without any trace of a convincing argument. See Virginia Wray, "An Authorial Clue to the Significance of the title *The Violent Bear It Away*," *Flannery O'Connor Bulletin* 6 (1977): 107–8.

15. John May raises this question of the direction for reading the epigraph, arguing that "the only reasonable way to proceed would seem to be from the novel and the author's world to the sense that she probably attributed to the text from Matthew." See John R. May, S.J., "*The Violent Bear It Away:* The Meaning of the Title," *Flannery O'Connor Bulletin* 2 (1973): 84. The obvious problem with this programmed direction of interpretation, which limits both texts by making one simply determine the meaning of the other, is that O'Connor is seen as an author speaking independently of the biblical tradition, rather than from within it.

16. Sumner Ferris identifies this translation as the Douai-Challoner Version, noting that the King James Version is not appreciably different. See Sumner J. Ferris, "The Outside and the Inside: Flannery O'Connor's *The Violent Bear It Away*," in *Critical Essays on Flannery O'Connor*, ed. Melvin J. Friedman and Beverly Lyon Clark (Boston: G. K. Hall, 1985), 88.

17. The parallels of Jesus and John to the habits of Mason Tarwater (as the glutton) and Rayber (as the extreme ascetic) are striking, especially in how Francis Tarwater resists both of them, for different reasons.

18. See Richard Giannone, *Flannery O'Connor and the Mystery of Love:* "But assuming responsibility for others, including one's assailant, is a paradoxical act of compassion. . . . Openness to suffering takes the narrative beyond the issue of human justice and transports the character beyond passive belief or unbelief to the sacramental foundation of faith" (xv).

19. It is worth noting here, in regard to the question of inward and outward violence, the example of Hazel Motes in *Wise Blood*. As I have argued above, the peni-

tential acts of O'Connor's characters are usually misunderstood by interpreters because of the assumption that these acts are the inward acts of renunciation and repentance. However, in this context, it seems more appropriate to say that those acts are still external, revealing more of Hazel's rebellion against the created order, rather than a willingness to bear the meaning and consequences of that order inwardly. This would instead entail a reorientation of his soul or heart, rather than a bloody mutilation of his body.

20. Desmond, "Violence and the Christian Mystery," 132.

21. Hawkins, *The Language of Grace,* 24.

22. This is a difficult position to maintain, of course, despite the fact that the word Manicheanism is often associated in this sense with O'Connor's thought. To offer just one example of her Augustinian account of the goodness of creation, both intellectually and physically, see her discussion in "Novelist and Believer" (*MM* 157).

23. Desmond, "Violence and the Christian Mystery," 130.

24. Ibid., 131.

25. There is another issue of "control" in Rayber's struggle, which he assumes to have been effected by Mason's emotionally charged religious indoctrination: his love for Bishop. Rayber recognizes the force of love, which "would overcome him" and rob him of control: "the love that appeared to exist only to be itself, imperious and all demanding" (*VBA* 113). But he dismisses it as an "affliction in the family" related to madness, not transcendence. In order to maintain control of himself, Rayber's response to this love for Bishop is to "anesthetize his life" (*VBA* 182). Rayber also refers to the lack of control over certain parts of the mind, presumably the "unconscious," which, he says to Francis, "works all the time, that you're not aware of yourself. Things go on in it. All sorts of things you don't know about." This does not interest Francis, who responds: "I don't care what my underhead is doing. I know what I think when I do it and when I get ready to do it" (*VBA* 171).

26. The voice that begins the discussion with Tarwater after his great-uncle's death can (among other possibilities) reasonably be assumed to be a form of Tarwater's self-consciousness and self-reflection. While the voice is often defined simply as the devil (especially given O'Connor's comments to this effect; see *HB* 359, 367), this should not preclude the fact that Tarwater is still, in fact, conversing with himself: "Only every now and then it sounded like a stranger's voice to him. He began to feel that he was only just now meeting himself, as if as long as his uncle had lived, he had been deprived of his own acquaintance" (*VBA* 35). The initial contact is strange and disagreeable, but eventually, as Francis senses that the voice is serving his best interests, it becomes his "friend." There is an interesting parallel between this experience of self-reflection and a devil character in Dostoevksy's *The Brothers Karamazov,* when Ivan Karamazov meets himself and/or the devil and finds him irritatingly aware of everything Ivan has thought about or written (see bk II, chap. 9).

27. Francis makes several critical comments directed toward Rayber's detached intellectual reasoning. When he observes Rayber's hearing aid, he queries, "Do you

think in the box? . . . or do you think in your head?" (*VBA* 105). And he comments on Rayber's inability to act: "He [Mason] always told me you couldn't do nothing, couldn't act" (*VBA* 169).

28. See John Desmond's insightful analysis in "The Mystery of the Word and the Act: *The Violent Bear It Away,*" *American Benedictine Review* 24 (1973), 343.

29. Ibid.

30. See Preston Browning, *Flannery O'Connor* (Carbondale: Southern Illinois University Press, 1974), 75. Browning describes the prophetic vocation as the novel's "most obvious motif," which is the focus of most interpretations, and he includes a brief overview of some of these interpretations.

31. O'Connor's sacramental vision, apparent in her fiction, essays, and letters, should challenge the pronouncement of her fiction and thought as dualistic, but this charge inevitably arises in the interpretation of her work. Joyce Carol Oates sees an inherent dualism in O'Connor's portrayal of the visible world. She refers to O'Connor's "essentially Manichean dualism of the Secular and the Sacred," in which "the natural ordinary world is either sacramental (and ceremonial) or profane (and vulgar)" (quoted in Hawkins, *The Language of Grace,* 23). Oates ignores the meaning of "sacramental" in order to import a secondary division into O'Connor's sacramental vision of the world by adding two further categories of "ceremonial" and "vulgar." This kind of reasoning results when it is assumed that O'Connor directs her work entirely at the secular, apostate world, as though it were a separate category and somehow sacramentally excluded. The supposition is that O'Connor's religious sentiments are divided, that she sees the world as sacramental, but only on her own religious terms, usually assumed to be rooted in Catholic doctrine. If one does not receive the sacraments, the world is not sacramentally received by that person. For O'Connor, the sacramental world is first known experientially. The sacraments are formal expressions and ritual enactments of that experience, but the only reason O'Connor can write novels and stories that revolve around specific sacraments (*The Violent Bear It Away* is O'Connor's minor hymn to the Eucharist) is because she sees them coming from something existentially deeper than doctrine. To accuse her of separating the religious sacramental experience from the secular, profane experience, is to misunderstand her sacramentalism entirely. She is explicit about this: "When I write a novel in which the central action is a baptism, I am very well aware that for a majority of my readers, baptism is a meaningless rite, and so in my novel I have to see that this baptism carries enough awe and mystery to jar the reader into some kind of emotional recognition of its significance. . . . I have to make the reader feel, in his bones if nowhere else, that something is going on here that counts" (*MM* 162).

32. Desmond, "The Mystery of Word and Act," 345.

33. The "violence of love" that Rayber feels is, in one sense, the powerful inner force that desires to love Bishop even though he cannot consider Bishop a complete human being. It can also be related to O'Connor's description of the "violence of love" expressed in Christ's words; that is, of giving more than the law requires. Rayber

experiences his love for Bishop violently because it demands something more of him; it pulls him toward something that he does not believe is real.

34. Giannone offers an interpretation of the rape in *Flannery O'Connor, Hermit Novelist:* "O'Connor's presentation of rape draws less on the modern understanding of rape as a political crime (with its attendant sympathy for the victim) and more on the timeless spiritual effects of this notorious weapon of degradation" (162–65).

35. Desmond, *Risen Sons,* 64.

36. The comparison is relevant and instructive on several levels, but especially with regard to judgment and punishment. Cain expresses his fear that, in his exile from God, those who know of his crime might slay him. God does not accept this as just punishment and prohibits any human hand from meting out God's own justice. He marks Cain instead, and in so doing he protects him from this kind of retribution.

CHAPTER FOUR.   **Purgatorial Visions**

An earlier version of this chapter appeared as "O'Connor and the Mystics: St. Catherine of Genoa's Purgatorial Vision in 'Revelation,'" *Flannery O'Connor Review* 2 (2003–4): 40–52.

1. Asals mentions the theme of purgation in O'Connor's work in *Flannery O'Connor: The Imagination of Extremity*: "Indeed, while the imagery of fire in O'Connor's fiction may be demonic, it is most often purgatorial, and what it signals is the infliction of a searing grace, the onset of a saving pain" (226).

2. See O'Connor's comment regarding these symbols: "Water is a symbol of purification and fire is another. Water, it seems to me, is a symbol of the kind of purification that God gives irrespective of our efforts or worthiness, and fire is the kind of purification we bring on ourselves—as in Purgatory. It is our evil which is naturally burnt away when it comes anywhere near God" (*HB* 387).

3. Catherine of Genoa, *Purgation and Purgatory, The Spiritual Dialogue,* trans. Serge Hughes (Mahwah, N.J.: Paulist Press, 1979), xvi. For the discussion that follows, references to this work will be noted in text by the page number.

4. In conjunction with the discussion in chap. 1 concerning the particular effects of the philosophical and biblical influences on O'Connor's work, it is worth mentioning that in the introduction to St. Catherine's writings, Benedict J. Groeschel identifies her three major literary sources: the Scriptures (especially Isaiah, the Psalms, the Pauline and the Johannine writings); the poems of Lodi of the Blessed Jacopone da Todi (1228–1306), "an ecstatic poet . . . who writes in the tradition of the Christian Neoplatonism of St. Augustine and especially of Dionysius"; and finally, a devotional treatise on Dionysius, as well as a translation and commentary of *The Mystical Theology and the Divine Names of Dionysius.* See Catherine of Genoa, *Purgation and Purgatory,* 23–24.

5. Rath, "Ruby Turpin's Redemption," 1; italics for "source" mine. Rath responds to the problem of polarity by suggesting that O'Connor was dramatizing the Thomistic "reconciliation of opposites" and that the "external objects" are "a means of tracking internal growth" (1). While the effort to diminish the polarity in this way is helpful, it still leaves Ruby separated from her experience and encourages the hierarchical division of the natural world and the supernatural. Understood in this way, the natural world becomes a "medium" through which the "higher truth" is perceived; and Ruby Turpin can only know through her senses rather than through her soul's ability to transcend the "natural-supernatural dialectic" through ascent and descent. Rath's account includes ascent only, since the material world is used only as a medium; consequently, the goal in ascending is to move "toward something fuller than the present life" (4). This assumption negates the purgatorial vision according to O'Connor and St. Catherine, which does not offer an escape to another world but a transformed vision of how to live better as a whole person within this world.

6. In *Flannery O'Connor,* near the end of his chapter "The Prophetic Imagination," Asals does acknowledge the human role in the transformative vision: "But although the awakening seems to come wholly from without, in O'Connor's work it comes from within also, for it entails the 'emergence of intuitions from below the threshold,' the 'openings of the soul's eye'" (231). But it seems that, because intuition comes "from below" and "consciousness has its roots deep in unconscious life," Asals has removed the possibility of an active, conscious, spiritual reordering in the revelatory experience. This type of one-sided interpretation of visionary experiences can ultimately be traced back to some of the reductive accounts of reason that were discussed in chap. 1, but for our purposes here it is worth noting that the primary emphasis is on a divine imposition of a religious vision rather than the experience and participation of the main character in the vision.

7. Asals, *Flannery O'Connor,* 222. Asals is referring to Abraham J. Heschel, *The Prophets* (New York: Harper and Row, 1962).

8. Ibid., 214.

9. Ibid., 225 (italics mine).

10. Ibid.

11. Ibid., 213, n. 15, referring to Victor White, O.P., *God and the Unconscious* (Chicago: Henry Regnery, 1953).

12. In one of her letters O'Connor makes a reference to her reading of the depth psychologists, including Jung, Erich Neumann, and Victor White, about which she says: "All this throws light momentarily on some of the dark places in my brain but only momentarily" (*HB* 103).

13. Asals, *Flannery O'Connor,* 213, quoting Aquinas.

14. Gentry, *Religion of the Grotesque,* 43.

15. Ibid.

16. Ibid., 48.

17. Ibid., 49.

18. Quoted in Anthony di Renzo, *American Gargoyles: Flannery O'Connor and the Medieval Grotesque* (Carbondale: Southern Illinois University Press, 1993), 216.

19. See the excellent article on another important biblical allusion in "Revelation" by Brian Britt, "Divine Curses in O'Connor's 'Revelation' and 2 Samuel 16," *Flannery O'Connor Review* 1 (2001–2): 49–55.

20. See Kahane, "Rage of Vision," 127; di Renzo, *American Gargoyles*, 210–11.

21. John R. May, e.g., says "Mary Grace, as her name itself suggests, announces the time of repentance" (John R. May, *The Pruning Word: The Parables of Flannery O'Connor* [Notre Dame, Ind.: University of Notre Dame Press, 1976], 12). See also, Norman McMillan, "Dostoevskian Vision in Flannery O'Connor's 'Revelation,'" *Flannery O'Connor Bulletin* 16 (1987): 18.

22. "Today's reader, if he believes in grace at all, sees it as something which can be separated from nature and served to him raw as Instant Uplift" (*MM* 165).

23. For a compelling discussion of how the desert father Dorotheos of Gaza speaks to the spiritual conflict that Ruby Turpin experiences here, see Giannone, *Flannery O'Connor, Hermit Novelist*, 232.

24. See J. Gerald Janzen's excellent commentary in *Job: A Bible Commentary for Teaching and Preaching* (Atlanta: John Knox Press, 1985), 2. The divine question Why are the righteous pious? raises the issue of the *motivation* for the piety, especially evident when the external rewards are absent or removed.

25. For example, Zophar the Na'amathite says, "Know then that God exacts of you less than your guilt deserves" (Job 11:6b).

26. Apparently, while Rembrandt was painting his *Belshazzar Sees the Writing on the Wall,* he had a neighbor in Amsterdam who was a rabbi and scholar, Manasseh ben Israel. This rabbi wrote a scholarly treatise in 1639 on the issue of the unintelligibility of the writing, where he argued that the wise men could not read the writing because it had been written from *top to bottom* rather than right to left as Hebrew is written. This is found in Richard Muehlberger, *The Bible in Art: The Old Testament* (New York: Portland House, 1991), 154. Ruby likewise sees human beings hierarchically ordered from top to bottom; this is at the heart of her inability to decipher the writing on the wall and to see where she stands in relation to the divine order.

27. See Philippians 2:3–8: "Do nothing from selfishness or conceit, but in humility count others better than yourselves. Let each of you look not only to his own interests, but also to the interests of others. Have this mind among yourselves, which is yours in Christ Jesus, who, though he was in the form of God, did not count equality with God a thing to be grasped, but emptied himself, taking the form of a servant, being born in the likeness of men."

28. In Matthew 19:17, Jesus responds to the man's question with "if you would enter *life,* keep the commandments." In other words, the emphasis is not the afterlife, but true eternal life.

29. See Ralph Wood's interpretation of "Revelation" as O'Connor's "comedy of grace": "The first and last words of the Gospel are hopeful rather than baleful. And

so are the beginning and the ending of this story. No one admitted entrance to purgatory can regress out of it. One's cleansing there may be greatly prolonged by one's own recalcitrant will, but there is no changing of direction. . . . However much they may differ about the doctrine of purgatory itself, classic Catholicism and classic Protestantism are here profoundly agreed: true faith is indelible and irreversible. Hence O'Connor's determination to embody, in this final scene of her finest story, the vision of an eschatological community that includes all of the redeemed" (Wood, *The Comedy of Redemption,* 131).

Conclusion

1. See Ivan's struggle to understand the unearthly obligation of love in "Rebellion," *The Brothers Karamazov.*

2. Eric Voegelin, quoted in Feely, *Flannery O'Connor,* 141. This passage was marked by O'Connor in her copy of Voegelin's *Israel and Revelation,* vol. 1 of *Order and History* (Baton Rouge: Louisiana State University Press, 1956).

3. I share this idea with other O'Connor scholars, notably, Richard Giannone (*Flannery O'Connor and the Mystery of Love* and *Flannery O'Connor, Hermit Novelist*) and John Desmond. See Desmond's conclusion in *Risen Sons,* 117–19.

BIBLIOGRAPHY

Works by Flannery O'Connor

Collected Works. New York: Library of America, 1988.

The Complete Stories. New York: Farrar, Straus and Giroux, 1971.

Flannery O'Connor: Spiritual Writings. Edited by Robert Ellsberg. Introduction by Richard Giannone. Maryknoll, N.Y.: Orbis Books, 2003.

The Habit of Being. Edited by Sally Fitzgerald. New York: Farrar, Straus and Giroux, 1979.

Mystery and Manners: Occasional Prose. Edited by Sally and Robert Fitzgerald. New York: Farrar, Straus and Giroux, 1969.

The Presence of Grace, and Other Book Reviews. Compiled by Leo J. Zuber. Edited with an introduction by Carter W. Martin. Athens: University of Georgia Press, 1983.

The Violent Bear It Away. New York: Farrar, Straus and Cudahy, 1960.

Wise Blood. New York: Farrar, Straus and Cudahy, 1962.

Works by Other Authors

Aquinas, Thomas. *Summa Theologiae.* Translated by the Fathers of the English Dominican Province. London: Burns Oates and Washbourn, 1934.

Asals, Frederick. "Differentiation, Violence and the Displaced Person." *Flannery O'Connor Bulletin* 13 (1984): 1–14.

———. *Flannery O'Connor: The Imagination of Extremity.* Athens: University of Georgia Press, 1982.

———. "The Limits of Explanation." In *Critical Essays on Flannery O'Connor.* Edited by Melvin Friedman and Beverly Lyon Clark, 49–53. Boston: G. K. Hall, 1985.

Balee, Susan. *Flannery O'Connor: Literary Prophet of the South*. New York: Chelsea House Publishers, 1994.

Bloom, Harold, ed. *Modern Critical Views: Flannery O'Connor*. New York: Chelsea House Publishers, 1986.

Brinkmeyer, Robert H. *The Art and Vision of Flannery O'Connor*. Baton Rouge: Louisiana State University Press, 1989.

―――. "Asceticism and the Imaginative Vision of Flannery O'Connor." In *Flannery O'Connor: New Perspectives*. Edited by Sura P. Rath and Mary Neff Shaw, 169–82. Athens: University of Georgia Press, 1996.

Britt, Brian. "Divine Curses in O'Connor's 'Revelation' and 2 Samuel 16." *Flannery O'Connor Review* 1 (2001–2): 49–55.

Browning, Preston M., Jr. *Flannery O'Connor*. Carbondale: Southern Illinois University Press, 1974.

Buber, Martin. *Eclipse of God: Studies in the Relation between Religion and Philosophy*. 1952. Reprint, New York: Harper and Brothers, Harper Torchbacks, 1957.

Byars, John. "Prophecy and Apocalyptic in the Fiction of Flannery O'Connor." *Flannery O'Connor Bulletin* 16 (1987): 34–42.

Catherine of Genoa. *Purgation and Purgatory, The Spiritual Dialogue*. Translated by Serge Hughes. Mahwah, N.J.: Paulist Press, 1979.

Coles, Robert. *Flannery O'Connor's South*. Baton Rouge: Louisiana State University Press, 1980.

Cook, Martha E. "Flannery O'Connor." In *American Women Writers*. Edited by Maurice Duke, J. Breyer, and M. T. Inge, 269–96. Westport, Conn.: Greenwood Press, 1983.

Copleston, F. C. *Aquinas*. London: Penguin Books, 1955.

Davies, Brian. *The Thought of Thomas Aquinas*. New York: Oxford University Press, 1993.

Desmond, John. "The Mystery of the Word and the Act: Flannery O'Connor's *The Violent Bear It Away*." *American Benedictine Review* 24 (1973): 342–47.

―――. *Risen Sons: Flannery O'Connor's Vision of History*. Athens: University of Georgia Press, 1987.

―――. "Violence and the Christian Mystery: A Way to Read Flannery O'Connor." *Literature and Belief* 17 (1997): 129–47.

Di Renzo, Anthony. *American Gargoyles: Flannery O'Connor and the Medieval Grotesque*. Carbondale: Southern Illinois University Press, 1993.

Dostoevksy, Fyodor. *The Brothers Karamazov*. Translated by Richard Pevear and Larissa Volokhonsky. New York: Vintage Books, 1990.

Driggers, Stephen G., Robert J. Dunn, and Sarah Gordon, eds. *The Manuscripts of Flannery O'Connor at Georgia College*. Athens: University of Georgia Press, 1989.

Driskell, Leon V., and Joan T. Brittain, eds. *The Eternal Crossroads: The Art of Flannery O'Connor*. Lexington: University Press of Kentucky, 1971.

Eggenschwiler, David. *The Christian Humanism of Flannery O'Connor*. Detroit: Wayne State University Press, 1972.

Elie, Paul. *The Life You Save May Be Your Own*. New York: Farrar, Straus and Giroux, 2003.

Farmer, David R. *Flannery O'Connor: A Descriptive Bibliography*. New York: Garland Publishing, 1981.

Feeley, Kathleen. *Flannery O'Connor: Voice of the Peacock*. New York: Fordham University Press, 1982.

Ferris, Sumner J. "The Outside and the Inside: Flannery O'Connor's *The Violent Bear It Away*." In *Critical Essays on Flannery O'Connor*. Edited by Melvin J. Friedman and Beverly Lyon Clark, 85–91. Boston: G. K. Hall, 1985.

Ficken, Carl. *God's Story and Modern Literature: Reading Fiction in Community*. Philadelphia: Fortress Press, 1985.

Fickett, Harold, and Douglas R. Gilbert. *Flannery O'Connor: Images of Grace*. Grand Rapids, Mich.: William B. Eerdmans, 1986.

Fitzgerald, Robert. "The Countryside and the True Country." *Sewanee Review* 70 (1962): 380–94.

Friedman, Melvin J., and Beverly Lyon Clark, eds. *Critical Essays on Flannery O'Connor*. Boston: G. K. Hall, 1985.

Friedman, Melvin J., and Lewis A. Lawson, eds. *The Added Dimension: The Art and Mind of Flannery O'Connor*. New York: Fordham University Press, 1977.

Gentry, Marshall Bruce. *Flannery O'Connor's Religion of the Grotesque*. Jackson: University Press of Mississippi, 1986.

Getz, Lorine M. *Flannery O'Connor: Her Life, Library and Book Reviews*. New York: Edwin Mellen Press, 1980.

———. *Nature and Grace in Flannery O'Connor's Fiction*. New York: Edwin Mellen Press, 1982.

Giannone, Richard. *Flannery O'Connor and the Mystery of Love*. Urbana: University of Illinois Press, 1989.

———. *Flannery O'Connor, Hermit Novelist*. Urbana: University of Illinois Press, 2000.

———. "Warfare and Solitude: O'Connor's Prophet and the Word in the Desert." *Literature and Belief* 17 (1997): 161–89.

Gilson, Etienne. *The Philosophy of St. Thomas Aquinas*. St. Louis: B. Herder, 1937.

Golden, Robert E., and Mary C. Sullivan. *Flannery O'Connor and Caroline Gordon: A Reference Guide*. Boston: G. K. Hall, 1977.

Gordon, Mary. "Flannery O'Connor: *The Habit of Being*." In *Good Boys and Dead Girls*, 37–44. New York: Viking Penguin, 1991.

Green, Gwendolen, ed. *Letters from Baron Friedrich von Hügel to a Niece*. Chicago: Henry Regnery, 1955.

Han, Jae-Nam. "O'Connor's Thomism and the 'Death of God' in *Wise Blood*." *Literature and Belief* 17 (1997): 115–27.

Hawkes, John. "Flannery O'Connor's Devil." *Sewanee Review* 70 (Summer 1962): 395–407.

Hawkins, Peter S. *The Language of Grace: Flannery O'Connor, Walker Percy, and Iris Murdoch*. Cambridge, Mass.: Cowley Publications, 1983.

Hendin, Josephine. *The World of Flannery O'Connor*. Bloomington: Indiana University Press, 1970.

Heschel, Abraham J. *The Prophets*. New York: Harper and Row, 1962.

Humphries, Jefferson. "Proust, Flannery O'Connor and the Aesthetic of Violence." In *Modern Critical Views: Flannery O'Connor*. Edited by Harold Bloom, 111–24. New York: Chelsea House Publishers, 1986.

Hyman, Stanley Edgar. *Flannery O'Connor*. Minneapolis: University of Minnesota Press, 1966.

Janzen, Gerald J. *Job: A Bible Commentary for Teaching and Preaching*. Atlanta: John Knox Press, 1985.

Jeffrey, David Lyle. *People of the Book: Christian Identity and Literary Culture*. Grand Rapids, Mich.: William B. Eerdmans, 1996.

Jones, L. Gregory. *Embodying Forgiveness: A Theological Analysis*. Grand Rapids, Mich.: William B. Eerdmans Publishing Co., 1995.

Kahane, Clare. "Flannery O'Connor's Rage of Vision." In *Critical Essays on Flannery O'Connor*. Edited by Melvin Friedman and Beverly Lyon Clark, 119–31. Boston: G. K. Hall, 1985.

Keane, Philip S., S.S. *Christian Ethics and Imagination*. Ramsey, N.J.: Paulist Press, 1984.

Kermode, Frank. *The Sense of an Ending: Studies in the Theory of Fiction*. New York: Oxford University Press, 1967.

Kessler, Edward. *Flannery O'Connor and the Language of Apocalypse*. Princeton, N.J.: Princeton University Press, 1986.

Kierkegaard, Søren. *The Sickness unto Death*. Translated by Howard V. Hong and Edna H. Hong. Princeton, N.J.: Princeton University Press, 1980.

Kinney, Arthur F. "Flannery O'Connor and the Art of the Holy." *Virginia Quarterly Review* 64, no. 2 (Spring 1988): 217–30.

———. *Flannery O'Connor's Library: Resources of Being*. Athens: University of Georgia Press, 1985.

Kreyling, Michael, ed. *New Essays on "Wise Blood."* Cambridge: Cambridge University Press, 1995.

Lee, Maryat. "Flannery 1957." *Flannery O'Connor Bulletin* 5 (1976): 39–60.

Littlefield, Daniel F., Jr. "Flannery O'Connor's *Wise Blood:* 'Unparalleled Prosperity' and Spiritual Chaos." *Mississippi Quarterly* 23 (1970): 121–33.

Magee, Rosemary. *Conversations with Flannery O'Connor*. Jackson: University Press of Mississippi, 1987.

Mallon, Anne Marie. "Mystic Quest in *The Violent Bear It Away*." *Flannery O'Connor Bulletin* 10 (1981): 54–69.

Maritain, Jacques. *Art and Scholasticism and the Frontiers of Poetry*. Translated by Joseph W. Evans. New York: Charles Scribner's Sons, 1962.

———. *Creative Intuition in Art and Poetry*. Cleveland: World Publishing, 1953.

———. *Range of Reason*. New York: Charles Scribner's Sons, 1961.

Martin, Carter W. *The True Country: Themes in the Fiction of Flannery O'Connor.* Nashville: Vanderbilt University Press, 1969.

Martin, Karl. "Flannery O'Connor's Prophetic Imagination." *Religion and Literature* 26, no. 3 (1994): 33–58.

May, Herbert G., and Bruce M. Metzger, eds. *The New Oxford Annotated Bible with the Apocrypha,* Revised Standard Version. New York: Oxford University Press, 1962.

May, John R. "The Methodological Limits of Flannery O'Connor's Critics." *Flannery O'Connor Bulletin* 15 (1986): 16–28.

———. *The Pruning Word: The Parables of Flannery O'Connor.* Notre Dame, Ind.: University of Notre Dame Press, 1976.

———. "*The Violent Bear It Away:* The Meaning of the Title." *Flannery O'Connor Bulletin* 2 (1973): 83–86.

Mayer, David R. "Apologia for the Imagination: Flannery O'Connor's 'A Temple of the Holy Ghost.'" *Studies in Short Fiction* 11 (1974): 147–52.

McMillan, Norman. "Dostoevskian Vision in Flannery O'Connor's 'Revelation.'" *Flannery O'Connor Bulletin* 16 (1987): 16–22.

Montgomery, Marion. "Flannery O'Connor's Sacramental Vision." *This World* 4 (1983): 119–28.

———. *Why Flannery O'Connor Stayed Home.* La Salle, Ill.: Sherwood Sugden, 1981.

Muehlberger, Richard. *The Bible in Art: The Old Testament.* New York: Portland House, 1991.

Muller, Gilbert H. *Nightmares and Visions: Flannery O'Connor and the Catholic Grotesque.* Athens: University of Georgia Press, 1972.

Orvell, Miles. *Flannery O'Connor: An Introduction.* Jackson: University Press of Mississippi, 1991.

———. *Invisible Parade: The Fiction of Flannery O'Connor.* Philadelphia: Temple University Press, 1972.

Quinn, John J., S.J., ed. *Flannery O'Connor: A Memorial.* Scranton, Pa.: University of Scranton Press, 1995.

Ragen, Brian Abel. *A Wreck on the Road to Damascus: Innocence, Guilt, and Conversion in Flannery O'Connor.* Chicago: Loyola University Press, 1989.

Rath, Sura P. Introduction. to *Flannery O'Connor: New Perspectives.* Edited by Sura P. Rath and Mary Neff Shaw, 1–11. Athens: University of Georgia Press, 1996.

———. "Ruby Turpin's Redemption: Thomistic Resolution in Flannery O'Connor's 'Revelation.'" *Flannery O'Connor Bulletin* 19 (1990): 1–8.

Reiter, Robert E., ed. *Flannery O'Connor.* St. Louis: B. Herder, 1968.

Rubin, Louis D., Jr. "Flannery O'Connor's Company of Southerners: or, 'The Artificial Nigger' Read as Fiction Rather Than Theology." *Flannery O'Connor Bulletin* 6 (1977): 47–71.

Scouten, Kenneth. "The Schoolteacher as Devil in *The Violent Bear It Away.*" *Flannery O'Connor Bulletin* 12 (1983): 35–46.

Shloss, Carol. *Flannery O'Connor's Dark Comedies: The Limits of Inference.* Baton Rouge: Louisiana State University Press, 1980.

Spivey, Ted Ray. *Flannery O'Connor: The Woman, the Thinker, the Visionary.* Macon, Ga.: Mercer University Press, 1995.

Stephens, Martha. *The Question of Flannery O'Connor.* Baton Rouge: Louisiana State University Press, 1973.

Trowbridge, Clinton. "The Comic Sense of Flannery O'Connor: Literalist of the Imagination." *Flannery O'Connor Bulletin* 12 (1983): 77–92.

Vawter, Bruce. *The Conscience of Israel: Pre-exilic Prophets and Prophecy.* New York: Sheed and Ward, 1961.

Voegelin, Eric. *Israel and Revelation.* Vol. 1 of *Order and History.* Baton Rouge: Louisiana State University Press, 1956.

———. "Reason: The Classic Experience." In *The Collected Works of Eric Voegelin,* vol. 12, *Published Essays, 1966–1985.* Edited by Ellis Sandoz, 265–91. Baton Rouge: Louisiana State University Press, 1990.

Von Hügel, Baron. *The Mystical Element of Religion: As Studied in St. Catherine of Genoa and Her Friends.* New York: Crossroad, 1999.

Weaver, Mary Jo. "Thomas Merton and Flannery O'Connor: The Urgency of Vision." In *Thomas Merton: Pilgrim in Process.* Edited by Donald Grayston and Michael W. Higgins, 27–40. Toronto: Griffin House Graphics, 1983.

Weinstein, Arnold. *Nobody's Home: Speech, Self, and Place in American Fiction from Hawthorne to DeLillo.* Oxford: Oxford University Press, 1993.

Westarp, Karl-Heinz, and Jan Norby Gretlund, eds. *Realist of Distances: Flannery O'Connor Revisited.* Aarhus, Denmark: Aarhus University Press, 1987.

White, Victor, O.P. *God and the Unconscious.* Chicago: Henry Regnery, 1953.

Whitt, Margaret Early. *Understanding Flannery O'Connor.* Columbia: University of South Carolina Press, 1995.

Wood, Ralph. "The Catholic Faith of Flannery O'Connor's Protestant Characters: A Critique and a Vindication." *Flannery O'Connor Bulletin* 13 (1984): 15–25.

———. *The Comedy of Redemption: Christian Faith and Comic Vision in Four American Novelists.* Notre Dame, Ind.: University of Notre Dame Press, 1988.

Wray, Virginia F. "An Authorial Clue to the Significance of the Title *The Violent Bear It Away.*" *Flannery O'Connor Bulletin* 6 (1977): 107–8.

INDEX

SUSAN SRIGLEY

is assistant professor of Religions and Cultures
at Nipissing University in North Bay, Ontario, Canada.